THE PURSUIT OF CRIME

THE PURSUIT OF CRIME

Art and Ideology in Detective Fiction

Dennis Porter

New Haven and London   Yale University Press

Published with the assistance of the Frederick W. Hilles publication fund.

Designed by Nancy Ovedovitz and set in Times Roman type.
Printed in the United States of America by The Vail-Ballou Press, Binghamton, N. Y.

Library of Congress Cataloging in Publication Data

Porter, Dennis, 1933–
   The pursuit of crime.

   Includes index.
   1. Detective and mystery stories—History and criticism. I. Title.
PN3448.D4P58   809.3′872   81-3399
ISBN 0-300-02722-2   AACR2

10   9   8   7   6   5   4   3   2   1

For Annick, Will, and Ann

Contents

Acknowledgments

The debts incurred by an author of a book such as this are manifold and not susceptible to telling. I can express my thanks only to those people and institutions who participated concretely in its production. I am therefore grateful to Peter Brooks and Richard Macksey, who read the manuscript in its unrevised form and gave encouragement when it was needed, to Richard Noland, whose knowledge of detective fiction is far broader than my own, to Ellen Graham and Sharon Slodki, whose sure editorial judgments made the finished work clearer and cleaner than it would otherwise have been, to Lucy Matteau, whose typing skills made it look like a book when it was still only a manuscript, to the National Endowment for the Humanities for a Research Fellowship in 1977–78 that enabled me to complete much preliminary reading and thinking, and to the University of Massachusetts at Amherst for sheltering a scholar in hard academic times. My greatest debt is to my wife, without whose enthusiasm for literature high and low it would never have occurred to me to play metasleuth.

Introduction

If the popular literature of our contemporary market economy has not yet achieved respectability, for some time now the academic study of it has. And the interest aroused in the academy can be accounted for on three fundamental grounds. In the first place, the tradition of folklore studies associated with the Russian Formalists and culminating in the work of Vladimir Propp has opened up a new approach to the study of literature especially well adapted to the analysis of large bodies of formulaic popular works. Since for the Formalists literature was "not a succession of masterpieces,"[1] the object of literary studies was not the great works of a canon but "literariness." And "literariness" is a quality displayed independently of aesthetic value by all specifically literary works, popular as well as highbrow.

Second, the popular literature of a consumer society in an age of mass literacy has long been regarded by critics of a broadly Marxian tradition as a reflector and valuable barometer of the society's ideological norms. The importance of popular works resides in their status as meaning-systems that embody implicit world views. Properly interpreted, therefore, they can provide important clues to the anxieties and frustrations, aspirations and constraints, experienced by the mass audience that accounts for their best-seller status.

Finally, and more parochially, the central place now occupied by American Studies in departments of literature in the United States, with its more egalitarian ethos and its interest in historical context,

---

1. See Victor Erlich, *Russian Formalism: History-Doctrine* (The Hague: Mouton, 1955), p. 261.

cultural continuity, and national myths, has inevitably led to the blurring of the frontiers between highbrow and lowbrow traditional in departments of English and foreign literatures. Until the commercial book trade became thoroughly product-oriented, at least, it was still possible to regard popular literature as opening a window directly onto the popular national soul. If the tales of frontier life from Puritan times on provided the first specifically American national myths for general consumption, the study of their character, influence, and persistence under changing historical circumstances was seen to be of great importance.

Yet perhaps the most compelling reason for paying attention to popular literature is its popularity. It is important to try to examine those intrinsic qualities of literary works which make them attractive to mass audiences. And of all the modern popular genres, the detective story as defined in its broadest sense, along with varieties of romance, has had the widest and most durable appeal. In spite of the spectacular rise of science fiction over the past two or three decades, detective stories continue to be written by successive generations of writers, not only for readers but also for movie and TV audiences that have never voluntarily cracked the back of any book. If, then, as the publishing industry tells us, the sales of Agatha Christie, Mickey Spillane, and Ian Fleming novels have run into the millions, it is essential to understand the objects of such massive cults. The genre's vitality is also confirmed by the fact that it is frequently parodied. The camp Holmeses and blundering Clouseaus as well as the cult of the greatest movie private investigator of them all, Humphrey Bogart, attest to a continuing fascination. Parody is, as we all know, a form of flattery.

In the eighties as in the twenties, the classic question remains, Why, at a time when so much solicits the attention, do great numbers of people still choose to read tales of crime and detection, if they read any books at all? Edmund Wilson's exasperated formulation of the problem "Who cares who killed Roger Ackroyd?" is pertinent but unhelpful. The implied answer—no one should give a damn—ignores the fact that millions do. His is the answer of an embattled literary pundit determined to defend high literary art against the various forms of philistinism operative in his time. Wilson's dismissive attitude toward Agatha Christie is probably standard among the great majority of contemporary critics,[2] who understandably object to formulaic literary works for reasons summed up by John G. Cawelti in a recent book. He writes of "their essential standardization and their primary relation to the needs of escape and relaxation."[3] What critics generally find in detective fiction are predictable problems of no intrinsic interest, stereotyped characterizations, and undistinguished writing—in short, a literature for puzzle addicts and thrill seekers produced at best by ingenious purveyors of commodities.

Yet the standard response of the higher criticism tends to overlook at least two interesting points. First, the combined influence of Russian Formalism, French Structuralism, and American myth criticism has been to demonstrate the formulaic component of all literature, high and low. Not only are those same critics who condemn the formulaic literature of popular mass culture often responsive to such literature when it takes the form of folk song and tale, they are also sensitive to the centrality of formulas in such elevated genres as comedy and tragedy. Consequently, it is no longer possible simply to dismiss a work on the grounds that it involves the application of a formula.

Second, the assertion that novels such as detective stories constitute a literature of "escape and relaxation" has remained relatively unexamined. "Escape" suggests, of course, a flight from something threatening, and "relaxation" an unwinding after a protracted period of unpleasurable effort or work. The interesting question that is often begged, however, is why people bother to escape into literature at all, if that is what they are, in fact, doing. They apparently do so not under compulsion, out of an urge for self-improvement, or with the hope of acquiring useful information—all reasons why people undertake certain kinds of reading—but in the expectation of pleasure. It is above all my purpose here to consider how a popular literary genre caters to reader pleasure. Why, in other words, do a great many people escape into detective novel reading as opposed, say, to other rec-

2. "Why Do People Read Detective Stories?" in *Classics and Commercials* (New York: Farrar, Straus, 1950), pp. 231–37, and "Who Cares Who Killed Roger Ackroyd?" in *The Art of the Mystery Story*, ed. Howard Haycraft (New York: Simon and Schuster, 1946), pp. 390–97.

3. *Adventure, Mystery and Romance* (Chicago and London: University of Chicago Press, 1976), p. 8.

reational activities such as making love, watching football, vacationing, buying clothes, listening to music, or simply walking the dog?

The following chapters make no effort to go over material by now familiar from a number of standard works concerning the history of the detective story genre.[4] Instead, they rely particularly on a limited number of well-known detective works mostly of novel length in order to isolate those genre characteristics that account for its popularity.

The definition of detective novel to be applied will be a broad one, broader than is customary in the standard histories and among those concerned with establishing a typology of the genre.[5] If the Detection Club of London has long admitted authors of spy intrigues and thrillers, I see no reason for academic critics to be more exclusive.[6] The attempt to devise strict categories and locate the by now vast corpus of published works within those categories is valuable only insofar as it draws attention to the range of possibilities in the genre and is a nuisance where it multiplies superficial differences. If we do hesitate between available terms in assigning a given work to a specific category such as mystery story, crime story, problem story, detective adventure story, police novel, thriller, or spy thriller, it is because in so many cases there is significant overlapping. I am, of course, aware that a classic golden age whodunit or problem story usually embodies an action sequence different from that of a detective adventure story or a spy thriller. Spy thrillers are typically pursuit dramas in which the identity of the criminal adversary is known from early on. The problem is to find him, and once having found him to penetrate into his fortified space in order to destroy him. Yet the great majority of detective stories have at least some features of the pursuit drama, as the classic example of Doyle confirms. The phase of the unmasking of the villain is so often followed by the phase of running down or preparing a trap for the now known criminal.

    4. Alme E. Murch, *The Development of the Detective Novel* (New York: Greenwood Press, 1958); Julian Symons, *Mortal Consequences: A History—From the Detective Story to the Crime Novel* (New York: Harper and Row, 1972); and Pierre Boileau and Thomas Narcejac, *Le Roman policier* (Paris: Petite Bibliothèque Payot, 1964).
    5. See Tzvetan Todorov, "Typologie du roman policier," in his *Poétique de la Prose* (Paris: Editions du Seuil, 1971), pp. 55–56.
    6. See Julian Symons, "The Detection Club," *The New York Times Book Review* (September 30, 1979), pp. 14 and 26.

"Detective novel" will therefore be employed here as the generic term for all novels whose principal action concerns the attempt by a specialist investigator to solve a crime and to bring a criminal to justice, whether the crime involved be a single murder or the endeavor to destroy a civilization. Neither the type of crime committed nor the type of legal or extralegal agent involved in pursuing the criminal determines a given novel's relation to the formula. It is the course of the action alone that does that. Because in the first part of the book I shall be focusing chiefly on the mechanisms that promote pleasure, and such mechanisms are to be found in a variety of human activities, the intention is less to point up differences than to establish the fundamental similarities that exist not only between detective novels and related genres but also between detective novels and all narrative fiction. An analysis of the detective genre is interesting not least for the light it sheds on the activity of novel reading in general.

A further premise of this study is that in spite of what hostile critics may think, there is an art of the detective novel that is not necessarily synonymous with literary art in Edmund Wilson's sense. Nevertheless, readers rely on such an art for their pleasure when they turn to detective fiction. The most interesting works in the genre are the products of craftsmen who have learned from the formula itself how to manipulate reader response to the ends of pleasure.[7] And an important element in that art is the power to make novel reading easy. At a time when "readability" has become an important critical issue, therefore, it is also worth exploring why detective stories pose so few problems of intelligibility. Finally, the fact that popular fiction is by definition a form of literature that does not offend the taste and values of its mass audience raises the issue of ideology. In order for a novel to be easily comprehensible and to please, a novelist has to go out of his way to avoid confusion and conflict in his reader. And he does so in

7. In his study of the circumstances that bear on the production of literary artifacts, Pierre Macherey remarks about a novel of Anne Radcliffe's that no work is "innocent"—"the apparent spontaneity of a simple book destined for immediate consumption presupposes the application of well-tried techniques, often borrowed from the most self-conscious of literary forms and passed from work to work by a secret literary tradition." *Pour une théorie de la production littéraire* (Paris: François Maspero, 1978), p. 39.

Unless otherwise indicated, translations from the French are my own.

part by creating a work that embodies in its structure ideological presuppositions that are likely to elicit the reader's recognition and approbation. Readability in a novel is dependent on a relationship of complicity between an author and a reader, involving the acknowledgment of shared community values as well as of fixed narrative norms. How, in the case of the detective story, that community of values was established historically is explored in part II; a full understanding of a literary genre requires an appreciation of the circumstances of its emergence as well as of its art.

Even if the vast majority of detective novels hardly merit in their own right the close scrutiny of traditional normative criticism, the questions they raise are important and various enough to invite a combination of critical approaches. However, if one assumes, as I do, that the most fruitful approach is to be derived from the character of the works themselves, then it is clear that in the case of the detective novel the Formalist / Structuralist method needs to be supplemented by a criticism more attentive to the reading experience. Given that detective novels consciously set out to please their readers in their own peculiar way, a reader-centered approach promises to illuminate more fully the genre's hold on the popular imagination.

The importance of reader-centered criticism, of the type associated in the United States with Stanley Fish and in France with Roland Barthes of *S/Z* and *Le Plaisir du texte*,[8] is that its concern is not with works regarded as static artifacts from the point of view of their end but with the complexity of the reading experience such works elicit. Structuralism, like more traditional criticisms, tends to ignore the reader's active role in the processing of a text, in the task of constructing, dismantling, and reconstructing hypotheses relative to the meaning and direction of the work in question. The approach of Fish, like that of Barthes, on the other hand, has the advantage of regarding meaning not as something present in a literary text to be extracted like ore from a mine but as located instead in the transaction occurring between a text and a reader, whenever a work is read.

And if such is the case for the major works of the literary canon, it is even more obviously so for the minor genre of the detective novel. The point of Stanley Fish's now celebrated title, *Self-Consuming Ar-*

8. (Paris: Editions du Seuil, 1970), and (Paris: Editions du Seuil, 1973).

tifacts,[9] is not only that works of literature use themselves up in the course of being read but also that reading itself is a form of consumption. And even more clearly than other narrative genres, the detective novel is created to feed an appetite in such a way that by the time it is read to the end nothing of the original novel remains except the paper it is written on and the memory of pleasure or disappointment. Detective novels are the most blatant examples of throwaway literature. They are books to leave behind in trains or vacation homes because in most cases their only "meaning" is in the first reading of them. If we are to explain the genre's hold over its vast public, therefore, we need to know *what* a work does to a reader while he reads it and *how* it does what it does.

Writing in the 1940s, Raymond Chandler sketched out the kind of work that was needed: "Neither in this country nor in England has there been any critical recognition that far more art goes into these books at their best than into any number of fat volumes of goosed history or social-significance rubbish. The psychological foundation for the immense popularity with all sorts of people of the novel about murder or crime or mystery hasn't been scratched. A few superficial and a few frivolous attempts but nothing careful and cool and leisurely."[10] And although there have been a number of interesting studies over the intervening decades,[11] it still seems to me true that the genre has not yet had the serious attention it deserves.

It is in any case in the spirit suggested by Chandler that the present work has been conceived. It is not necessarily designed for fans of detective stories and it does sometimes employ a critical vocabulary not usually associated with histories of the genre. However, the interest of the approach adopted resides, I hope, in the suggestion that so many human activities normally considered in isolation are associated

9. *Self-Consuming Artifacts: The Experience of Seventeenth Century Literature* (Berkeley: University of California Press, 1972).

10. Quoted by Frank MacShane, *The Life of Raymond Chandler* (London: Jonathan Cape, 1976), p. 138.

11. Apart from the works by Cawelti, Murch, Symons, and Boileau-Narcejac, there is David I. Grossvogel's recent book, *Mystery and Its Fictions: From Oedipus to Agatha Christie* (Baltimore: The Johns Hopkins University Press, 1979). As his title suggests, however, he is concerned only tangentially with detective stories, and apart from brief chapters on Agatha Christie and Edgar Allan Poe, he concentrates on works from the highbrow canon.

at deeper levels. The books we read, the movies we watch, the games we play, and the research we engage in all afford insights into certain constants of our affective life. In short, reading fiction is mysterious not least because, like sex, war, science, and chess in their more specific ways, it stimulates physiological reactions that range from the tears of popular romance to the tumescence of pornography.

PART I:
ART

1

Crime Literature

Historians of detective literature may be differentiated according to whether they take the long or the short view of their subject. Those taking the long view claim that the detective is as old as Oedipus and serendipity or at least eighteenth-century China.[1] Those maintaining the short view assume that detective fiction did not appear before the nineteenth century and the creation of the new police in Paris and London, that its inventor, in the 1840s, was Edgar Allan Poe, and that it reached its golden age in the opening decades of the twentieth century with the nonviolent problem novel.

Clearly a case may be made for both views that chiefly depends on the preliminary definition adopted, but the view preferred will also be conditioned by the way one evaluates the representation of crime in literature. In order to understand the significance of detective literature, it is therefore useful to consider briefly its relationship to the much larger and vaguer category of crime literature.

Some confusions may be cleared up at the outset by acknowledging that the crime represented in literature takes two fundamentally different forms, a circumstance confirmed by the fact that to speak of crime in our modern generic sense before the eighteenth century is in itself to be guilty of an anachronism.[2] The kind of "crime" associated with

1. A French critic, Fereydown Hoveyda, concludes that the origins of the genre "are lost in the mists of time" and finds elements of the detective story in the early Hebrew tradition, in Bedouin and American Indian legends, Celtic folklore, Herodotus, and *The Thousand and One Nights. Histoire du roman policier* (Paris: Les Editions du Pavillon, 1965), pp. 38–40.

2. See G. Elton's essay, "Crime and the Historian," in *Crime in England*, ed. J. S. Cockburn (London: Methuen, 1977), pp. 38–40.

Oedipus Rex and Greek tragedy in general is mythic crime. And the same is true of Elizabethan or seventeenth-century classical theater, of Shakespeare and Racine. Incest, murder, rape, and maiming in such literary traditions occur in a context defined by the sacred. That is to say, the crimes committed by an Oedipus, a Macbeth, an Othello, or a Phèdre have the unexpungeable character of sins or of transgressions against a suprahuman order. The deeds represented are the work of legendary figures whose exemplary destinies are designed to illuminate human limits and hidden cosmic purposes. Such characters, in any case, have the stature of demigods, remote in time and place, rank and experience, from the lives of the audiences who witness their fates. Their deeds may inspire dread and have archetypal significance; they do not touch average lives directly in the same way as does that profane crime encountered on country highways and city streets.

A literature that took profane crime as its sole subject matter had, of course, flourished alongside the canonical works of our literary tradition as ephemeral popular pieces, which in the seventeenth and eighteenth centuries took the form of street ballad, broadsheet, and chapbook.[3] At the same time, from the sixteenth century on the representation of mundane criminal activities also achieved the dignity of printed books as occasional episodes in a picaro's progress. Rogue literature, however, celebrated not so much the criminal as the trickster, the man who lives narrowly within the margins of the law but who, in his determination to survive in a harsh world, trades deceit for deceit and in the end gives more than he gets. The picaro is the Renaissance prototype of the modern confidence man rather than a criminal as such. Moreover, his female equivalent was the resourceful whore. And in such subtly censored avatars of the whore's progress from *Moll Flanders* and *La Vie de Marianne* to *Manon Lescaut*, the European novelists celebrated the energies of lives lived either within or on the margins of crime.

In eighteenth-century England the criminal careers of Jonathan Wild and Jack Sheppard, Dick Turpin and Dick King, furnished material for the literary representation of real crime at all levels, from that of Defoe, Fielding, and Gay down to broadsheet and ballad. In the latter

---

3. See Victor E. Neuburg, *Popular Literature: A History and Guide* (London: Penguin Books, 1977), chaps. 2 and 3.

form such works supplemented the still popular romances of Robin Hood and gave rise to a comparable notoriety for their subjects. In the present context, the significance of such criminal heroes resides in the fact that they have recognizable local origins and that, in the case of the highwaymen, their legendary status is founded to a large extent on their resistance to constituted authority. Hence they have something of the character of social bandits in the sense Eric Hobsbawn has given to the term,[4] that is to say, of rebels against what was widely perceived to be an unjust social order.

In the serious literature of the romantic period the representation of crime appears in three fundamentally different forms. First, there is the demonic crime of the gothic tradition, crime that is only apparently supernatural in character and occurs preferably in isolated, medieval sites. Second, there is the continued representation of sacred crime in the figures of such reevaluated mythic rebels as Cain and Prometheus. And finally there is a kind of profane crime that is quasi-political in character. From Schiller's *Robbers* to Hugo's *Hernani*, romantic poets dramatized the careers of heroes who made themselves social bandits as acts of political protest. In the latter case, the outlaws involved are typically neither rogues nor sadistic monsters nor common criminals but nobles or noble souls who are victims of usurpations or other acts of injustice. Their purpose is the overthrow of tyranny. The representation of the lives of common criminals at a level above that of the broadsheet or *The Newgate Calendar* had to wait both for the effects of the new humanitarianism of the late eighteenth and early nineteenth centuries to be absorbed, and for the coming of the protorealism that flourished in the 1820s and 1830s in France and England in the form of sketches of average life. But before I look briefly at two such representative writers of the new democratic age in literature as Dickens and Victor Hugo, it is worth considering William Godwin's *Caleb Williams* as an example of the way in which late eighteenth-century English radical thought shaped a crime novel to its vision. In its handling of the themes of crime, punishment, and the

4. " . . . peasant outlaws whom the law and the state regard as criminals, but who remain within peasant society, and are considered by their people as heroes, as champions, avengers, fighters for justice, perhaps even leaders of liberation, and in any case as men to be admired, helped and supported." *Bandits* (New York: Delacorte Press, 1969), p. 13.

law, not only does Godwin's novel provide a striking contrast with the detective fiction of the following century, it also sums up some important late eighteenth-century attitudes.

Published in 1794, *Caleb Williams* is a hybrid work that combines some of the characteristics of a radical social novel with elements of the gothic and the picaresque in its settings, and of melodrama in its situation. As Godwin himself acknowledged in a subsequent preface, it was originally conceived as a tale of persecution that found a model for its plot and its strong effects in the Bluebeard story.[5] Moreover, it was deliberately constructed to promote the kind of suspense later associated with melodrama. Yet unlike most melodrama it finds motivations for its effects in class codes of conduct and in the sociopolitical institutions of eighteenth-century England. Godwin's work is important in the present context because it is a crime novel in the sense I have given to that term here. That is to say, it adopts the point of view not of the pursuing agents of law enforcement but of their wrongly accused quarry; it takes the form of a pursuit drama in which the hero, who is also the narrator, is an innocent if overcurious victim, forced to flee the persecutions of a secret murderer. The work's sociopolitical dimension is to be found in the circumstance that makes the victim a member of the educated servant class and the criminal tormentor his employer and member of the English landed gentry.

Godwin's radicalism appears in his representation of that "Tory despotism" which had obtained in the English countryside since the Tudors. Thus Godwin represents the experience of prison life in order to inveigh against an unequal justice that is indifferent to human suffering: " 'These, said I, 'are the engines that tyranny sets down in cold and serious meditation to invent. This is the empire that man exercises over man' . . . 'Thank God,' exclaims the Englishman, 'we have no Bastile! Thank God, with us no man can be punished without a crime!' Unthinking wretch! Is that a country of liberty, where thousands languish in dungeons and fetters?'' (p. 209).

Because of his social station Mr. Falkland is able to manipulate the forces of the law in order to have the possessor of his guilty secret,

---

5. See "Godwin's Own Account of *Caleb Williams*," in *The Adventures of Caleb Williams or Things as They are*, ed. George Sherburn (New York: Holt, Rinehart and Winston, 1965), p. xxix.

the young Caleb Williams, first incarcerated and then pursued from hiding place to hiding place. As a result, not only does Godwin's novel have the gripping character of nightmare, it also sets out to expose the machinery of eighteenth-century English law enforcement in its various elements from the class character of the judgments of the justices of the peace and the slowness and expense of the processes of law, to the squalor of prison life and the criminal connections of those "thief-takers" who in the days before the creation of a professional police constituted along with parish constables the sole agents of the law. Godwin's work is interesting not least because it suggests both the scorn widely felt for those forerunners of the detectives, the "thief-takers," and the sympathy experienced for the class of outlaw who lived outside the law because of the blatant injustice of the law. On the one hand, there is the disgraced member of a robber band, Gines, who turns from "the liberal and manly profession of a robber" to "the sordid and mechanical occupation of a blood-hunter" (p. 303). And, on the other hand, there is Captain Raymond, the chief of the robber band himself, who speaks with the authentic voice of social banditry in the tradition of Robin Hood: " 'We, who are thieves without a license, are at open war with another set of men, who are thieves according to law! . . . Since by the partial administration of our laws, innocence, when power was armed against it, had nothing better to hope for than guilt, what man of true courage would fail to set these laws at defiance, and, if he must suffer by their injustice, at least take care that he had first shown contempt of their yoke?' " (pp. 251, 256).

Finally, *Caleb Williams* also suggests the form taken by the popular literature of crime in the age before penny dreadfuls and dime novels. Godwin makes it the fate of his hero to become a legend in his time, like Don Quixote. He learns "from the mouth of a hawker who was bawling his wares" that he has become the notorious protagonist of ballads and broadsheet literature: " 'Here you have the MOST WONDERFUL AND SURPRISING HISTORY, AND MIRACULOUS ADVENTURES OF CALEB WILLIAMS: you are informed how he first robbed, and then brought false accusations against his master; as also of his attempting divers times to break out of prison.' " (pp. 311–12).

By grafting a social novel of upper-class crime onto a plot of melodrama, Godwin suggested the form a more serious kind of popular literature might take. In his handling of the theme of crime, he reveals himself to be related to that tradition of Enlightenment and utilitarian thought which came to regard the law itself, the severity of its penal code and its institutions, not as a defense against crime but as its cause. On the other hand, missing from Godwin's novel is the impulse to represent lives lived at all levels of the social order in the cities of the new industrial society. The turn toward a new urban realism, not only of the middle and lower-middle classes but also of the lower depths, had necessarily to wait for the effects of industrialization and the attendant population explosion to become fully manifest. And such was obviously the case by the 1820s and 1830s in London and Paris. In the decades succeeding the French Revolution, the increasing concentration of lower-class and potentially dangerous populations in urban centers was a matter of widespread anxiety on both sides of the channel. But for those writers sympathetic to the sufferings and aspirations of urban workers and the shiftless poor, these lives constituted new and potentially explosive material for their art. With novelists like Hugo and Dickens, therefore, criminal activity could come to be represented in a different light. Novels like *The Last Day of a Condemned Man* and *Oliver Twist* constitute a new kind of gallows literature that forces a radical rethinking of societies at whose center stood the guillotine of *la place de la Grève* or the gibbet of Newgate. Moreover, the criminal underworlds both novelists evoke are threatening in ways that the delinquent milieus of rogue literature never were. The crime of Hugo and Dickens is the profane crime close to home of a desacralized reality; its perpetrators are mostly ordinary, unheroic people for whom crime is an alternative to pauperism. Godwin's focus on law enforcement as a sociopolitical issue is joined to a realist preoccupation with the culture of poverty and the criminal underworld.

If I have singled out Hugo and Dickens as examples of the entry of the subject matter of crime into popular literature of a new and more serious kind—*Les Misérables* is, of course, the tale of a "criminal" that was one of the most popular novels of the century in any language—their works are no more than representative of a wide variety of crime literature. From early on in the nineteenth century, a preoccupation with the collective violence of war, revolution, rebellion, repression, and public execution, with crimes by and against the state, existed alongside anxiety at the random, individual violence of murder, rape, abduction, burglary, and street theft. And both kinds of violence are reflected in the popular literature of the time from the street ballad, the *faits divers* of the expanding popular press and such specialist journals as *The Newgate Calendar* [6] and the *Gazette des Tribunaux*—both of which furnished accounts of the lives, trials, and deaths of notorious criminals—to memoirs of such eminent French crime fighters as François Eugène Vidocq and Louis Canler or the public executioner Charles Henri Sanson. There also flourished the sensation novels in which such friends of Dickens as Ainsworth and Bulwer-Lytton specialized, and the *romans feuilletons* of an Eugène Sue and even a Balzac.

What in any case emerges from the mass of literary materials is a widespread preoccupation in European society with violent crime of all kinds, a preoccupation that was stimulated by the new technology of printing and distribution and that goes a long way toward explaining how the notoriety of criminals great and small would lead in the following decades to the appearance of a literary antidote in the form of the Great Detective. Before going on to consider the emergence of that heroic type in Western literature, however, it is important to remember the form a radical crime novel of the early nineteenth century could take in the hands of Dickens and Hugo. An instructive contrast may be drawn between the view of crime and law enforcement embodied in *The Last Day of a Condemned Man* and *Oliver Twist*, on the one hand, and in the detective story that first appeared in the 1840s, on the other.

Dickens, of course, was born of lower-middle-class parents whose solvency was frequently threatened and whose incompetence was expressed most clearly in his own eyes by their apparent willingness to abandon their son to life in a London workshop. As a result, his sense of the precariousness of average human lives and his own closeness to London street life, both as a boy and later as a law clerk and appren-

6. The full title of an early nineteenth-century edition is *The Newgate Calendar; Comprising Interesting Memoirs of the Most Notorious Characters Who Have Been Convicted of Outrages on The Laws of England Since The Commencement of the Eighteenth Century; With Occasional Anecdotes and Observations, Speeches, Confessions, And Last Exclamations of Sufferers.* By Andrew Knapp and William Baldwin, Attorneys at Law (London: J. Robins and Co., 1824).

tice journalist assigned to the law courts, quickly matured into an open hostility to the institutions of established society and a sympathy for its victims. In *The Sketches by Boz*, written by Dickens at the beginning of his career, the celebrated comic verve of some episodes is balanced by other far more somber images of England during the early industrial age. Such is the case in the sections entitled Gin-shops, The Pawnbroker's Shop, The Criminal Courts, and A Visit to Newgate.

Oliver Twist, Dickens's tale of an orphan boy, is a social novel contained in a fairy story. Yet its qualities as fairy story do nothing to undermine its power as a social novel; on the contrary, they enhance it. In this case, those childhood anxieties of abandonment by parents, which are commonly translated into the universal language of fairy tales, are given a concrete social dimension in the workhouse system created by the Poor Law Act of 1834. One historian has described the goal of the new law as follows: "Henceforth, 'out relief' would not be given to able-bodied males who, it was assumed, if out of work, were so for willful reasons. Relief was to be given only in workhouses, where the conditions were to be as 'disagreeable as consistent with health.' "[7]

And beyond the workhouse Dickens finds real analogues for the threats of starvation and exposure to witches or child-abusing adults in such contemporary social phenomena as the pauperization of the English working classes and the criminalization of abandoned children in city "rookeries." Dickens's novel is above all a crime novel to the extent that it represents the milieus and institutions of criminal society in ways recognizable from such roughly contemporary accounts as those by Patrick Colquhoun and Henry Mayhew. For long stretches of his work, Dickens draws on material similar to that found in the *Newgate Calendar* or the sensation novels of his friends and contemporaries. Yet he endows that material with a new seriousness by combining it with the realism of his popular sketches, and generates a dramatic intensity completely absent from the *Newgate Calendar*. The terror the novel promotes has nothing to do with gothic supernatural but unites instead the force of childhood nightmare with an imaginative sympathy for those threatened by violence, including certain

---

7. Ben C. Roberts, "On the Origins and Resolution of English Working-Class Protest," in *Violence in America: Historical and Comparative Perspectives*, ed. Hugh Davis Graham and Ted Robert Curr (New York: Signet Books, 1969), p. 259.

death. To reread the descriptions of the murder of Nancy, the hunting down of Bill Sikes, and Fagin's arrest and vigil in the condemned cell is to be made aware that the potency of Dickens's art is designed to confront evil with evil. By adopting the point of view of Sikes for a time, Dickens submits his reader to the strong material of sensation literature, but he does so in a spirit of moral seriousness absent from popular melodrama and penny dreadfuls. The representation of first a horrible murder and then a quasi-lynching of the murderer engenders an ambivalence of feeling that disconcerts. And a similar ambivalence attaches itself to Fagin, once the evil child-snatcher is transformed into a hunted creature gone to ground in Newgate's condemned cell.

Images of the mob that claws at Fagin and corners Sikes, like those of Newgate itself, linger beyond the epilogue of a reconstructed family and an idyllic rural retreat. Dickens incorporates into *Oliver Twist* a visit to the prison that had previously been evoked in *The Sketches by Boz* with the expressed intention of obliging his reader to reflect on its significance: ''Those dreadful walls of Newgate, which had hidden so much misery and such unspeakable anguish, not only from the eyes, but, too often, from the thoughts of men, never held so dreadful a spectacle as that. The few who lingered as they passed, and wondered what the man was doing who was to be hanged tomorrow, would have slept but ill that night, if they could have seen him.''[8]

In the age of Dickens, public executions, even if they had retreated from Tyburn to Newgate, still lent a dimension of reality to an act that was to become invisible by the century's end. It is noteworthy that no writer of detective fiction will face his readers with the spectacle of judicial punishment in the same way that Dickens does in *Oliver Twist*: ''Day was dawning when they again emerged from Newgate. A great multitude had already assembled; the windows were filled with people, smoking and playing cards to beguile the time; the crowd were pushing and quarreling, joking. Everything told of life and animation, but one dark cluster of objects in the centre of all—the black stage, the cross-beam, the rope, and all the hideous apparatus of death'' (p. 409).

A similar determination to confront his public with the reality of judicial murder characterizes Victor Hugo's *Last Day of a Condemned*

---

8. *The Adventures of Oliver Twist* (London: Oxford University Press, 1949), p. 408.

Man. The work is a long monologue that describes the feelings a condemned man undergoes on a journey from the pronouncement of the sentence of death down to the moment, some weeks later, when he is about to mount the scaffold, his hair cut in preparation and his collar removed. When compared with Dickens's work its effect on the reader is perhaps vitiated by the fact that, apparently in order to enhance the reader's sympathy for his condemned man, Hugo never discloses the nature of the murder beyond implying it was somehow justifiable homicide. And he chooses a criminal hero who in all other respects appears to be the essence of bourgeois respectability. Nevertheless, Hugo is even more direct than Dickens in confronting his reader with the evil of capital punishment: "Wretched man! what a crime I have committed and what a crime I cause society to commit!"[9]

Hugo's purpose is then to stir the conscience of the reading public. Like Dickens again, however, he also arouses widely pervasive fears. The most memorable scenes of *The Last Day of a Condemned Man* are probably those which describe the ceremony of inspecting and chaining the convoy of prisoners to be dispatched to the prison hulks in Toulon. Apart from the spectacle of the shackling of men in irons itself, what such scenes suggest so potently is the solidarity of a criminal countersociety whose existence constitutes a permanent threat to civilized order. Linked together by hand in the courtyard of Bicêtre, the five gangs of chained men begin to dance and sing: "They were singing a song of the convict galleys, a ballad in slang, to a tune that was by turns plaintive, wild and gay; and from time to time one could hear sharp cries and broken, panting outbursts of laughter blend with the mysterious words, followed by fierce applause. And all the time the rhythmic clanking of chains served as an orchestra to the song that was even harsher than the sound of the chains. If I were looking for an image of a witch's sabbath, I would not find one that was either better or worse" (p. 308).

The threat posed here is the threat of the *bas-fonds*, of that criminal underworld evoked in a somewhat different way via Fagin's den in *Oliver Twist*. It is noteworthy that not only do both authors describe

---

9. *Le Dernier Jour d'un condamné* in *Oeuvres complètes,* vol. 2 (Paris: André Martel, 1948), p. 339.

different aspects of the criminal institutions and manners of their times, they also introduce examples of underworld slang into their novels. The harsh wit of the invented language manages to suggest the degree of alienation from the values of respectable society—"My father married the widow [was hanged] and I am retiring at Mount Regretfully [the scaffold of the guillotine]" (p. 335).

Of the two novels, that of Dickens is, of course, a much broader social novel—Hugo was subsequently to produce a similar kind of social crime novel with *Les Misérables*. The strategy of adopting the point of view of an orphan boy for large sections of his novel enables Dickens to shift between two societies, that of the respectable world and that of the criminal underworld, and to suggest at the same time how the institution of the new workhouse effectively promoted the criminalization of the indigent. Insolvency, pauperization, the waiting criminal underworld, and the shadow of Newgate and its gallows come to appear as a threat that hangs over child and adult alike, a threat from which the melodramatic plot involving Oliver's half-brother Monk is largely an irrelevance, although it does provide a mechanism for furnishing Oliver with surrogate parents at the end. What Dickens suggests most memorably to his middle and lower-middle-class public is the evil of criminal society on the one hand, and on the other, the complicity of established society in expanding it by means of its social doctrines, laws, and institutions. *Oliver Twist* in particular embodies a critique of the prevailing social opinions of that established society in the turbulent early decades of the nineteenth century, opinions that one historian has summarized as follows:

> Englishmen and other Europeans of the time developed a set of beliefs that is still widespread today, essentially equating the "working classes" with the "dangerous classes" and arguing that misery, crime, personal disorganization, and rebellion sprang from approximately the same causes, and occurred in approximately the same segments of the population. The causes were the breakdown of traditional social arrangements and the demoralizing overpopulation of the great cities.[10]

In spite of its happy ending, therefore, *Oliver Twist* is a crime novel of a consciously discomforting kind because in representing both

10. Charles Tilly, "Collective Violence in European Perspective," in *Violence in America*, p. 21.

crime and its punishment, it raises questions about the existing social order, its laws, and its conception of social justice of a kind that detective fiction proper never will, at least until the American hard-boiled school of the 1920s. That moral seriousness which expressed itself in the political radical's sympathy for the victims of society's laws and institutions finds no echo in the central tradition of the detective story.

An important clue to the very different moral ambience of the detective genre is to be found in De Quincey's celebrated essay of 1827, "On Murder Considered as One of the Fine Arts." The relevant point in De Quincey's satirical piece is that it is a witty document of the early aesthetic movement which teases the bourgeois by divorcing the cult of art from morality in the most sensitive of areas. It purports to reprint one of the monthly lectures of a Society of Connoisseurs in Murder: "They profess to be curious in homicide; amateurs and dilettanti in the various modes of bloodshed; and, in short, murder fanciers. Every fresh atrocity of that class which the police annals of Europe bring up, they meet and criticize as they would a picture, statue or other work of art."[11]

What De Quincey does for the idea of the supreme crime of murder is to detach it from the social circumstances in which it is rooted in the romantic realism of Hugo and Dickens and isolate it as literary subject matter capable of sustaining the play of wit and irony. De Quincey legitimates the idea that discriminating pleasure may be obtained not from the sight of inflicted pain—he is no Sade—but from the spectacle of an artist at work in a medium that includes the human body. The shock of murder is no longer in the act but in its aesthetic treatment. The kind of literary murder De Quincey praises is the kind that appeals not to "old women" or "the mob of newspaper readers"—"they are pleased with anything provided it is bloody enough" (page 365)—but to amateurs of ideas and formal perfection.

In short, De Quincey expresses a way of regarding the commission of crime that in 1841 Edgar Allan Poe applied to the technique of uncovering the cause of crime. With "The Murders in the Rue Morgue," Poe invented the fine art of detection as a counterpart to

11. *Romances and Extravagances, De Quincey's Writings,* vol. 11 (Boston and New York: Houghton Mifflin, 1977), p. 529.

the fine art of murder. Dupin, too, is a connoisseur of crime, but his hobby is the production of elegant solutions. On the evidence of the most celebrated works in the genre, one might conclude that the appearance of the detective story had as much to do with late romantic attitudes and the aesthetic movement as with changing social realities and the new police. To conclude thus, however, would be to ignore the fact that the two are closely related.

2

Backward Construction and the Art of Suspense

Poe's first Dupin story, "The Murders in the Rue Morgue," constitutes the celebrated prototype of detective fiction as problem story for a number of reasons, two of which are crucial. In the first place, as I noted in chapter 1, it established the principle of the detective hero as amateur of genius, who is drawn to the solution of mysterious crimes as to a superior form of ratiocinative play. And in the second place, it furnishes a model of narrative art in which the denouement determines the order and causality of the events narrated from the beginning.

There is a wide gap between the social crime novel as practiced by Dickens and Hugo and the detective story of Poe. Apart from the whole question of the aesthetics of the novel versus that of the short story, there is the fundamental shift in content and point of view from the commission of crime and the criminal to the adventure of explaining crime and pursuing its perpetrator. Furthermore, Poe's influence on the direction taken by the genre is important because of his late romantic conception of literature and its function. His own aesthetics is a combination of philosophic idealism, whose interpreter for the English-speaking world was Coleridge, a consequent protosymbolist cult of art, and a hostility to democratic attitudes in all spheres, including the political. Such a combination of values appears most clearly in Poe's detective stories in the figure of his heroic investigator, Claude Dupin.

It is no accident that from his vantage point in Jacksonian America Poe makes his detective French and sets him down in the civilized cityscape of Paris. Dupin is neither a vulgar policeman like Vidocq

himself or his fictional equivalents in Poe's tales, nor is he comparable to the simple-minded newspaper editors of "The Mystery of Marie
Roget." He is fashioned, rather, in the image of the artist hero—solitary, studious, given to wandering the city streets by night, and above
all a thinker whose ratiocinative powers have been honed on higher
things than murder. If the Dickensian crime story derives from a humanitarian's interest in social problems and a realist's concern to explore the circumstances and possibilities of less than average life, the
origins of the main nineteenth-century tradition of the detective story
are to be found in a late romantic preoccupation with the nightside of
the soul and with the cultivation of the powers of mind beyond what
is normally thought possible. Dupin's super-rationality borders on the
supernatural. There is in other words continuity between Poe's gothic
mystery and romantic horror stories, on the one hand, and his detective tales of ratiocination, on the other. Both kinds of story usually
expose the reader to the strongest of effects, but whereas the former
is calculated to chill the reader's blood by exposing him to the experience of murder ("The Tell-tale Heart") or torture ("The Pit and the
Pendulum"), the latter employs the material of horror fiction with an
ironic matter-of-factness in order to celebrate the triumph of a superior
mind. Poe's first detective story inverts De Quincey's aesthetics of
murder by imagining a comparable art of detection, but in both cases
the central unsettling irony is in the simultaneous presence of extreme
brutality and an unusual refinement of taste and perception.

The importance of "The Murders in the Rue Morgue" from the
point of view of the art of fiction is that it established the precedent
for the genre in which the denouement determines the order and causality of all that precedes. It is a peculiarity of detective fiction that the
story of an investigation is made gradually to uncover the story of the
crime which antedates it. And the business of uncovering is made to
proceed via a series of steps that are carefully calculated with a view
to their effect on a reader. The writing process Poe describes in "The
Philosophy of Composition" in connection with his ballad, "The
Raven," was clearly applied to the elaboration of his first detective
story. He opens the essay by quoting Dickens on the subject of *Bar-
naby Rudge*, a strange novel that itself has elements of a murder mystery as well as of a novel of popular violence: "By the way, are you
aware that Godwin wrote his *Caleb Williams* backwards? He first in-

volved his hero in a web of difficulties, forming the second volume, and then, for the first, cast about him for some mode of accounting for what had been done."[1]

While doubting the truth of the case Dickens cites,[2] Poe accepts the principle involved: "Nothing is more clear than that every plot must be elaborated by its *dénouement* before anything be attempted with the pen. It is only with the *dénouement* constantly in view that we can give a plot the indispensable air of consequence, or causation, by making the incidents, and especially the tone at all points, tend to the development of the intention" (p. 453).[3] The primacy of plot in such a conception of the art of composition is clear. Yet the plot is not important for its own sake but for the emotions it enables an author to excite in a reader. Poe sought effects that were "novel" and "vivid." And to achieve such effects the author had to be aware of what the climactic moment of his poem / tale was to be, so that he could build toward it: "the poem may be said to have its beginning—at the end, where all works of art should begin" (p. 459).[4]

"The Murders in the Rue Morgue" is interesting because through the association of a theory of composition with a particular kind of material, a value system, and a heroic type, it made possible the rise of a new popular genre. Nevertheless, although Poe's tale is written backward in conformity with his theory—all the details of the double murder could not have been set down before the author had first determined the nature and method of his murderer—his view of "backward construction" is different from that of Godwin, and it is Poe's

1. Edward H. Davidson, ed., *Selected Writings of Edgar Allan Poe* (Boston: Houghton Mifflin, 1956), pp. 452–53.

2. Poe was, in fact, wrong and Dickens right: "I formed a conception of a book of fictitious adventure, that should in some way be distinguished by a very powerful interest. Pursuing this idea, I invented first the third volume of my tale, then the second, and last of all the first." "Godwin's Own Account of *Caleb Williams*," p. xxv.

3. Godwin's own version of Poe's point reads as follows: "I felt that I had a great advantage in thus carrying my invention from the ultimate conclusion to the first commencement of the train of adventures upon which I proposed to employ my pen. An entire unity of plot would be the infallible result; and the unity of spirit and interest in a tale truly considered, gives it a powerful hold on the reader, which can scarcely be generated with equal success in any other way" (p. xxvi).

4. Pierre Macherey sums up the result as follows: "its composition depending on a secret, the work is not at all what it appears to be—full of deception it presents itself as the opposite of its real meaning." *Pour une théorie de la production littéraire*, p. 33.

practice that was destined to become the prototype of classic detective fiction. After the prologue devoted to a discussion of analytical thought, it is "the web of difficulties" in all their circumstantiality with which Poe immediately confronts his reader. Accounting for those difficulties occupies the pages that follow down to the climactic moment of the unmasking of the murderer and the final explanations of the denouement. The effects achieved are both "vivid"—the murders involved are sufficiently gory to fix the attention and sufficiently mysterious to stimulate the fantasy—and "novel"—the detective is the first in a long line of artist / thinkers, the locked room provides a model puzzle for the genre, and the choice of murderer, an orangutan, has rarely been more outrageous. Yet none of these features would carry the strong charge they have in the story if Poe had not contrived to set them in a composition that plays upon the reader's sensibilities by first arousing his morbid curiosity, and having toyed with it for an appropriate length of time, by satisfying it in a wholly unexpected way. Apart from everything else, Poe taught his successors how to make their readers wait before providing the solution to a mystery and how valuable for achieving the effect of surprise was a first-person narrator who was not himself the detective.

Just as the example of Vidocq was not to be followed as an appropriate method for the investigation of crime,[5] Poe's art of composition also implies that Vidocq's memoirs are a poor model in the aesthetic sphere. The loosely combined series of episodes that constituted the popular police literature of Poe's French predecessor recalls the picaresque adventure novel rather than a taut tale of detection constructed around a single incident. In spite of Poe's having invented the formula however, it is clear why among his short works of detective fiction only "The Murders in the Rue Morgue" has been genuinely popular. Both "The Mystery of Marie Roget" and "The Purloined Letter" are either too painstakingly circumstantial and theoretical or too cerebral and lacking in action to appeal to popular taste—a stolen letter, as Poe himself was undoubtedly aware, does not excite an interest compara-

---

5. In "The Murders in the Rue Morgue" Dupin criticizes the Parisian police for their lack of method, and he comments: "Vidocq, for example, was a good guesser, and a persevering man. But, without educated thought, he erred continually by the very intensity of his investigation. He impaired his vision by holding the object too close." *Tales* (New York: Dodd, Mead and Co., 1952), p. 494.

ble to that of the death of a beautiful woman, an event that for him was "unquestionably, the most poetical topic in the world" (p. 458).[6] Poe showed how in fiction crime might cease to be regarded as a social problem in order to become a philosophic and even aesthetic one. Moreover, by putting the emphasis on the emotions to be aroused in a reader through the compositional manipulation of the material, Poe made explicit the aesthetics not only of detective fiction but also of popular literature in general down to *Goldfinger* and *Love Story*.

Yet he did not go on to explore more fully the possibilities of the genre he inaugurated with "The Murders in the Rue Morgue." And he was, therefore, a less popular writer than either of his two principal successors in the genre, Emile Gaboriau and Conan Doyle. Nevertheless, if from the point of view of the development of detective fiction the latter turned out to be by far the more interesting of the two, it is because he is the one who most thoroughly assimilated Poe's technique of composition. Whereas Gaboriau is closer to the example of Vidocq and the sprawling *feuilleton* novel of writers such as Eugène Sue, Doyle's well-told tales suggest what was possible in the genre when practiced by a writer more attuned to popular taste in his time than Poe had been in his. It is noteworthy in this connection that before he ever attempted to write a detective work of novel length, Doyle followed Poe's preference for short works of high intensity by writing five volumes of stories.

Apart from a type of heroic detective, what Doyle acquired above all from Poe was an art of narrative that promotes the reader's pleasure through the calculation of effects of suspense on the way to a surprise denouement. Moreover, the effects of suspense involved depend on the step-by-step process of rational inquiry. The traditional suspense of fear—either fear of threatened disaster, which characterizes tragedy or melodrama, or fear of love unfulfilled, which is central in romance or romantic comedy—is largely supplanted in "The Murders in the Rue Morgue" by the suspense of an unanswered question. Mysterious circumstances are adduced right at the beginning in order to trigger the reader's desire to know the cause. Except in the most cerebral and nonviolent works in the genre, however, there is some combination of the two forms of suspense; the desire to know "whodunit"

6. *Selected Writings*, p. 458.

is excited alongside the fear that whoever it was might repeat his crime.

All narrative, from the most popular to the most subtle, from Ian Fleming to Henry James, traditionally depends for its success with a reader to some extent on its power to generate suspense. Suspense involves, of course, the experience of suspension; it occurs wherever a perceived sequence is begun but remains unfinished. And it may be present in verbal forms at all levels, from a sentence to a full-length novel—something that accounts for the urge felt by listeners to complete other people's dangling sentences. Suspense, as we know from the example of a rhythmically dripping tap, is a state of anxiety dependent on a timing device. And the particular device employed in the detective story is related to its peculiarity of structure mentioned above. In the process of telling one tale a classic detective story uncovers another.[7] It purports to narrate the course of an investigation, but the "open" story of the investigation gradually unravels the "hidden" story of the crime. In other words, the initial crime on which the tale of detection is predicated is an end as well as a beginning. It concludes the "hidden" story of the events leading up to itself at the same time that it initiates the story of the process of detection.

Consequently, there is involved one of those displacements of chronological time which for the Russian Formalists distinguished the art of plotting from the raw material of fable. The effect of the crime is revealed before the statement of its causes. This means that detective fiction is preoccupied with the closing of the logico-temporal gap that separates the present of the discovery of crime from the past that prepared it. It is a genre committed to an act of recovery, moving forward in order to move back. The detective encounters effects without apparent causes, events in a jumbled chronological order, significant

---

7. Raymond Chandler made the point in an essay first published in the *Saturday Evening Post* on March 11, 1939: "Yet, in its essence the crime story is simple. It consists of two stories. One is known only to the criminal and to the author himself. It is usually simple, consisting chiefly of the commission of a murder and the criminal's attempts to cover up after it. . . . The other story is the story which is told. It is capable of great elaboration and should, when finished, be complete in itself. It is necessary, however, to connect the two stories throughout the book. This is done by allowing a bit, here and there, of the hidden story to appear." Frank MacShane, ed., *The Notebooks of Raymond Chandler* (London: Weidenfeld and Nicolson, 1976), p. 42.

clues hidden among the insignificant. And his role is to reestablish sequence and causality. Out of the *nouveau roman* of the offered evidence he constructs a traditional readable novel that ends up telling
the story of the crime.

A classic detective novel may be defined, then, as a work of prose
narrative founded on the effort to close a logico-temporal gap. Writing
about the gothic tradition, Macherey observes, "The movement of the
novel is double, since it must first hide before it reveals its mysteries.
Right until its end the secret must weigh on the imagination or the
reason of its hero, and the whole course of the story concerns the description of this wait as well as its creation" (p. 40). The appeal of
both gothic and detective novels, on the other hand, depends on the
fact that closure of the logico-temporal gap referred to does not occur
right away but only after significant delay. That state of more or less
pleasurable tension concerning an outcome, which we call suspense,
depends on something not happening too fast. In other words, the detective story formula offers a remarkably clear example of the crucial
narrative principle of "deliberately impeded form."[8]

The sharpness of the anxiety felt by the reader of a novel as a consequence of an unresolved and therefore suspenseful situation varies
enormously. It depends on such factors as the length of time elapsed
between the initial moves in a sequence and the approach to a conclusion, the sympathy evoked for the characters concerned, the nature of
the threat represented by the obstacles, or the desirability of the goal.
There is obvious suspense as long as imminent danger goes uncon-
tained, but there is also suspense where an orphan is without parents,
a lover without his loved one, or a problem without a solution. The
need for the relief from tension which comes with a concluding term
is felt in such situations just as much as in those that threaten violence
or death.

If, of all the literary genres, detective fiction, along with melodrama
in general, depends for its success primarily on the power to generate
suspense, it is also clear that the key device employed in its production is a form of impediment. More obviously than most other fiction
or drama, a detective novel is composed of two contradictory impul-

---

8. See Victor Erlich's discussion of this concept in *Russian Formalism*, p. 178.

ses. On the one hand, it is made up of verbal units that combine to close the logico-temporal gap between a crime and its solution. On the other hand, it also contains at least an equal number of units that impede progress toward a solution. Like all fiction, detective novels are constructed of progressive and digressive elements; they are at the same time concentrated and diffuse. There must be a journey but it must be circuitous and preferably strewn with obstacles: "The crooked road, the road on which the foot senses the stones, which turns back on itself—this is the road of art."[9] Without a journey you have *Tristram Shandy*, a riotous milling about among overlapping digressions, a tour de force of diffusion that has the form of a shaggy dog story. Yet with mere progression there is simply a rush to the pleasure of a denouement that turns out to offer no pleasure at all. Furthermore, the progression / digression dichotomy, which is as old as Laurence Sterne, has been revived by Formalists and structuralists. Boris Tomashevsky distinguished between "bound motifs"—those units of plot which form themselves into indispensable logico-temporal sequences—and "free motifs"—"those which may be omitted without disturbing the whole causal-chronological course of events."[10] Umberto Eco, on the other hand, writes of "fundamental moves" and "incidental moves."[11]

That an appropriately rich emotional response to dramatic and narrative works alike depends on some combination of the two elements may be illustrated from no less a source than Aristotle's *Poetics*. If the chief articulatory moments out of which a detective novel is constructed may still be usefully defined by the critical concepts of peripeteia, recognition scene, and scene of suffering, it is because these concepts are important examples of the contradictory impulses referred to. The first signifies, of course, a reversal, or the sudden tak-

9. Viktor Shklovsky, "The Connection between Devices of Syuzhet Construction and General Stylistic Devices (1919)," in *Russian Formalism: A Collection of Articles and Texts in Translation*, ed. Stephen Bann and John E. Bowet (Edinburgh: Scottish Academic Press, 1973), p. 48.

10. "Thematics," in *Russian Formalist Criticism: Four Essays*, ed. Lee T. Lemon and Marion J. Reis (Lincoln: University of Nebraska Press, 1965), p. 68.

11. "The Narrative Structure in Fleming," in *The Bond Affair*, ed. O. del Buono and Umberto Eco (London: Macdonald, 1966), pp. 53–56.

ing off of the action in an unexpected direction; the second, the passage from ignorance to knowledge; and the third, "a destructive or painful action, such as death on the stage, bodily agony, wounds and the like."[12] The end of a traditional detective novel is the recognition scene in the form of an unmasking and, in a manner to be discussed in a later chapter, the scene of suffering. Together they constitute the desired goal or solution. Peripeteia, on the other hand, refers to what is, in effect, a device of retardation on the level of the action, as Viktor Shklovsky noted: "the fundamental law of peripeteia is that of retardation: of the braking of recognition" (p. 66).

In a detective story peripeteia implies the sudden and unexpected postponement of the apparent approach to a solution. The gap that seemed to be closing opens again. Yet without such an alternate approach to and retreat from a recognition scene there is no suspense. It is therefore a central paradox not only of detective fiction but also of dramatic and narrative literature in general that pleasure results to a large degree from the repeated postponement of a desired end.

Of the many devices of retardation employed in detective novels, some are also features of other narrative genres and others are peculiar to the process of criminal investigation. Among those occurring in the detective novel but not necessarily exclusive to it are the following:

1. On the level of plot, there is peripeteia itself. That is to say, a discovery or event involving a deflection or rebound from progress toward resolution. Examples of this are parallel intrigues, including rival investigations or love motifs that intermittently suspend the principal investigation, and false trials and false solutions, i.e., solutions that apparently account for the data and are offered by a foil to the Great Detective or are assumed by him for a time to be accurate.

2. On the level of roles, there is the antidetective or criminal, who may remain passive and not impede the Great Detective's search or actively intervene in a variety of ways to prevent unmasking and capture. There are also other blocking figures, such as recalcitrant or confused witnesses, false detectives like Watson or Lestrade, who take time misrepresenting the evidence, and false criminals or suspects.

12. Quoted by Geoffrey Hartman, "Literature High and Low: The Case of the Mystery Story," in his *The Fate of Reading* (London and Chicago: University of Chicago Press, 1975), p. 203.

These figures first have to be unmasked before they can be proved innocent and the real criminal can be concentrated on.

3. On the level of character types, there are typically the taciturn Great Detective—in the interest of suspense his thought processes are not disclosed until the recognition scene itself—the garrulous assistant, and the more or less large cast of "characters" or grotesques, whose very oddness makes them for a time impenetrable.

4. On the level of content, there are the episodes themselves, which, as in adventure novel or odyssey, intervene in greater or lesser numbers between a given point of departure and a fixed destination. And there are also the false clues, which mixed together with the true clues make unraveling more complex.

5. On the level of formal elements, finally, apart from plot, it seems that almost any device in a verbal artifact may be employed to perform at a given moment the delaying function, from the episodes themselves conceived as formal units to the employment of a "perpetual idiot" as a narrator, passages of description or dialogue, narrative commentary, and authorial interventions.

The above list is not intended to be exhaustive, but it does suggest in ways not usually acknowledged that the art of narrative is an art of misleading or of tactical retreat before an advancing reader. Moreover, although a number of the devices are already present in Poe's first tale of ratiocination, others are exclusive to works of novel length. In order to illustrate some of the theoretical propositions made here, therefore, I should like to focus on three detective novels by way of example, only the second of which, Doyle's *Hound of the Baskervilles*, may be said to be directly inspired by Poe's story. Wilkie Collins's *Moonstone* derives from a hybrid Dickensian tradition, of a kind that combines a plot of mystery with social commentary, and Raymond Chandler's *The Big Sleep* owes a debt not only to that same nineteenth-century English tradition but also to various nineteenth and twentieth-century American writers in ways that will be discussed later. If detective novels are constructed backward and are made up of progressive and digressive elements for the purpose of producing suspense, how this operates in practice is best shown by reference to concrete cases that have the advantage of being both familiar and generally acknowledged as minor classics of the genre. They are in addition works that are sufficiently different in terms of period, narrative method, and length to encompass some of the genre's variety. Wilkie Collins's mid-Victorian novel runs to over five hundred pages in the Penguin edition, whereas Conan Doyle's Edwardian tale is a very slim volume and Raymond Chandler's late-1930s work is not much longer than two hundred pages. Finally, all three novels also illustrate that success in the field is not a matter of the mechanical combination of devices but of the purposeful rethinking of a formula.

The *Moonstone* begins and ends with the frame story of the diamond itself, its history, vicissitudes, loss, and restoration to a Hindu sect. The tale of the diamond contains that of its acquisition, troubled possession, and loss by the Herncastle family. And this story in its turn frames the central story of the jewel's inheritance by the Herncastle niece, Rachel Verinder, its theft, and the long frustrated effort to account for the mystery of its theft. At the same time, linked to the story of crime and investigation conducted under the shadow of a double curse—that of the Hindu god and the wicked uncle—is the motif of the interrupted courtship of Rachel Verinder by Franklin Blake. The disappearance of the gem drives them apart, and the explanation of its loss and its brief reappearance on its passage back to India make possible their reconciliation. In the end Collins's novel ironically reverses the action pattern of traditional folk fairy tales by making happiness dependent not on an act of repossession but on a release dependent on a definitive loss. The action pattern involved is that of the curse story.

Such a brief outline of the novel's principal motifs and structure suggests the work's complexity. And the complexity is increased still further by a narrative apparatus of astonishing cumbersomeness. The Victorian novelist has his story told by no fewer than five different narrators and fills out the remaining details by means of six further letters and statements. The effect is certainly one of looseness and bagginess of the kind Henry James deplored in a novel. Yet the cumbersome structure is also instrumental in generating the work's peculiar form of suspense. By fragmenting and deploying the material of his story in such a leisurely fashion, Collins paradoxically shows how self-conscious his narrative art is. His novel's structure is determined by the form of the double story. But the investigative task of closing the gap between the discovery of the theft and the known events of the previous evening is made more difficult than usual because there is more than one investigator. The "hidden" story of what led up to the theft and of the scene of suffering, constituted by the events of the mysterious night in the young woman's room, takes a long time to get told because the story's progressive elements are for long periods overwhelmed by digressive elements of all kinds. Detection has never been made to appear more difficult than in the novel that T. S. Eliot held to be "the first and greatest of English detective novels."[13]

The devices of retardation employed by Collins include most of those listed above. On the level of the plot, there are too many peripeteias to need emphasizing here, but it will be recalled that *The Moonstone* contains one of the most unexpected recognition scenes in detective writing since *Oedipus Rex,* namely Franklin Blake's discovery that he himself is apparently guilty of the theft whose perpetrator he was pursuing. And there is also the important subplot of the interrupted courtship, which ironically provides the motive for bringing the investigation to a close at the same time that it postpones closure by virtue of the space occupied by its narration. Finally, still on this level, there are the various false solutions proposed to account for the apparent facts, including that of the blundering local policeman, Superintendent Seegrave—it was the Indian jugglers aided by an inside accomplice—that of the great Sergeant Cuff—it was Rachel Verinder herself helped by her maid and ex-thief, Rosanna Spearman—and that of Rachel Verinder—it was her cousin, Franklin Blake, which though literally true is morally false, since he was unconscious of his actions at the time.

On the level of roles, there are the false detectives (Seegrave and Cuff as well as the various narrators who function as interpreters of events), the false criminals, whose mysterious conduct makes their innocence difficult to establish (the Indians, Rosanna Spearman, Rachel Verinder, Franklin Blake), and the recalcitrant witnesses (Rosanna Spearman, Rachel Verinder, and Doctor Candy).[14] As for the large and varied cast of characters, many of them have that Victorian large-

13. "Wilkie Collins and Dickens," in *Selected Essays*, ed. (London: Faber, 1951), p. 464.

14. It is, of course, possible for a given character to perform more than one role, as Vladimir Propp shows in *Morphology of the Folktale* (Bloomington: Indiana Research Center in Anthropology, 1958). His term for the phenomenon is "assimilation."

ness one might expect from a close friend and collaborator of Dickens.

One of the most original features of Collins's novel, however, is the way he combines the portrayal of character with the formal problem of narration. If the story of the investigation takes so long to get told in *The Moonstone,* it is partly because Collins enjoys employing naive narrators, of whom the two most notable are the Shandean figure of the loyal family retainer, Betteredge, and the evangelical Miss Clack. Betteredge in particular is equipped with many of the qualities of Sterne's Tristram, including garrulousness, a tendency to ride hobbyhorses, a fondness for digression, and a preoccupation with the difficulty of story telling. The usefulness of the device of the naive narrator is that it provokes reader impatience by means of a legitimized waywardness.[15]

What chiefly sets *The Moonstone* apart from the tradition of the detective story developed by Poe and Doyle, however, is the fragmentation of both the narrator's and investigator's roles. Instead of a single elucidating intelligence placed at the center of the work and set off against one or more obfuscating foils, there are a number of figures who share the detective's role. And various limited narrators are made responsible for reporting sections of a whole that no single omniscient point of view can encompass. Both the story and the conduct of the investigation have an atypical complexity that largely justifies the postponement of the denouement for an unusually long period.

The technique employed by Collins, with his parade of more or less interesting, comic, and loquacious witnesses, is reminiscent of that staple of TV melodrama, the criminal trial. The advantage of the structure of the trial from a dramatic point of view is in the formal order it imposes on the raw material of crime and investigation. Not only does it involve the effort on the part of an investigator to establish the guilt of a criminal, the rules of due process function as so

---

15. The following is a characteristic passage of Betteredge's musings: "I wonder whether the gentlemen who make a business and a living out of writing books, ever find their own selves getting in the way of their subjects, like me? If they do, I can feel for them. In the meantime, here is another false start, and more waste of good writing-paper. What's to be done now? Nothing that I know of, except for you to keep your temper, and for me to begin it all over again for the third time." Wilkie Collins, *The Moonstone* (London: Penguin Books, 1966), p. 45.

many devices of retardation. A trial is a form of theater characterized by piecemeal revelation and the potential for startling peripeteias right down to the denouement of the verdict. Above all, its power of generating suspense derives from the measured and circumlocutionary processes of the law themselves. And Collins's success in *The Moonstone* largely depends on his having found narrative equivalents for those processes.

Compared with the circuitous trail followed by *The Moonstone,* the path from crime to solution recorded in *The Hound of the Baskervilles* is relatively straight but still crooked enough to excite suspense about the outcome. It has the typical shape of the classic problem detective novel and is narrated in the first person by Doctor Watson as observer and confidant of the great Holmes in action. It begins and ends in Holmes's rooms in London, involves for the most part an excursion to a particularly charged location, Dartmoor, and has a limited cast of characters from among whom the detective has to choose his criminal. Furthermore, after an opening chapter reintroducing the reader to the Great Detective, his manner and method, the problem in hand is posed swiftly in the second and third chapters; the specialist in mysterious crimes is confronted with a fresh mysterious crime. And, as in *The Moonstone,* the paraphernalia of the supernatural and the threat of a curse are employed to stimulate anxiety and point to the cause of crime in the false solution of the extrarational itself.

The Hound of the Baskervilles is thus structurally simpler than *The Moonstone* because it has a single narrator of fixed value throughout and because it has a single elucidating intelligence at its center. Nevertheless, in Doyle's 1904 novel, too, the telling is partly fragmented in the interest of the kind of creative deformation that produces suspense. As well as the simple first-person account by Watson as eyewitness, the fiction also involves him in the writing of letters to Holmes and in the keeping of a diary. And Watson's records are supplemented by an ancient manuscript and a newspaper report.

The functional significance of Watson in the Holmes stories generally resides in his performance of the dual role of naive narrator and false detective, or "perpetual fool." In the former role the limited range of his awareness is important for the coup de theatre of the recognition scene. Watson's average man's chattiness is the appropriate foil to the taciturnity of the detective genius. That is to say, what are referred to as the characters of "Watson" and of "Holmes" are to an important degree derivations from the functions they perform.

At the same time, in the role of false detective, Watson's presence is required to entertain and distract while the real business of detection is carried on offstage, either in Holmes's impenetrable mind or literally somewhere else. The most original device employed by Doyle in *The Hound of the Baskervilles,* therefore, is that of the absent detective. By having the false detective Watson assume the real detective's role throughout the middle chapters of the novel, Doyle ironically contrives to let confusion multiply and the threats mount right up to the surprise reappearance of Holmes in the guise of "the other man."

The absent detective is the most obvious device used to delay unmasking in *The Hound of the Baskervilles,* but many of the other devices typical of the genre are also employed. There is, for instance, the unfulfilled promise of a romance between Sir Henry Baskerville and Stapleton's supposed sister. But it is the pursuit of false criminals, chiefly by Watson, that is most important here. And as in most detective fiction the evidence is first made to point in the direction of a given character until a sudden reversal proves his innocence. Thus in Doyle's novel the butler—Barrymore—and his wife, the escaped convict, and "the other man" on the moor, who turns out to be Holmes, all come under suspicion and are then cleared of guilt either by dying or by being unmasked.

In spite of its slimness, then, *The Hound of the Baskervilles* affords a characteristic mix of digressive and progressive elements, including among the former the blind alleys and constructed anticlimaxes typical of detective adventure stories. Like *The Moonstone,* it is also characterized by a scene of suffering that is reenacted in order to catch the criminal. In both novels this scene precedes the recognition scene proper and makes possible the exorcism of the supernatural threat; through the reenactment of a painful experience a mystery is made to yield once more to science. In *The Moonstone* the long delayed surprise is in the demonstration of how under the influence of drugs an apparently guilty man may be morally innocent. In *The Hound of the Baskervilles* there is a similar demonstration of how an ordinary animal may be made to resemble an infernal beast. Reenactment of the original scene of suffering, but with blank bullets, also occurs in the penultimate chapter of Raymond Chandler's 1930s thriller, *The Big*

Sleep, as part of the shock denouement. And in the approach to denouement also, behind the new surface of hard-boiled realism, the basic elements of the detective formula persist.

The Big Sleep embodies the inherited detective formula because it narrates the story of a criminal investigation that fills a gap in time. It begins with the mystery of blackmail and of a disappearance and proceeds with great deliberateness through a series of peripeteias to a reenacted scene of suffering and a recognition scene with the power to shock. Although not so marked as in *The Moonstone,* the distance opened up between the crime and its solution is relatively wide in *The Big Sleep.* Consequently, it offers another, somewhat different example of the variety of rhetorical choices available to a novelist who sets out to sustain narrative suspense.

Of the three novels, *The Big Sleep* has the least complicated narrative apparatus, but it also has a plot involving multiple murders of a complexity at least equal to that of *The Moonstone.* Thus the novel is simpler than *The Hound of the Baskervilles* to the extent that it is narrated throughout in the first person by Chandler's Californian version of the literary detective, Philip Marlowe, but of greater aesthetic cunning because it takes the ironic form of an unnecessary journey.[16] It opens and concludes with a scene situated on the Sternwood estate in order to reveal that Marlowe need have looked no further for his criminal than the first character he meets after the butler on entering the Sternwood mansion, namely General Sternwood's psychopathic younger daughter, Carmen. The crooked path in this case turns out to double back on itself; the way out of the investigative maze proves to be right next to the way in. The important difference is that by the end the investigator's point of view on the scene he confronts has been profoundly modified. The journey may have been unnecessary as part of the effort to capture the criminal—Carmen even pretends to faint into Marlowe's arms in that first scene—but it is made indispensable for the moral education of the investigator and, even more importantly, for the appropriate aesthetic experience of the reader.

---

16. In describing the critical approach dominated by what he calls the "normative illusion"—"the normative illusion would like a work to be different from what it is" (p. 27)—Macherey comments, "The story appears literally superfluous because it exists finally in order to hide a secret with whose revelation it is fulfilled or annulled." *Pour une théorie de la production littéraire,* p. 28.

After Dashiell Hammett, Chandler constructs a novel that has the obvious form of a hunt or chase insofar as it follows the trail of clues in an unbroken chain from person to person and from place to place through the urbanized landscape of Southern California. From its beginning in *The Red Harvest*, the form taken by the hard-boiled detective novel suggests the metaphor of the spreading stain. The initial crime often turns out to be a relatively superficial symptom of an evil whose magnitude and ubiquity are only progressively disclosed during the course of the investigation. An important formal consequence of this is apparent in a work such as *The Big Sleep*, which has a large cast of characters, rapidly shifting locations, and an intricately plotted but episodic narrative structure. Philip Marlowe is always on the move, always encountering fresh situations and new characters that hamper his progress toward the solution of crime. In other words, among the principal devices of retardation employed by Chandler are stunning peripeteias and the proliferating episodes themselves. And the agents of his plot are blocking figures of all kinds, from the professional criminals and their hit men to corrupt cops, siren women, and that most recalcitrant of witnesses, a dead man.

It is hardly a matter of hard-boiled realism, in fact, if there are no fewer than six murders in *The Big Sleep*, two of which at least are committed for the sake of thrilling peripeteias by characters who have the smallest of parts. From the point of view of the art of narrative, the functional value of the discovery of a corpse is that it often represents the most brutal of reversals—murder, in spite of its repetition in detective novels, is always produced as a surprise—and the deadest of dead ends. After a death the investigative task often has to begin again. And similar peripeteias are produced by the blow from behind or the drugged drink which delivers the detective into the hands of his adversaries. One of the reasons why Chandler's plots are so complicated, in fact, is that in order to refocus suspense, Philip Marlowe's search is often broken off and relies on an outstanding clue or the surfacing of a fresh face before it can be resumed.

In Chandler's hands, then, the detective novel is seen to break down more clearly than in the formal detective story into a succession of independent episodes linked by an investigative purpose and a point of view. And it is because of its fundamentally episodic structure that a novel like *The Big Sleep* illustrates the apparent paradox that the progressive and digressive units of a narrative sequence are often one and the same. Every action sequence that occurs in a detective novel between a crime and its solution delays for a time that solution even when it appears logically required by it. Down to the level of a sentence, all telling involves the postponing of an end simply because articulate speech is linear and expresses itself in the dimension of time. It is a situation that the most interesting authors of detective novels have knowingly exploited.

More obviously than other narrative genres, the detective novel promotes the myth of the necessary chain. It implies that the only path to the destination that is the solution of a mystery is the step-by-step path of logico-temporal reconstruction. But the only genuine necessity in a detective novel is that minimum of impediments required for the production of the thrills of suspense and for the experience of sudden insight after blindness. Along with *The Moonstone* and *The Hound of the Baskervilles, The Big Sleep* confirms how the best detective novels are constructed backward and in the knowledge of the paradox that the circuitous and even painful path in fiction—"a detour that might be avoided"[17]—is also the path of pleasure. Thus in Chandler's novel the disclosure of Carmen Sternwood's guilt at the outset would short-circuit the whole reading experience designed by the author. Philip Marlowe is the necessary principle which joins all the intermediary links of the chain that brings the reader by a roundabout route back to the point of departure viewed now with new knowledge. For the novelist, to make his reader go the long way round is to make him feel something he would not otherwise feel. It is also, if more rarely, to make him learn something impossible to learn any other way, that is, by the experience of having lived through it.

Unlike the works of the two English authors, *The Big Sleep* appears to be in the mainstream of a twentieth-century American realism. It dispenses with the suggestion of the supernatural, situates criminal activity where it mostly occurs, in modern urban settings, points to the psychological and even socioeconomic causes of crime, and employs a tough-minded contemporary vernacular. In its technique, too, it shows a preference for dramatized scenes, dialogue, and description over narrative summary that is also characteristic of modern American

17. *Pour une théorie de la production littéraire*, p. 29.

realism. Yet what Chandler's example allows us to perceive is that even the familiar story-telling devices of realism are far from "natural" vehicles for the communication of meaning. The calculated narrative art of *The Big Sleep* makes clear how such apparently progressive features as description and dialogue are also digressive and manipulatory. That this is the case may be illustrated by a brief analysis of a scene from Chandler's novel. But first a word about description and dialogue in general.

Although the narrative techniques of the three novels under discussion vary in ways already touched on, the use made of description is similar, apparently because the character and function of descriptive passages in prose narrative remain relatively fixed. Unlike a painting, which may be said to "describe" a scene by presenting a spectator immediately with the impression of the whole before he is able to distinguish the parts, a verbal description offers the successive parts out of which the reader has to construct his own impression of the whole. We have to wait in order to find out whether the first details evoked will be extended, confirmed, or contradicted by what follows. That is, a verbal description has a temporal dimension and can be assimilated only by being read line by line down the page. By virtue of the fact that a reader has to wait for an end, a passage of description in a novel induces an element of suspense in the same way that a novel as a whole does.

Further, a passage of description is generally assumed to have a mimetic function. Yet unlike a painting, again, a descriptive passage is not framed and complete in itself. On the contrary, it occupies space in a developing narrative and therefore has the effect of preparing or delaying as well as of disclosing something. In other words, its role is at least as rhetorical as it is representational. Unlike a person or place described in an ordinary conversation, a character or scene evoked in a novel is in the first place a narrative device employed in order to get a story told in a particular kind of way. It is a verbal construct within a larger verbal construct and therefore can be made to signify in a variety of ways within the complex system of verbal cross-references that is a novel.

Traditionally, under the guise of simply denoting, descriptive passages have been made to connote. They do not represent so much as produce an image charged with a cultural meaning, an image designed to trigger recognition and efface itself instantly for the sake of its meaning.[18] In different ways, depending on whether they evoke persons, places, animals, or things, descriptions have for referents such abstract qualities as menace, cruelty, egotism, gentleness, sexuality, eccentricity, naivety, innocence, corruption, or nobility. And in detective stories in particular they are used especially to make the reader properly responsive to a promise or threat. The descriptions of the Shivering Sands in *The Moonstone* and of Dartmoor in *The Hound of the Baskervilles* are calculated to suggest the presence of supernatural forces and to stimulate a shudder of foreboding. In other words, as has been clear at least since John Ruskin, descriptions always orient the reader's feelings.

Nevertheless, in his discussion of the significance of realist description in "Un Coeur simple," the "effet de réel" essay,[19] Roland Barthes has argued that those descriptive details, such as Madame Aubain's barometer, which resist all attempts at critical recuperation into a theory of given work's symbolic order, are simply present to signify reality. They are there, so to speak, *because* they don't mean anything; they are examples of what Philippe Hamon has called a "thématique vide."[20] Whatever the status of such evoked objects in a realist tale, however, their function in a detective story is clear. Everything that is described or merely mentioned is significant because it has the status of a potential clue. Thus, where on the mimetic level a described thing may simply imply the density of unrecuperable reality, as Barthes suggests—"l'effet de réel"—on the hermeneutic level it is always either a clue or a false clue. It either contributes to the solution of the enigma or delays the solution by diverting attention. From the point of view of the art of narrative, nothing in a detective story is insignificant because at worst it will mislead. That is why descriptions which are not intended to reveal truths may have instead the function of hiding them. Whole passages such as those already referred to, describing the Shivering Sands and Dartmoor, as

18. Stephen Heath puts it this way: "The wealth of detail that constitutes a description in a Balzac text has for its final purpose a self-effacement before the social meaning that it is its function to signify." *The Nouveau Roman: A Study in the Practice of Writing* (Philadelphia: Temple University Press, 1972), p. 78.

19. *Communications* 2 (1968):84–89.

20. "Qu'est-ce qu'une description?" *Poétique* 12 (1972):465–85.

well as the opening description of the Sternwood estate in *The Big Sleep,* have the status of false clues. In the first two cases, the suggestion of unimaginable horrors is largely belied by the return to rationality at the denouements. And in the case of Chandler's novel, the opening scene is deliberately deceptive in the opposite sense; the vision of early innocence yields to the discovery of ultimate corruption.

Two representative examples of descriptions of characters may serve to illustrate some of the points made here. The first is taken from *The Moonstone* and concerns the great Sergeant Cuff, the second is a description of General Sternwood, Philip Marlowe's client in *The Big Sleep.*[21]

> A fly from the railway drove up as I reached the lodge; and out got a grizzled, elderly man, so miserably lean that he looked as if he had not got an ounce of flesh on his bones in any part of him. He was dressed all in decent black, with a white cravat around his neck. His face was as sharp as a hatchet, and the skin of it was yellow and dry and withered as an autumn leaf. His eyes, of a steely grey, had a very disconcerting trick, when they encountered your eyes, of looking as if they expected something more from you than you were aware of yourself. His walk was soft; his voice was melancholy; his long lanky fingers were hooked like claws. He might have been a parson—or an undertaker—or anything else you like, except what he really was. [p. 133]

> Here, in a space of hexagonal flags, an old Turkish rug was laid down and on the rug was a wheel chair, and in the wheel chair an old and obviously dying man watched us come with black eyes from which all fire had died long ago, but which still had the coal-black directness of the eyes in the portrait that hung above the mantel in the hall. The rest of his face was a leaden mask, with the bloodless lips and the sharp nose and the sunken temples and the outward turning earlobes of approaching dissolution. His long narrow body was wrapped—in that heat—in a traveling rug and a faded red bathrobe. His thin clawlike hands were folded loosely on the rug, purple-nailed. A few locks of dry white hair clung to his scalp, like wild flowers fighting for life on a bare rock. [pp. 5–6]

In all fiction of a broadly realist tradition, the portrait is a relatively fixed, conventional form. It usually appears when a new character is

21. Raymond Chandler, *The Big Sleep* (1939; reprint ed., New York: Ballantine Books, 1971).

introduced and may be defined as a verbal construct designed to leave the reader with a strong impression of a human or social type. It presupposes the selection of certain widely recognizable cultural signs that enable the reader to make the appropriate determinations. Depending to some extent on the importance of the character in the story, it runs to roughly a paragraph in length. It also usually fulfills the expectation that it will communicate certain kinds of information about sex, age, physique, size, taste and social situation, as well as some insight into moral character. Above all, a portrait in the realist tradition, like descriptive passages in general, strives to be memorable, something that, given the length of an average novel, is not easy to achieve. A portrait is a small block of prose competing for the reader's attention with an abundance of detail spread over two to five hundred pages of other prose. Both passages quoted above show the devices employed to achieve such goals.

In order to fix in the reader's memory the illusion of character, both authors resort to insistence and repetition. As Stephen Heath has noted about Balzac's descriptions, it is not so much a matter of "exaggeration, but rather an overabundance of sense" (p. 78, n. 23). Both Collins's and Chandler's descriptions employ a language that is rich in epithets and adjectival phrases and moves typically into hyperbole and metaphor in order to make itself visible—conventional metaphors in the case of Collins's Betteredge and more original ones in the case of Chandler's Marlowe. As a result, the two characters described are stimulants for the fantasy; they possess the storybook quality of the marvelous. In the first case, great age is combined with the idea of an ascetic leanness and colorlessness in order to connote the legendary wisdom of the seer or wizard. In the second case, age connotes the physical decadence and clear-sighted remorse of a life on the edge of death. Both figures are Dickensian grotesques who combine the cadaverous and the sinister in order to stimulate a reaction of fear and wonder. They appear early in their respective novels, and their function is clearly to embody the promise of revelations to be made— What enigma could resist the powers of divination of the strange and wonderful Cuff? What horror explains the expression of those "coal-black" eyes in the wasted body of General Sternwood? Both descriptions oblige the reader to linger over the possibilities they point to and function as important units in the hermeneutic code.[22] The careful but insistent detailing whets the appetite for disclosures that as a consequence may be indefinitely postponed. Yet descriptions are considered unpopular because they stop something from happening. They are regarded by a certain class of reader as obstacles to be circumvented or skipped on the way to the action. Nevertheless, sustained suspense relies on the frequent recurrence of this device of realist technique. Another such device is dialogue. It, too, takes the crooked path to knowledge.

Dialogue is employed at certain points by the three writers under discussion, but in relation to the length of their novels, it is used most extensively by Chandler. Dialogue is a principal device of narrative technique in the modern American realist novel chiefly for two reasons. First, it is believed to create an effect of greater dramatic immediacy than does reported speech or narrative summary. Second, it is considered to be an important feature of realist aesthetics because it performs a mimetic function. It represents directly the speech of characters interacting in a situation. Nevertheless, the legitimate realist endeavor to imitate levels of contemporary speech is subordinated to narrative ends in novelists like Hemingway.

In a detective story a dialogue most commonly takes the form of an interrogation of a potential suspect or witness by an investigator. As such it is an exercise ostensibly undertaken in the interest of truth and involves a stylized series of question and answers interspersed with narrative commentary, asides, and brief evocations of scene. Consequently, from a rhetorical point of view it embodies the principal of gradualness. Information emerges slowly, as the result of a step-by-step process of probe and response. The varieties of popular speech, like the different human, social, and regional values associated with them, are entertaining distractions that also postpone access to the knowledge desired. The frequent waywardness of ordinary conversations may be made to serve a delaying function, as Collins in particular shows. Garrulous or laconic interlocutors are as valuable as naive narrators in preventing a tale from getting told too rapidly for reader

---

22. In the theory of narrative codes outlined in *S/Z* Barthes defined the hermeneutic code as "the voice of truth." Its function in a traditional text was "to formulate the enigma and to lead to its solution." (Paris: Editions du Seuil, 1970), p. 24.

pleasure. In the detective novel the advantage of dialogue as a narrative device is, therefore, twofold. Not only does it enhance verisimilitude by emphasizing the mysterious opacity of people and the difficulty of detection, it is also another important means of promoting suspense.

The way in which the various devices of realist narrative technique may be successfully combined in a detective novel in the interest of suspense is apparent from a great many scenes in *The Big Sleep*. Chandler's novel makes particularly clear that satisfactory telling is an art of delaying which subtly disguises its effects. The short scene in Chapter 26 that narrates the poisoning of the small-time crook, Harry Jones, by the hired killer, Canino, illustrates the point very well. The scene is also a remarkable example of the apparent "naturalness" of Chandler's story-telling method.

In the first place, much of the scene's power derives from the adoption of the limited point of view of Philip Marlowe. As a result, the reader is put in the position of eavesdropping on a murder that takes place on the other side of a glass partition. The narrator is restricted to the reporting of effects perceived indirectly, leaving room for the play of the reader's fantasy and the drawing of appropriate inferences.

The scene opens slowly with the careful description of a run-down commercial building, the function of which is to connote squalor and charged menace.

> There was a tarnished and well-missed spittoon and a gnawed rubber mat. A case of false teeth hung on the mustard-colored wall like a fuse box in a screen porch. . . . The fire stairs hadn't been swept in a month. Bums had slept on them, left crusts and fragments of greasy newspaper, matches, a gutted imitation-leather pocketbook. In a shadowy angle against the scribbled wall a pouched ring of pale rubber had fallen and had not been disturbed. A very nice building.

There follows Marlowe's arrival outside an office and the overhearing of Harry Jones's voice:

> I froze. The other voice spoke. It had a heavy purr, like a small dynamo behind a brick wall. It said: "I thought you would." There was a vaguely sinister note in that voice.
>
> A chair scraped on linoleum, steps sounded, the transom above me squeaked shut. A shadow melted behind the pebbled glass. [pp. 158–64]

The passage is in itself a notable example of the way in which Chandler promotes suspense out of a mosaic of narrative devices. In sentences marked by their rhythmic variety, he alternates spoken phrases with sharp descriptive detailing, narrator commentary ("There was a vaguely sinister note in that voice"), and a suggestive simile in order simultaneously to foreshadow and to retard a violent denouement that the reader is led to expect, although he is surprised and shocked by the form it finally takes. Involved is a type of action writing designed to arouse a disturbingly mixed response. Placed in the position of a voyeur at a murder, the reader is submitted to the characteristic form of Chandler's hard-boiled irony that is wit in a context of cruelty.

The idiom employed in the dialogue itself is a picturesque and alien vernacular—alien at least to any reader likely to read to the end such stylistically sophisticated fiction—of the marginal world of gangsters and petty hoodlums. Apart from the standard "punks," "dough," and "blonde broads," there are words of criminal period slang such as "gat," "shill," "twist," and "Chicago overcoat," and phrases like "tapping the peeper" and "dummying up to you." But the entertaining novelty of the language is largely effective in the dramatic context because it functions as euphemism. What is overheard implies something like the opposite of what actually happens.

Chandler's art consists primarily in taking the conventional devices of narrative realism and infusing them with a tension-producing ironic power by his mastery of pace, style, and tone. He is unusual among writers of detective novels because he is aware that the most satisfactory way of impeding the rush to the denouement is to force the reader to pay attention sentence by sentence by virtue of the precision and energy in the prose—that "lightning struck on every page" of which Billy Wilder spoke.[23] The closing lines of the poisoning of Harry Jones by Canino provide a characteristic example of the rich texture and careful shaping to be found in Chandler's writing.

The little man begins by responding to the killer's apparent effort at reconciliation:

---

23. Miriam Gross, ed., *The World of Raymond Chandler* (London: Weidenfeld and Nicolson, 1977), p. 47.

"No," Harry Jones said. "No hard feelings, Canino."

"Fine. Let's dip the bill. Got a glass?" The purring voice was now as false as an usherette's eyelashes and as slippery as watermelon seed. A drawer was pulled open. Something jarred on wood. A chair squeaked. A scuffing sound on the floor. "This is bond stuff," the purring voice said.

There was a gurgling sound. "Moths in your ermine, as the ladies say."

Harry Jones said softly: "Success."

I heard a sharp cough. Then a violent retching. There was a small thud on the floor, as if a thick glass had fallen. My fingers curled against my raincoat.

The purring voice said gently: "You ain't sick from just one drink, are you, pal?"

Harry Jones didn't answer. There was labored breathing for a short moment. Then thick silence folded down. Then a chair scraped.

"So long, little man," said Canino. [p. 163]

The narrative elements of the passage are by now familiar. The actual dialogue largely consists of a few fixed phrases of Canino's normally employed to express conviviality but sadistically ironic in the context. The narrator's interventions, on the other hand, are limited to the precise notations of perceived phenomena, chiefly heard sounds, and to reminding the reader of his presence through the use of two ostentatious, hard-boiled similes that also confirm the approaching treachery. But for the most part the passage is constructed out of short declarative sentences ("A drawer was pulled open. Something jarred on wood.") that constitute a form of action commentary and that, as in a radio sportscast, give a blow-by-blow account of an event with a feared but long postponed outcome. The violent climax is made to appear all the more chilling because it is experienced only indirectly. Apart from the purring voice, the killer remains unknown and the killing itself is confirmed only when Marlowe examines the body and smells the cyanide.

The point of the whole scene is not what happens in it—the fate of Harry Jones, for example, is of no significance for the plot—but how Chandler makes it happen for the reader. The significance is in obliging the reader to play the role of reluctant voyeur, forced to await a violent climax. The scene embodies a remarkable lesson of how not to make something happen too quickly, if you want to elicit the reader's involvement. The spareness of action writing that hides the cunning of its craft clearly derives from the tradition of Hemingway. Yet the terse wit that defines the evil and makes the waiting pleasurable as well as painful is pure Chandler.

The power of promoting the suspense of fear is common to all forms of popular literature, dramatic as well as narrative. It is, for instance, acknowledged to be one of the chief defining characteristics of stage and film melodrama from the genre's beginnings in the French revolutionary period down to James Bond. One of the crudest examples of a device of retardation is found in early film melodrama. It involved typically alternating images of a young woman lashed to a track, on the one hand, with those of an approaching locomotive and a galloping posse, on the other. However crude the technique, it does indicate the indispensable element of all suspense in film or literature, namely that of witnessing an action evolve along a time-line toward a fixed point in the future that will signify salvation or rescue for the characters concerned.

One of the best-known applications of the cinematic technique of cutting to promote suspense is in *High Noon*. Fred Zinnemann's formal frame, reminiscent of Collins's broken courtship in *The Moonstone*, is provided by the motif of the interrupted wedding. Sexual consummation is made dependent on the successful resolution of an unequal combat in the street between gladiators, thus furnishing a double focus for suspense. But between the wedding ceremony and the postponed departure for the honeymoon, there occurs the relentless countdown to the shoot-out with the famous alternation of images of railroad station, hotel, sheriff's office, clock, and train. The rhythmic cutting that in this case was deliberately heightened by the music protracts the waiting and brings out into the open the patently erotic structure of melodrama.

Similarly, in the detective novels discussed in this chapter the various narrative devices have the primary function of preventing premature disclosure in the interest of suspense. Only a story that embodies an appropriate quantity of resistance in its telling is experienced as satisfactory; the longest kept secrets are the ones we most desire to know. It is a circumstance that probably explains why the short story has never achieved such widespread popularity as longer fiction or serial narrative; the reader's desire is gratified too quickly for the pleasure to be particularly intense.

Finally, what an analysis of detective novels also helps us realize is the centrality of suspense in novel reading generally. Reading fiction of all kinds is an activity which generates tension that can be relieved only through the experience of an end. All story telling involves the raising of questions, the implied promise of an answer, and, in traditional narrative at least, the provision of that answer in time. When the proper time for the provision of an answer will be in a given story obviously depends on a number of factors among which the most crucial is probably the writer's capacity to sustain suspense while convincing the reader that his digressions are pleasurable and purposeful in themselves. The shortest version of *The Hound of the Baskervilles,* one wholly devoid of digression, would be no longer than a grammatically complete sentence—''The murder of Sir Charles Baskerville and the attempted murder of Sir Henry Baskerville by a relative seeking to inherit the family fortune were solved by the distinguished amateur detective, Mr. Sherlock Holmes, assisted by his friend, Dr. Watson.'' Whatever else Doyle puts into his novel adds nothing to the announcement of a crime and the naming of a criminal, although it does involve the reader in the experience of strange and chilling possibilities. In other words, a detective novel's length is determined less by a supposed organic necessity inherent in the material itself than by the need to promote in a reader the excitement of some combination of the suspense of fear and the suspense of an unanswered question. Consequently, whether or not the length of a book is felt to be appropriate will depend on such extraneous factors as reading habits and the prevailing conventions in book production as well as on an author's skill. The minimum appropriate length is that required to generate the experience of suspense; the maximum appropriate length is that which is compatible with the maintenance of a reader's concern about an outcome without loss of his interest on the way to it.

What emerges most clearly from an analysis of detective fiction as opposed to that of most other kinds of novels is, then, that the art of narrative is always the art of withholding as well as of giving information. It is an art of timing that because of the nature of the novel as book is an art of spacing. Everything in a satisfactory traditional novel is placed by the author at a certain point between covers usually containing somewhere between fifty to one hundred thousand words, in order to be discovered there by a reader at the appropriate moment.

And in this connection, reading narrative fiction can be seen to involve a form of participation different from that of looking at a painting or even listening to music.

Reading a novel is an activity of decipherment and discovery that involves the physical task of following the printed sentence down the page with one's eyes and of turning over the successive pages. It is a painstaking search for revelations that may occur at any point on the way to a culminating revelation. Whatever a given work's subject matter, therefore, reading it always takes for its reader the form of the special kind of adventure that is a treasure hunt. With the turning of each fresh page, there is communicated the thrill of exposure to the unknown, to the possibility of danger or of reward. With each fresh paragraph, new clues may appear that lead on, however circuitously, to the buried treasure of the denouement. It is perhaps no more than a happy accident of Western technology that a novel in our culture has the physical form of a shallow box which opens from the side. A certain feeling for a book's buried treasure must have been felt by those who once arranged to have their own books equipped with clasps and keys. It is in any case the desire to discover the nature of a given novel's secrets that often drives us to complete it, frequently in the face of considerable odds.

3

Detection and Digression

There is ample testimony to support the view that readers of popular literature in general and detective novels in particular read compulsively. W. H. Auden claimed, "For me as for many others, the reading of detective stories is an addiction like tobacco or alcohol," an addiction he recognized through "the intensity of the craving."[1] And Roland Barthes implied something similar about the way readers read detective fiction in *Le Plaisir du texte*.[2] In that work Barthes distinguished between two major categories of texts, the *texte de plaisir* and the *texte de jouissance,* and made a passing reference to a third category, the *texte de désir,* which he mentions only to dismiss. It is to this despised third category that along with other forms of popular literature he assigns detective stories. They are *textes de désir* to the degree that they exploit the linear nature of narrative in order to stimulate end-oriented desire in a reader. From Barthes's point of view a run-of-the-mill detective novel permits none of the verbal excess or the play of the text which is the sign of a *texte de plaisir.* According to Barthes, the reader of a detective novel tends to behave like a schoolboy at a burlesque show; he is so aroused in his desire to see the female sex organ that he is tempted to rush the stage in order to help the stripper strip faster. Such a reader is therefore interested only in the plot articulations, in those major progressive elements, or bound motifs, which drive the story forward. Digressive effects, or free motifs, supposedly only bore him.

Yet, as was suggested in the previous chapter, suspense, which is

1. "The Guilty Vicarage," in his *Dyer's Hand* (London: Faber and Faber, 1963), p. 146.
2. (Paris: Editions du Seuil, 1973).

crucial to the pleasure of reading detective fiction, depends on devices of retardation that in many cases take the form of digressive effects. In fact, such classics in the genre as the three works discussed above achieve their status precisely because they possess some of the features Barthes looked for in a *texte de plaisir*. A reader is less interested in the truth that is behind the ambiguous appearances and will eventually be revealed than in the surface show. "The hidden beyond of things is less attractive than the fragile surface which never ceases to deceive," comments Macherey. And he adds, "The novel lasts as long as it manages to maintain appearances and thus denounces its true nature; it emerges from a highly ephemeral interval and is no more than an intermediary, an interlude, a *divertissement*" [p. 41]. The actual business of detection may imply narrow concentration on a task and end-oriented urgency. Its literary representation, however, functions only as a source of pleasure when the task in hand is constantly interrupted by a variety of devices and diverting features that are experienced as more or less pleasurable in themselves.

Moreover, it is on the basis of such features as well as on the compositional cunning discussed earlier that we make judgments of aesthetic quality. In his *Morphology of the Folktale*[3] Vladimir Propp ignores what he himself refers to as the aesthetic elements of the corpus of tales he analyzes, and the reason for this is clear. In order to uncover so convincingly the structural identity of all the tales on the level of the functions of the *dramatis personae,* he found it necessary to ignore all superficial differences. The result, as Levi-Strauss showed,[4] is that Propp's morphology is limited to the demonstration of similarity. His approach provides no critical tools for the analysis of difference. And such a lack is particularly evident in the structural analysis of a formulaic genre such as the detective story because the differences are precisely what appeal to connoisseurs. In the language of the Formalists, one important source of literary pleasure is in the artful deviation from the norm. In this respect, therefore, a detective novel is not less literary than a major work of the highbrow culture but more so. No other genre is more conscious of the models from which it borrows and from which it knowingly departs.

3. (Austin and London: University of Texas Press, 1968).

4. "L'Analyse morphologique de contes russes," *International Journal of Slavic Linguistics and Poetics* 3 (1960):122–49.

From Wilkie Collins and Conan Doyle down to Raymond Chandler, Georges Simenon, and Ian Fleming, the most interesting detective fiction is read in large measure for its differences, for its capacity to remain faithful to a tradition at the same time that it reinvents it in unexpected ways. As a consequence, given that crime and its investigation remain largely fixed, most of the novelty is to be found not in the progressive sequences of actions but in the digressive effects. As often as not, detective novels are appreciated for their free motifs more than for their bound ones. But it is important to realize that a successful novel is inconceivable without the presence of both. The art of literary detection depends largely on the manner in which we are diverted while we wait for the inevitable denouement. Crime solving is a vehicle making possible a journey whose stopovers are frequently more enjoyable than the purposeful approach to a destination itself.

Near the beginning of the second chapter of *The Maltese Falcon,* Dashiell Hammett devotes a passage to the description of Sam Spade rolling a cigarette.

> Spade's thick fingers made a cigarette with deliberate care, sifting a measured quantity of tan flakes down into curved paper, spreading the flakes so that they lay equal at the ends with a slight depression in the middle, thumbs rolling the paper's inner edge down and up under the outer edge as forefingers pressed it over, thumbs and fingers sliding to the paper cylinder's ends to hold it even while tongue licked the flap, left forefinger and thumb pinching their end while right forefinger and thumb smoothed the damp seam, right forefinger and thumb twisting their end and lifting the other to Spade's mouth. He picked up the pigskin and nickel lighter that had fallen to the floor, manipulated it, and with the cigarette burning in a corner of his mouth stood up.[5]

The questions raised by such careful reporting of a mundane act relate to its significance in the context. What possible purpose can such a description serve in a novel ostensibly devoted to the story of a criminal investigation?

It is perhaps surprising that at least four reasons may be adduced for its presence in the text. On one level, it performs the delaying function necessary for the production of suspense—it intervenes between the announcement of a death and Spade's departing to investi-

---

5. (1930; reprint ed., New York: Vintage Books, 1972), pp. 10–11.

gate it. Second, it is a minor example of a mimetic effect designed, because of its sheer banality, to induce the illusion of reality. Third, it contributes, as an element of montage, to the construction of a character called Spade—expertise in the rolling of one's own cigarettes connoting in industrial society the preference of the individualist and folksy do-it-yourselfer for the handmade. Finally, and most importantly, it is a passage that can be enjoyed in its own right independently of contextual function. It is an example of playful excess in Barthes's sense. On the level of representation, the description is conducive to reader pleasure simply because it evokes a manual dexterity satisfying to observe, and, on the level of pure language, it sets in motion a play of echoing lexemes and self-reflexive phonemes. In a single complex sentence Hammett finds a combination of words that mimic the adroitness of fingers performing a practiced task and the agreeable physical sensations excited by anticipation in a smoker through the concrete references to "tan flakes," "curved paper," "damp seam," a tongue that licks, and forefingers and thumbs that pinch, smooth, and twist. But it is important to realize that such enjoyment is also the enjoyment of language itself, which in this case is rich in echoing monosyllables—"tongue licked the flap"—and present participles—"sifting . . . spreading . . . rolling . . . sliding . . . pinching . . . twisting . . . lifting."

The paragraph, chosen more or less at random from Hammett's novel, is an example of a narrative unit of dubious structural significance. Yet it is clearly not redundant from an aesthetic point of view and by no means presents an obstacle to reader pleasure. Moreover, it is a narrative unit of a kind that occurs frequently in the better detective novels of all types. The authors of popular detective fiction are only rarely single-minded historians of actions. Like all popular writers, they are in the first place entertainers. And the quality and forms of entertainment they provide within the broad limits imposed by the genre vary enormously.

In this connection, it is important to remember that, in the English-speaking sphere, if Poe created the prototype of the short work of detective fiction, it was Collins who created a model for the detective novel, even if his particular kind of complexity appears unrepeatable. *The Moonstone* is remarkable because in it Collins invented a way of sustaining the reader's interest in his principal action sequence while at the same time serving up the heterogeneous incidental pleasures of the typical Victorian novel. And he did so by combining the forms and material of romantic comedy, comedy of manners, and mystery novel with those of the detective novel. *The Moonstone's* tortuous plot is unwound at such a leisurely pace, in fact, that the work's long delays are only occasionally interrupted by its strategically placed revelations. Like many an English detective novel since, it shifts for long periods out of the threat of an unknown evil into tenderness and satiric observation. *The Moonstone* is so constructed that the reader can have it both ways. It is a detective novel that is both container and contained. Like melodrama, at least temporarily it "reasserts the presence in the world of forces that cannot be accounted for by the daylight self and the self-sufficient mind."[6] Unlike melodrama, it also distances the menace of such forces through the play of irony. If Collins's work is more than a facile thriller, it is because evil, mystery, and horror are for long stretches dissipated by generosity, love, and humor. The threat of India and its sacred mysteries still hovers at the end, but it is a threat that is distanced. In the English foreground there is a victory for science and for benevolence.

No novel illustrates better the notion that tales of crime are read at least as much for their free motifs as for their bound ones than Wilkie Collins's *Moonstone*. It has an appropriate quota of crimes—apart from the all-important theft of the gem itself, there are a suicide and a murder—and its principal action concerns the investigation of crime. Yet Collins takes over five hundred pages to narrate a story whose chief events could be outlined in a paragraph. The obvious conclusion is that neither the criminal acts nor their solution constitute in themselves the work's raison d'être. On the contrary, the latter is located partly in the pleasurable / painful experience of suspense and partly in those many features of narrative that are without relevance to crime.

Along with manners, probably the primary digressive pleasures provided by Collins in *The Moonstone* relate to the representation of "character." If not an invention of Victorian fiction—the looming example of Shakespearean tragic and comic heroes is the most obvious model—"character" assumed an importance there of a kind that could

6. Peter Brooks, *The Melodramatic Imagination: Balzac, Henry James, Melodrama, and the Mode of Excess* (New Haven and London: Yale University Press, 1976), p. 19.

confuse the whole aim of the novel with the creation of ''character'' as such. And the reason for this is not hard to find. The representation of ''character'' may be made a vehicle for the ever-popular marvelous as well as for an extroverted and optimistic humanism that finds confirmation for its faith in great individuals. As Dickens showed most memorably, ''character'' is the expression of superabundant energy; human idiosyncrasy is the sign of the creativity of a nature that is rich and various, if sometimes sinister. In fiction it was above all ''character'' that was the focus of life's vitality, pathos, and humor.

The Moonstone is a novel of memorable characters not only in its principal narrators, Betteredge, Clack, and Franklin Blake, and its young lovers—who are enriched with temperaments and educations calculated to differentiate them from the stock figures of romantic comedy—but also in its other roles. The most memorable are Godfrey Ablewhite, the villain of the work and a nineteenth-century Tartuffe in the guise of a fashionable philanthropist; Rosanna Spearman, the reformed thief, who is also a deformed and rejected lover; Sergeant Cuff, the fallible but humane Great Detective; and Ezra Jennings, another victim of life and society's prejudices in the shape of a dark-skinned outsider and explorer of the nightside of the human psyche.

It is, however, chiefly in his narrators, Betteredge and Miss Clack, that Collins exploits the contemporary taste for the foibles of ''character.'' His narrative technique permits him to combine the pretense of functionality—each narrator supposedly makes his own contribution to the unfolding of the tale on the basis of his direct involvement in the events—with the intrinsic interest generated by stubborn human variety. As with the great Shandy, the reader's interest is divided between the story of the teller and of the telling, on the one hand, and the story he or she has to tell, on the other. In delivering their testimony, the two narrators are set up as representative types of a nineteenth-century English society rich in the endearing or vicious grotesqueries so central to the Victorian imagination. They are comparable comic types to the extent that they both embody a manic single-mindedness whose emblem in both cases is a single, very different book. Betteredge's cherished *Robinson Crusoe* is made to stand for the quality of generous faith that defines him, and Miss Clack's Bible for the antithetical quality of bigotry.

The pleasure Collins provides is especially in a humor that comments and evaluates. The level of that humor may be gauged from the following two short passages. The first is a projection of the persona of the amiable Betteredge, of "a sleepy old man, in a sunny back yard," reflecting on the married state. The second is the unctuous voice of Miss Clack commenting on the news that her beloved Christian philanthropist, Godfrey Ablewhite, is not to marry Rachel Verinder after all.

> We were not a happy couple, and not a miserable couple. We were six of one and half-a-dozen of the other. How it was I don't understand, but we always seemed to be getting, with the best of motives, in one another's way. When I wanted to go upstairs, there was my wife coming down; or when my wife wanted to go down, there was I coming up. That is married life, according to my experience. [pp. 43–44]

> And it was equally easy to recognise the welcome reappearance of his own finer nature in the horror with which he recoiled from the idea of marriage with Rachel and in the charming eagerness which he showed to return to his Ladies and his Poor.
>
> I put this view before him in a few simple and sisterly words. His joy was beautiful to see. He compared himself, as I went on, to a lost man emerging from the darkness into the light. When I answered for a loving reception of him at the Mothers' Small-Clothes [Conversion Society], the grateful heart of our Christian Hero overflowed. He pressed my hands alternately to his lips. Overwhelmed by the exquisite triumph of having got him back among us, I let him do what he liked with my hands. I closed my eyes. I felt my head, in an ecstasy of spiritual self-forgetfulness, sinking on his shoulder. In a moment more I should certainly have swooned away in his arms, but for an interruption from the outer world, which brought me to myself again. A horrid rattling of knives and forks sounded outside the door, and the footman came in to lay the table for luncheon. [pp. 298–99]

Both passages invite the reader's complicity in recognizing very different human qualities in the voices of the two narrators. The first finds a language to express an attitude of chastened folk wisdom of a kind that can proclaim, "I am (thank God!) constitutionally superior to reason" (p. 208). The second is a tour de force of satirical writing that appeals to the reader by employing the vocabulary of Victorian piety against itself.

What the above suggests, in fact, is that among other things *The Moonstone* is a remarkable comic novel. And as such it is typical of an important tendency in a genre characterized by an unusual degree of self-mockery.[7] It is, for instance, notable that *The Maltese Falcon* incorporates an important element of self-parody into its structure only a year after the hard-boiled novel tradition had been successfully launched with *Red Harvest*. John G. Cawelti has pointed out that Hammett's story material of a search for long lost treasure suggests an adventure story for boys rather than a contemporary crime story. But, more importantly, *The Maltese Falcon* has something of the character of a parody that possesses elements of Marx Brothers slapstick, as even some of the chapter titles suggest—"G in the Air," "Horse Feather," "The Fat Man," "Merry-Go-Round." If we are to believe Hammett's own account, in fact, the novel's title contains a sly reference to another bird book, *The Wings of the Dove*.[8] Thus *The Maltese Falcon* was apparently conceived as a hard-boiled thriller and as a send-up of Henry James at the same time.

The freakish gang of criminals constituted by Joel Cairo, Caspar Gutman, and Wilmer are, in effect, comic bunglers over whose physique and acts Hammett allows himself to linger indulgently. The foppish Cairo's attempts to play the heavy as well as his spats with Brigid O'Shaughnessy are particularly memorable. And the tension the novel generates is dissolved in laughter before the end, when the seventeen-year quest ends with the discovery that the bird is fake. If Collins invented the comic detective novel of manners, therefore, Hammett was the earliest exponent of the comic thriller. Both writers show how the free motifs of comedy could be made compatible with the bound motifs of a crime plot. Laughter, as we have since learned from Hitchcock, is by no means incompatible with suspense. Some sixty years after Collins, in any case, Hammett revealed how in a twentieth-century American idiom it was possible to have it both ways with gusto.

7. See George Grella's convincing discussion of the formal detective novel as "one of the last outposts of the comedy of manners in fiction." "Murder and Manners," *Novel* 4, no. 1 (1970):30–48.

8. William F. Nolan, *Dashiell Hammett: A Casebook* (Santa Brabara: McNally and Loftin, 1969), p. 61.

As well as being a detective novel, *The Moonstone* is a monument to Victorian taste and a compendium of Victorian attitudes, not least because unlike Poe's more sharply focused tales it allows the business of detection to be overwhelmed by heterogeneous background material and a satirical point of view. Apart from anything else, it is rich in asides and even disquisitions on such subjects as India and its faiths, English values, philosophical and cultural attitudes, religious beliefs, race and class prejudices, medical science, and experiments in psychic research. Clearly, it was written for a public more tolerant of leisurely paced fiction than is our own. But if it is still enjoyable at all, it is chiefly because its author was prepared to indulge in digression for its own sake. *The Moonstone* is successful because it joins manners to murder in the effort to promote pathos and laughter, outrage, fear, and faith. Crime is the pretext for a survey of the range and variety of contemporary life.

From an aesthetic point of view, the appeal of *The Moonstone* is similar to that of a rambling Victorian mansion. It is oversized, asymmetrical, full of surprising twists and turns, and highly decorative. As such, it suggests the loss as well as the gain resulting from the campaign conducted from the late nineteenth century on to raise the status of the novel to that of high art. The examples of first Flaubert and then James have been taken to signify that a serious novel must appear to have no visible irrelevances and that all its parts must be submitted to the discipline of a controlling design.[9] A novel should always be far more than a lose chain of episodes or a parade of characters. The hidden metaphor presiding over such a theory of the novel is clearly the organic one ultimately derived from Aristotle. But it was updated in the nineteenth century through the influence of the plastic arts. The model for the novel became not so much the body as figurative sculpture. Nevertheless, the belief persisted that just as superfluous organs constitute a scandal in nature—the monstrous appendix—so in art and

9. For a modern critical reaction to the recent orthodoxy, see Jonathan Culler's study, *Flaubert: The Uses of Uncertainty* (Ithaca: Cornell University Press, 1974). Roland Barthes sums up the significance of Flaubert in this respect in a single verbless sentence: "Flaubert: a way of interrupting and of making holes in discourse without making it meaningless." *Le Plaisir du texte*, p. 18.

literature every scene, figure, and texture has to pass the stern test of aesthetic function.

Precisely why the novel as sculpted object should have come to appear as the ideal for all fiction has its origins in mid-nineteenth-century taste and in the aesthetic movement. It is important to realize, however, that this ideal is not particularly helpful in understanding a great many novels animated by different conceptions of themselves. Not only does it promote various kinds of misreadings, especially of works from the past, it fails to account for some of the kinds of pleasure derived from novel reading. And this is particularly true of a genre like the detective novel.

An older, antithetical model for narrative fiction has been that of the journey, and it is a model that represents more accurately the kind of experience a reader undergoes when he reads a great many works written before the modern period. From Homeric odyssey to picaresque progress, from folk fairy tale and knightly quest to detective, Western, and spy story, narrative fiction has involved a setting out, a passage through the world, and the eventual arrival at a destination, which may or may not be a return to the point of departure. Probably the most common model for narrative is, in fact, that of the difficult journey through a country without maps. Its pleasures derive from obstacles overcome and from encounters with the strange and marvelous. That is why, alongside the novel, travel journals of various kinds have enjoyed such widespread popularity for so long. The best of them have the appeal of plotless novels, as Paul Theroux's recent *The Great Railway Bazaar* confirms. The narrative art there is not in the delivery of the aesthetic experience of organic wholeness but in the creation of memorable episodes, including especially the savoring of the odd and the exotic. The pleasure is taken en route without any necessary reference forward or backward; except in heroic explorers' tales of the Stanley and Captain Scott variety, the destination counts for nothing.

If *The Moonstone* has something of the character of a leisurely journey through Victorian English civilization, Raymond Chandler's novels take even more obviously the form of a Californian odyssey in which the episodes bulk larger than the whole. On the circuitous routes to their denouements 65,000 words later,[10] Chandler's works

10. "Plan a length of 75,000 words because all publishers love to cut and 65,000 is about the right length." *The Notebooks of Raymond Chandler*, p. 13.

reveal a similar taste for halting investigations that generate a variety of grotesque characters and novel encounters. The line that in England goes back at least as far as Fielding, if not Chaucer, and passes through Dickens and Collins, was extended in the 1930s as far as the American West Coast. However much Chandler learned from Dashiell Hammett, his fiction confirms the knowledge to be derived from his biography that he also had a solid classical English education and aspired to be an English man of letters long before he ever reached California.[11] In any case, his example suggests that the gap between the hard-boiled school and the detective novel of manners, at least as practiced by Collins, is not necessarily as wide as is usually assumed. Chandler is the sardonic chronicler of Californian taste, speech, and attitudes in his time even before he is an action writer for pulp magazines.

The convention of the private eye provided talented writers like Chandler and Hammett with the freedom to wander and enter associated with the picaresque hero. And the realist aesthetic itself constituted excuse enough for the more or less detailed evocation of new scenes that indulge the author's fondness for interior or exterior cityscapes connoting metonymically great wealth and moral corruption, seediness, and evil. But if Chandler in particular lingers over descriptions of decor and atmosphere, it is in order to offer consciously worked-up tableaux on a guided tour through the luxury and seaminess of a half-savage country, tableaux that ask to be appreciated in their own right. His works are Southern Californian journeys that invite the reader to stop and enjoy the strangeness, viciousness, and luxuriance of the region's flora and fauna.

Thus, on the way to the solution of the mystery of Rusty Regan's disappearance in *The Big Sleep,* there are stopovers at the millionaire's estate of the Sternwoods, at a pornographic lending library, a homosexual's pad done in a 1930s Chinese style, the hall of justice, a petty hoodlum's apartment, a gangster's elegant casino, a remote garage by night, and assorted hotels and offices. But perhaps the most celebrated example of Chandler's rich digressive effects in the novel is the description of the hothouse inhabited by the dying General Sternwood: "The air was thick, wet, steamy and larded with the cloy-

11. See chap. 1 of *The Life of Raymond Chandler.*

ing smell of tropical orchids in bloom. The glass walls and roof were heavily misted and big drops of moisture splashed down on the plants. The light had an unreal greenish color, like light filtered through an aquarian tank. The plants filled the place, a forest of them, with nasty meaty leaves and stalks like the newly washed fingers of dead men. They smelled as overpowering as boiling alcohol under a blanket'' (p. 5). The excess here is verbal. The passage is a typical piece of ornamental writing that in the end relies on the most self-conscious of rhetorical figures, the simile, for its strong effects. But the kind of excitement it generates recalls the pleasure Barthes found in language: "I am interested in language because it hurts me or attracts. It is perhaps a form of class eroticism.''[12]

The most characteristic mark of a Chandler novel is, in fact, a quality of extravagance that is present not only in the evocation of decor as here but also in the description of character, in the pungent dialogue, and in the general texture of his prose as well. Such a style applied to characters gives rise to the creation of grotesques often equal in their vividness to those of the great Victorian novelists. In *Farewell, My Lovely,* for example, Philip Marlowe encounters a rich and varied series of more or less minor figures that include the amorous thug, Moose Molloy ("a big man but nor more than six feet five inches tall and not wider than a beer truck''[13]), and his vicious little Velma; the sleepy black hotel porter; the alcoholic old slut, Mrs. Florian; the effete Harvard boy, Marriott; and the fat police chief, John Wax. But perhaps the most memorable of all is Chandler's 1940s Indian.

> The Indian smelled. He smelled clear across the little reception room when the buzzer sounded and I opened the door between to see who it was. He stood just inside the corridor looking as if he had been cast in bronze. He was a big man from the waist up and he had a big chest. He looked like a bum.
>
> He wore a brown suit of which the coat was too small for his shoulders and his trousers were probably a little tight under the armpits. His hat was at least two sizes too small and had been perspired in freely by somebody it fitted better than it fitted him. He wore it about where a house wears a

---

12. *Le Plaisir du texte*, p. 62.
13. *Farewell, My Lovely* (1940; reprint ed., London: Penguin Books, 1949), p. 7.

wind vane. His collar had the snug fit of a horse-collar and was about the same shade of dirty brown. A tie dangled outside his dirty jacket, a black tie which had been tied with a pair of pliers in a knot the size of a pea. Around his bare and magnificent throat, above the dirty collar, he wore a wide piece of black ribbon, like an old woman trying to freshen up her neck.

He had a big flat face and a high-bridged fleshy nose that looked as hard as the prow of a cruiser. He had lidless eyes, drooping jowls, the shoulders of a blacksmith and the short apparently awkward legs of a chimpanzee. I found out later that they were only short.

If he had been cleaned up a little and dressed in a white nightgown, he would have looked like a very wicked Roman senator.

His smell was the earthy smell of primitive men, and not the slimy dirt of cities. [pp. 123–24]

Chandler's Indian, like Moose Molloy, the black hotel porter, the alcoholic old woman, and the fat police chief, are intended to make indelible impressions in the space of a paragraph or so. They are the fauna of his Southern Californian urban scene in the thirties and forties, offered up to a reader appetite for the marvelously grotesque. In other words, in his portraits of "characters" Chandler sets himself the literary task of finding new combinations of words to express models of ugliness, corruption, squalor, evil, and eroticism. The goal is not so much mimesis as astonishment. His example reminds us that the traditional pleasure of novel reading derives above all else from the "vivid" and the "novel," in encountering figures, places, and situations that burst through ordinariness. What we enjoy most in comedies and novels of manners is not the familiar average but eccentricity, the banal made strange.

That Chandler's descriptions often have only a tenuous connection to the plot of detection is confirmed by the passage just quoted. If its length is out of all proportion to the minor strong-arm role played by the Indian in the story—he almost strangles Marlowe to death bare-handed—it is because description here is an end in itself. It is indulged in less for the traditional narrative purpose of character creation than for the sake of its sentences. The Indian is an idea that permits Chandler to produce prose for an ideal reader who is a connoisseur of verbal wit and fine, figurative writing of a new kind. Toward the end of his life he wrote, "My whole career is based on the idea that the formula doesn't matter, the thing that counts is what you do with the formula; that is to say, it is a matter of style."[14]

Further, it is no accident if the hallmark of the Chandler style is the arresting simile, because the simile is the most decorative of rhetorical figures. On the two pages following the hothouse passage from *The Big Sleep* quoted above, for example, three similes occur. The first describes the general's remaining locks of white hair—"like wild flowers fighting for life on a bare rock"; the second, the way he uses his remaining strength—"as carefully as an out of work show-girl uses her last good pair of stockings"; and the third, his reaction to Marlowe's cigarette—"he sniffed at it like a terrier at a rat-hole" (pp. 6–7). And such more or less memorable similes may be found scattered throughout the pages of his novels as well as collected in his notebooks. The fact that Chandler kept a notebook of similes with the apparent intention of working them into future novels confirms an attitude toward writing which may be characterized as that of the aesthete. Among the most suggestive in the notebooks are expressions like "lower than a badger's balls," "smart as a hole through nothing," "a face like a collapsed lung," "a mouth like a wilted lettuce."[15] And what they suggest is that in Chandler's case there is something like an inversion of the way in which novels are popularly assumed to be composed. Instead of the words of each sentence being selected simply as the means through which plot is fleshed out into story, the plot itself has the character of the means, since it provides a justification for the presence on the page of inventive wordplay and arresting images.[16]

In his critical biography Frank MacShane makes the point that Chandler's earliest novels began as rewrites of a number of short stories that had already appeared and disappeared in the pulp magazines.

14. Quoted by Frank MacShane, *The Life of Raymond Chandler*, p. 63.
15. MacShane, p. 64.
16. Chandler's attitude is made clear in a letter to Hamish Hamilton which expresses astonishment at the idea that there are writers who hate the process of writing sentence by sentence: "But a writer who hates the actual writing, who gets no joy out of the creation of magic by words, to me is simply not a writer at all. The actual writing is what you live for. The rest is something you have to get through in order to arrive at that point. . . . How can you hate the magic which makes a paragraph or sentence or a line of dialogue or a description something in the nature of a new creation?" Quoted by MacShane, *The Life of Raymond Chandler*, p. 209.

He also emphasizes how Chandler did not regard himself as a natural storyteller: "He found it hard to tell a story and therefore used a method similar to that of a playwright who has in mind a number of scenes he wants to string together" (p. 67). What both this and the notebooks suggest is that for Chandler the parts of his novels always preceded the whole. His art takes and gives pleasure at the level of scene, paragraph, and sentence, and to some extent allows the plots to take care of themselves—an art, in other words, which is close to being the antithesis of that of an Agatha Christie.

Chandler himself explained his priorities in the following way:

> A long time ago when I was writing for the pulps I put into a story a line like this: "He got out of the car and walked across the sun-drenched sidewalk until the shadow of the awning over the entrance fell across his face like the touch of cool water." They took it out when they published the story. Their readers didn't appreciate this sort of thing, just held up the action.
>
> I set out to prove them wrong. My theory was that readers just *thought* they cared about nothing but the action; that really, although they didn't know it, they cared very little about the action. The things they really cared about, and that I cared about, were the creation of emotion through dialogue and description. The things they remembered, that haunted them, were not for example that a man got killed, but that in the moment of death he was trying to pick a paper clip off the polished surface of a desk, and it kept slipping away from him.[17]

The significance of Chandler's example is that it illustrates a form of irony common in the detective novel genre. It is not so much the evocation of a death that is experienced as disturbing or memorable but the conjunction of death and a paper clip. Chandler invents situations and phrases that both shock and amuse because, like surrealist metaphors, they bring together such disparate elements. The piquancy here is in the juxtaposition of a mundane object and the most extreme of human experiences.

The quintessence of Chandler's style is what has come to be known as a "Chandlerism," that is, a sardonic one-liner which may or may not take the form of a hard-boiled conceit. Whenever it does, the second term of the comparison, like the paper clip in the presence of

---

17. Quoted by MacShane, p. 51.

murder, is a pleasurable digressive effect that derives from a tradition
of wit. The thrill of reading Chandler is less often in the experience
of suspense than in the discovery of a collapsed lung in a face or a
wilted lettuce in a mouth. He puts his personal cachet on the genre by
combining the epigramatic flourish of Oscar Wilde with the moral environment of "The Killers."

In "Twelve Notes on the Mystery Story" Chandler distinguishes
four categories of readers of detective novels, namely, the puzzle addict, the sensation hunter, the sentimental "worrier-about-the-charac-
ters," and the "intellectual literate reader who reads mysteries because they are almost the only kind of fiction that does not get too big
for its boots." He recognizes that there is likely to be something of
the four types in any given reader, but he also acknowledges that it is
impossible to interest each type equally in a single novel without contradiction. Chandler's solution was to ignore the first category and to
appeal over the heads of the second and third to that fourth category
of reader, who "savors style, characterization, plot twists, all the vir-
tuosities of the writing much more than he bothers about the solution."[18] Thus if Chandler is still read, it is not for ingenuity in the
plotting of enigmas but for character, scene, dialogue, and above all
verbal texture.

Not the least interesting aspect of Chandler's fiction is, finally, that
it is founded on a paradox. Its highly self-conscious artistry is deployed on material that had previously been associated with the most
meretricious of popular genres, namely, the hard-boiled action thriller
of the pulp magazines. Significantly, the paradox is already encountered in the works of another aesthete masquerading as a realist,
Flaubert himself. In both cases there is a characteristic tendency of the
prose to issue in decorative simile, and much of the pleasure of the
novel resides in a visible ironic relationship between style and content. The tawdriness of represented life is an opportunity for the display of a flamboyant verbal artistry.[19]

18. MacShane, ed., *The Notebooks*, p. 39.
19. The poignancy of his situation is suggested by his comments on a work of Max
Beerbohm's: "I found it sad reading. It belongs to the age of taste, to which I once
belonged. It is possible that like Beerbohm I was born half a century too late, and that
I too belong to an age of grace. I could so easily have become everything our world has
no use for. So I wrote for *Black Mask*. What a wry joke." Quoted by MacShane, *The
Life of Raymond Chandler*, p. 76.

Both Collins and Chandler confirm in different degrees that apart from suspense itself the features that are conducive to pleasure in the best detective fiction are such digressive effects as the representation of manners, "character," and decor, and humor, wit, and stylishness in the prose. They offer what even Edmund Wilson conceded as characterizing at least some of the classics in the genre: "The old stories of Conan Doyle had a wit and a fairy-tale poetry of hansom cabs, gloomy London lodgings and lonely country estates that Rex Stout could hardly duplicate with his backgrounds of modern New York."[20]

Furthermore, their works are also reminders that popular literature has always catered to a taste for picturesque extremes. Like fairy tale and melodrama, the popular novel deals in the polarities of innocence and evil, wealth and poverty, beauty and ugliness, youth and age, obesity and leanness, cunning and gullibility. It also shows a fondness for larger than life characters and threatening or grandiose locales, for the Falstaffs, Micawbers, and Old Goriots as well as for castles, jails, tunnels, mansions, and tenements. If popular literature in general has an aesthetic, in fact, it is founded on the notion of "the human comedy" in a more general sense than that intended by Balzac. Its ideal is perhaps best suggested by *The Canterbury Tales* insofar as that work combines the characteristics of a colorful pageant with those of an interrupted journey. It is a journey, moreover, that in Chaucer's work functions openly as a device for getting the rich intercalated material narrated. The work's containing frame makes possible an anthology of episodes that span the whole spectrum of human behavior from the bawdy, the hypocritical, the lascivious, and the evil to the noble, the patient, and the pious. At the same time, as in the finest narrative works, Chaucer's "poetry" is the end of which it is also the means.

Within their far narrower limits both Collins and Chandler combine some of the polarities of the Chaucerian "human comedy" with the suspense of mystery. Collins was plainly influenced by the tradition of the mystery novel itself as well as by the Victorian novel of manners. And there is in the lurid decorativeness of many of Chandler's scenes the quality of California gothic. Both writers rely for much of their appeal on the representation of extravagant life and spectacular evil.

20. "Why Do People Read Detective Stories?", p. 233.

The interest of a very different writer like Simenon, on the other hand, resides largely in his discovery of suggestive digressive effects for the detective novel in the material of traditional French realism. He is a quieter writer whose art relies on a Balzacian sense of place and a feeling for French social types. He situates the unspectacular adventures of a middle-aged bureaucrat in milieus that constitute in their own right *Scènes de la vie parisienne* or *Scènes de la vie de province*. And his characters embody an idea of average Frenchness at a variety of social levels. The Maigret novels are without the mood of menace, the formidable "characters," the dazzling verbal effects, or the wit and humor displayed to varying degrees by the two writers of the Anglo-American tradition. What Simenon is invariably praised for, on the other hand, is his power to evoke "atmosphere."

In a perceptive essay entitled "The Geography of Simenon," the British historian Richard Cobb writes: "Simenon's endless attraction is his sensitive rendering of atmosphere, of the feeling of a locality, and the acuity of his social observation."[21] Although Cobb approaches Simenon as a social historian and connoisseur of French life, it is nevertheless revealing that in three essays devoted to Simenon he scarcely mentions the fact that the works he is writing about are mostly detective novels. Those free motifs that are the fruits of social observation and of notations from recognizable French life are what attract Professor Cobb. For the fan, the pleasures of the master's works are to be found not in the cunning of the plot, the melodrama of violence, brilliant ratiocination, eccentric manners, or the style of wit, but in the savoring of ordinariness. Simenon's appeal derives from his capacity to revive and extend the reader's knowledge of familiar scenes and places. All his works contain examples of his power to trigger the reader's recognition.

The opening paragraph of *Les Vacances de Maigret,* with its description of a French provincial town, is typical of a great many openings. With Simenon as with Balzac, in the beginning is a place: "The street was narrow, like all the streets in the old quarter of Sables d'Olonne, with uneven cobblestones and side-walks that you had to step down off whenever you met an approaching pedestrian. The door in the corner was a magnificent double-door that was painted in a dark

---

21. Richard Cobb, *Tour de France* (London: Duckworth, 1976), p. 188.

rich green and gleamed in the light. It had two highly polished brass door-knockers of a kind that you only see on the houses of provincial lawyers or at the entrance of a convent."[22] The notations are brief but sufficient to connote the unevenness, narrowness, order, and mellow age associated with French provincial towns. And as well as appealing to a shared cultural knowledge—"of a kind that you only see"—the last sentence has a characteristically pleasing precision of sensuous detail. Like a painting by a Dutch master, Simenon's door invites the reader to enjoy the material spectacle of prosperous bourgeois life.

The example of the short passage suggests that Simenon's famous "atmosphere" is largely a matter of reminiscing delicately about places calculated to appeal to the reader's nostalgia and of finding images that speak directly to the senses. Thus, a little further on in the same novel, he does for a small provincial police station what he did for the provincial street in the passage just quoted: "Moreover, there was a smell that Maigret sniffed at happily, a good heavy smell that you could cut with a knife and that was made up of the leather of shoulder straps, the wool of uniforms, bureaucratic forms, cold pipes and of those poor devils, too, whose rear-ends had polished smooth the two wooden benches in the waiting room" (p. 28). Simenon's pleasure in the acuity of his hero's sense of smell is also the reader's. The appeal is in the precision of concrete detail that translates here the nostalgia of the Parisian outsider for the lost paradise of provincial simplicity and humanity.

If Maigret's journeys are through the familiar territory of metropolitan France, they are nevertheless memorable because at their best they encapsulate the peculiar charm of the Frenchness of things French. Simenon's novels are certainly among the slowest paced of the best-known detective fiction of recent decades because he invents as a central reflector not a brilliant supersleuth or a tough athlete but a quiet observer of the human scene. Maigret is a literary device for making things visible that derives from the long line of Parisian *flâneurs*. He remains a walker of city streets, a habitué of old-fashioned zinc bar cafés, a connoisseur of the variety of urban neighborhoods at a time when many of his literary peers have taken to fast cars and intercontinental travel. As far as France is concerned, Simenon is a tour

22. *Les Vacances de Maigret* (Paris: Presses de la Cité, 1948), p. 7.

guide of last resort. Maigret, writes Richard Cobb, is "endlessly excited by the prospect of smelling out the ambience of a *quartier* never previously visited, or neglected for many years. And it is pleasant for the reader who is thus taken well off the routes of any guide."[23]

Among the newer writers of detective fiction, Nicolas Freeling is closest in spirit to Simenon, and his appeal is obviously to a similar class of reader. His originality lies largely in shifting the locale of his action from Paris to Amsterdam, from France to Holland, and in equipping his detective hero, Van de Valk, with a set of cosmopolitan Dutch attitudes. The difference between the two writers' works is significant, however, precisely to the extent that Freeling opens up a distance between his hero and "Dutchness" in a way that Simenon never does between Maigret and French life. If one of the incidental pleasures of Freeling is in his representation of the social life of the new Holland of sixties affluence, it is a pleasure noticeably more satirical in character than is usual in Simenon. Therefore, placing Van de Valk in the situation of a bureaucratic policeman, putting him on a bicycle, and fitting him out with a French wife tends only to emphasize the difference of tone between the two writers.

Freeling's most successful novel is probably *The King of the Rainy Country,* a work that quickly abandons Amsterdam in order to make a swift guided tour of Europe that takes in *Fasching* in Cologne, win-

---

23. Cobb is particularly impressed with Simenon's qualities as a connoisseur of place: "Simenon, too, is constantly and attractively reminding one that history should be walked, seen, smelt, eavesdropped, as well as read: he seems to say that the historian must go into the streets, into the crowded restaurant, to the central criminal courts, to the *correctionnelles* (the French equivalent of magistrates' courts), to the market, to the cafe beside the canal Saint-Martin, a favourite hunting ground, to the jumble of marshalling yards beyond the Batignolles, to the backyards of the semiderelict workshops of the Rue Saint-Charles, to the river ports of Bercy and Charenton, as well as to the library. There is a real quadrilateral in Paris: it's bounded by the Rue des Archives, Rue de Turenne, Place des Vosges, Rue du roi de Sicile, Quartier Saint-Paul, Rue Vieille du Temple, making up the old faubourg Saint-Antoine and the Marais, on the Right Bank, beyond the Hotel-de-Ville. This is where he likes to place his lonely, secret little people, because he knows it is, or was, a quartier *de petits* [*sic*] *gens* and of Jewish immigrants. He is as fond of it as of Maubert-Mouffetard, on the Left Bank, in the Ve *arrondissement*, the ancient centre of poverty and of the Paris tramp; as fond of it as he is of the XIIe, in the wastes of the Avenue Voltaire, to the east of the Marais, or the lock at Conflans, the place where the Oise joins the Seine." "Maigret's Paris," in *Tour de France*, p. 180.

ter sports in Innsbruck, the Vosges Mountains, Strasbourg, Biarritz, and the Basque country. In other words, although Freeling also provides his reader with the interest of such traditional realist detailing as a tour of the home of a rich Amsterdam lady (she puts her money in bathrooms) and of a working man's cottage in the Vosges, his choice of digressive elements is much more attuned to the taste of the affluent sixties than is that of Simenon. His appeal is quite consciously to the reader as tourist, as the following passage suggests.

> The tourist, getting the quick rundown on Rembrandt, is told that what makes the city of Amsterdam notable is, firstly, twice as many waterways and bridges as Venice and, secondly, the very fine seventeenth-century architecture. It is true that at a time when the glories of Paris and Vienna were still to come, when the political capital of the world was Madrid and the diplomatic and artistic capital was Venice, Amsterdam was the world's commercial and banking capital. The tourist seeing little evidence of all this, is inclined to be sceptical. For with less intelligence than Venice, less than Innsbruck, less even than St. Malo, the city fathers have allowed the automobile full liberty and destroyed practically all the beauty.[24]

And the description of old Amsterdam goes on to contrast modern squalor with past elegance. The narrator's role here has become that of an environment-conscious tour guide who lets his audience into the secrets that other tour guides fail to reveal. The reader is expected to take his pleasure in the cultural information passed on about one of the world's great cities and in the acerbic voice of a narrator of the world.

Writers of detective novels are in the realist tradition insofar as they have always tended to anchor crime in a specific location and in certain milieus and social strata. Originality in the genre has often amounted to no more than a freshness of decor, accent, and attitude. Yet detective fiction is read for that freshness as much as for anything else. Doyle's London, Chandler's Southern California, and Simenon's Paris are mythic worlds evoked in order to excite the reader with an inventory of their magical or malignant possibilities. Similarly, the interest aroused by a novel of Dorothy L. Sayers or Dick Francis is due in large part to the entrée afforded the average reader into worlds remote from his everyday experience. An Oxford college, a London

24. *The King of the Rainy Country* (London: Penguin Books, 1968), p. 18.

club, an advertising agency, and a racing stable are from the point of view of the general public closed institutions. Their lore and ambience, like those of a prison, a barrack room, a hospital, or a monastery, are therefore a matter of curiosity. Apart from any violence, the character of life in such communities is intrinsically fascinating, as the success of endless TV documentaries attests. Up to a point, arcane information about bell ringing in East Anglia or a steeple chase jockey's preparation for a race is not simply tolerated but enjoyed, since it satisfies the reader's curiosity about what goes on behind the scenes. An actor's dressing room or a pilot's cabin communicates something of the thrill of a secular holy place.

The modern writer who best illustrates the indispensable component of free motifs in any popular detective story and the changing taste in such motifs is probably Ian Fleming. Although his works belong to the separate category of the spy thriller, their connection with the American hard-boiled tradition, especially with Micky Spillane, is equally as marked as their derivation from the Doyle, Rider Haggard, and John Buchan adventure story. The vogue of James Bond extended from the early fifties into the late sixties and was during those years an international phenomenon much commented on by intellectuals in several countries.

Fleming's novels are noteworthy because he takes the original detective story material of mystery with violence, combines it with the explicit sex interest of the hard-boiled tradition, invokes the conflict between big power ideologies, and goes beyond the atmospheric evocation of place associated with Doyle, Chandler, and Simenon into the world of the new tourism. Like Hammett and Chandler, alongside his detective Fleming puts into his novels an exciting woman or two and various "characters" in minor roles, as well as villains who are the embodiment of the grotesque. Dr. No and Goldfinger are monsters of evil who are more threatening and drawn with less wit than the Joel Cairo and Casper Gutman of *The Maltese Falcon,* but who nevertheless feed a similar popular taste for sinister freaks. Fleming updated all this, however, chiefly because he was alert to the appeal in the fifties and sixties of the contemporary upper-middle-class pleasures of jet age travel and the life-style associated with it. Next to Hammett's ascetic private investigator, Fleming's hero resembles an international playboy who has the depersonalized ethics of the organization man.

In the essay referred to above, Umberto Eco touches on a feature of Fleming's novels that he has trouble accounting for within the framework of his critical method: "In fact, what is surprising in Fleming is the minute and leisurely concentration with which he pursues for page after page descriptions of articles, landscapes and events apparently inessential to the course of the story; and conversely the feverish brevity with which he covers in a few paragraphs the most unexpected and improbable actions."[25] The lengthy descriptive passages are further defined by Eco as examples of "high technical skill which makes us see what he is describing, with a relish for the inessential, and which the narrative mechanism of the plot not only does not require but actually rejects." Involved is a "technique of the aimless glance" (p. 66).

What Eco does not point out, however, is that the presence of such passages is justified largely on the dual grounds of pleasure and functionality. Not only do Fleming's descriptions play an important delaying function in the promotion of suspense, they contribute to the reader's enjoyment in their own right. The aimlessness of the glance is only apparent. Like the rolling of Sam Spade's cigarette, what Fleming describes is important because it is calculated to stimulate the senses and appeal to the reader's fantasy. His descriptions are typically of beautiful women, vintage cars, memorable meals, and the scenery of exotic places. And among these it is women and cars that recur most frequently for the obvious reason that they are the sexiest machines of the age. In other words, as Eco notes, such passages are not intended to communicate information but to be "evocative," although he does not say what they are evocative of.

In fact, Fleming makes his readers' mouths water for sun-soaked tropical beaches and vintage wines as well as for those more traditional fictional pleasures associated with gorgeous blondes and macho trials of strength. As the following description of the girl Bond encounters on Dr. No's Caribbean island makes clear, it is no accident that the vogue for Fleming's novels coincided with the rapid expansion of the *Club Méditerranée*.

25. "The Narrative Structure in Fleming," p. 65.

It was a naked girl with her back to him. She was not quite naked. She wore a broad leather belt around her waist with a hunting knife in a leather sheath at her right hip. The belt made her nakedness extraordinarily erotic. She stood not more than five yards away on the tideline looking down at something in her hand. She stood in the classical relaxed pose of the nude, all the weight on the right leg and the left knee bent and turning slightly inwards, the head to one side as she examined the things in her hand.

It was a beautiful back. The skin was a very light uniform café au lait with the sheen of dull satin. The gentle curve of the backbone was deeply indented, suggesting more powerful muscles than is usual in a woman, and the behind was almost as firm and rounded as a boy's. The legs were straight and beautiful and no pinkness showed under the slightly lifted left heel. She was not a coloured girl.

Her hair was ash blonde. It was cut to the shoulders and hung there and along the side of her bent cheek in thick wet strands. A green diving mask was pushed back above her forehead, and the green thong bound her hair at the back.[26]

The complete scene also entails an empty beach and a green-blue ocean, so that it naturally suggested to the writer Botticelli's Venus. The comparison is significant because it shows that if the author lingers over such descriptions—"The skin was a very light uniform café au lait with the sheen of dull satin"—it is because he sees himself as a connoisseur of art and beauty writing for an audience of connoisseurs. A more honest comparison, however, would have been with a recipe from a gourmet cookbook. Fleming's description of a naked white woman gone savage—with a belt and a hunting knife—has in the context the power of a recipe because when you have read it and savored in anticipation its ingredients, you want to try it.

If Honeychile Rider has the status of a consumable object in *Doctor No,* she is not alone. The verbal image Fleming paints is only the most sensuously rich among a great many choice objects that he sets before his reader, beginning with the splendor of the Jamaican landscape in the opening paragraph. Fleming's works serve, in fact, to remind us of something already touched on, namely, that even in the realist tradition the description of objects is often in itself a source of pleasure. The antique shops of two such masterworks of phantasmagoric realism as Balzac's *Wild Ass's Skin* and Dickens's *Old Curiosity*

26. *Doctor No* (New York: New American Library, 1959), p. 69.

Shop are stuffed by their authors with strange and ancient objects, which constitute themselves into prose poems designed to feed the fantasy. And even Madame Aubain's unexceptional barometer, which puzzled Roland Barthes, has in ''A Simple Heart'' a stolid verbal presence redolent of bourgeois interiors and therefore amounts to a flavor to be tasted alongside others. As Roland Barthes once noted, a reader is sometimes more interested in a description of the weather than in a writer's thoughts.[27] It seems that even the petty details of our human existence, both past and present, familiar and strange, may possess an unexpected power of suggestion when fixed in a block of prose.

Ian Fleming constructs objects that appeal to a strictly contemporary taste for the good life. In *Doctor No,* for example, there is a description of the ultimate bathroom.

> There was everything in the bathroom—Floris Lime bath essence for men and Guerlain bath cubes for women. He crushed a cube into the water and at once the room smelled like an orchid house. The soap was Guerlain's Sapoceti, *Fleurs des Alpes.* In a medicine cupboard behind the mirror over the washbasin were toothbrushes and toothpaste, Steradent toothpicks, Rose mouthwash, dental floss, Aspirin and Milk of Magnesia. There was also an electric razor, Lentheric after-shave lotion, and two nylon hairbrushes and combs. Everything was brand new and untouched. [p. 119].

As so often in fairy tales, the reader is invited to enjoy the fantasy of luxury inside the wicked palace, but luxury here is of a kind that contemporary society does make available to a glamorous few. The brand names are important because they are testimony both to discriminating taste and to conspicuous consumption. The description of Dr. No's guest bathroom provides Fleming with the opportunity to indulge in the poetry of consumerism.

That ''relish for the inessential'' (p. 66) to which Eco refers, then, is one of the principal sources of Fleming's popularity. He is not read for his ratiocinative plots any more than Hammett is, nor for the kind of digressive effects associated with Wilkie Collins and Chandler. He is read, rather, for his power to sustain excitement concerning an outcome while at the same time he feeds the reader's appetite with evocations of figures and places that embody mythic polarities. His digres-

27. *Le Plaisir du texte,* p. 85.

sive effects are calculated to appeal alternately to fantasies of oral, anal, and genital eroticism. Thus in the James Bond novels traditional motifs are rendered modish, not simply through the allocation of roles according to the anxieties of the age of the cold war—having Russians and communists taking over the villains' roles from Nazis or mobsters—but also through the invention for the old motifs of new and fabulous fifties costumes. It should be remembered that *Casino Royale* was published in 1953, that is, in the continuing period of postwar European austerity as well as of the cold war.

Under the circumstances, it is curious that Eco should attribute the interest of Fleming's descriptions to their evocation of objects and situations familiar to his readers: "Fleming does not describe the sequoia that the reader has never had a chance to see. He describes a game of canasta, an ordinary motorcar, the control panel of an aeroplane, a railway carriage, the menu of a restaurant, the box of a brand of cigarettes available in any tobacconist" (p. 67). And it is true that few novels take up so much space describing their hero entering and leaving hotel rooms, showering, dressing, reading menus, ordering meals, eating, drinking, playing various games, driving cars, or lounging on beaches. What makes such activities different in a Fleming novel is the level at which James Bond operates, the savoir faire with which he carries out ordinary activities. In *Casino Royale,* for instance, the reader learns that Bond's cigarettes are "a Balkan and Turkish mixture made for him by Morlands of Grosvenor Street."[28] The game he plays in the elegant casino of the title is not canasta but baccarat. And when he returns to his hotel he calculates he has twenty-three million francs, or roughly fifty thousand dollars at his disposal.

Furthermore, the backdrops for adventure are such fashionable resort areas as the Côte d'Azur and the Caribbean, along with the grand hotels and airports of the world's capital cities. A model for the spy thriller of the James Bond type had, of course, been provided by John Buchan's *Thirty-nine Steps,* which was first published in 1915, and in film by the Hitchcock spy thrillers that took their cue from Buchan's novel. Buchan's work is essentially a pursuit drama that involves its

28. *Casino Royale* (1953; reprint ed., New York: Bantam Books, 1971), p. 21.

hero in a flight as well as in a hunt, an assassination, and an attempt to prevent the leak of naval plans. As far as its digressive effects are concerned, however, along with a series of more or less comic encounters with "characters," it also makes use of trains and fast cars, and with its background of the Scottish Highlands establishes the precedent of the importance of locale in the spy thriller. What Buchan did close to home and on a relatively modest scale with Scotland, Fleming does with the world's beauty spots. At a time when mass tourism was still in its infancy, he provided his readers with fabulous journeys through the playgrounds of the jet set. If Paul Theroux's *Great Railway Bazaar* offers the pleasures of the plotless novel, therefore, Fleming's works often have the appeal of a plotted travelogue of a kind that finds its ultimate expression in *Moonraker*, in what was until recently the most exotic of journeys, namely a voyage to the moon. In that novel, however, Fleming pushes beyond the traditional limits of the spy thriller into the strange adventure novel of Jules Verne and science fiction.

At a time that was not yet an age of affluence, then, Fleming's works first appealed to a hunger for luxury, travel, and fast living. This is confirmed by the relative speed with which his novels have become dated. It is, of course, a tendency of most popular literature in mass consumer society to date very rapidly because the public for such literature is conditioned to expect the traditional sex and adventure to be dressed in the most advanced fashions of the day. Its reflex is always to move on, to reject last year's novels with last year's slang and last year's hemlines. Bond's fifties flamboyance therefore has about it what we now recognize as a period flavor. In their time the appeal of the James Bond novels was largely in the detailed account they provided of a mythically glamorous life-style. To his average readers Fleming offered behind-the-scenes glimpses of a society that was high, fast, sexy, and dangerous. To his minority of upper-middle-class readers, on the other hand, he provided flattering confirmation of the fact that they frequented the right kinds of places and drank, smoked, ate, dressed, drove, and made love in fashionable ways.

The eclipse in popular appeal of the detective novel by the spy thriller is to be explained in large part, in fact, by the greater opportunities the latter affords for travel to exotic locations and for expense-account living. The explanation of the James Bond phenomenon lies above all, then, in the power it possessed to communicate a *frisson nouveau*. Fleming's digressive effects are calculated to submit his readers to the experience of the ultimate polarity of sybaritism and torture as well as to many of the more conventional stations in between. To a degree unusual even in the toughest hard-boiled writers, bodies in Fleming's novels are alternately assaulted or caressed; intense pleasure for his secret agent is the reward for extreme pain.

In Fleming as in all the writers discussed, the detective plot furnishes the vehicle which makes possible a whole range of pleasures, including those traditionally associated with comedy and romance, satire, fantasy, and realism. That those people who are fans of detective fiction in the broad sense used here do not have to be coerced into their reading is therefore not surprising. From Collins to Fleming the most memorable works in the genre embody an acute awareness of the mechanisms of pleasure. And in this context crime itself is no more than an instrument for focusing the reader's attention, the means by which he is made docile and willingly led. In other words, detective novels are read less for their structural constants than for their decorative variables. As Geoffrey Hartman has noted in the essay quoted above, "In a B movie, we value less the driving plot than moments of lyricism and grotesquerie that creep into it; moments that detach themselves from the machine narrative."[29]

It is remarkable, for instance, that if one eliminates the violent encounters from a James Bond novel, one is still left with the bulk of the fictional material. That is to say, equally as much as in *The Moonstone* the background has invaded the foreground, but it is a background largely constituted by the representation of the leisure activities of the contemporary middle to upper-middle classes. Apart from the peripeteias of the manhunt itself, one encounters lengthy descriptions of those activities that along with the popular arts of cinema, TV, and literature are themselves the favorite pastimes of the modern age, including in particular random sex, exotic tourism, gourmet cooking, and the kind of play, ranging from bridge, baccarat, and golf

29. "Literature High and Low: The Case of the Mystery Story," in *The Fate of Reading*, p. 218.

to sports car driving and skindiving, associated with the new affluence. In other words, Fleming's example makes very clear some of
the variety of levels on which detective fiction makes its hedonistic
appeal. The traditional association between vacations and detective
novels of all kinds is no coincidence; both connote a time for anti-
work, self-indulgence, and sensuous gratification. In this case, the
goal of the reading is in the pleasures of the trip; the novel is a vacation in itself.

4

The Detective Novel as Readable Text

The question of the progressive and digressive elements of detective fiction and the pleasures deriving from them leads to the further and related question of "readability." The detective novel has remained a highly popular genre because, above all, it is enjoyable to read, but it would not be considered enjoyable by most people unless it were also easy to read. If, for the vast majority, the end of novel reading is pleasure, the prerequisite for pleasure through narrative is "readability" in both meanings of that word. To say that a novel is "readable" is to mean either that it is worthy of being read for the pleasurable feelings it stimulates or that it is not difficult to follow. Conversely, to declare a given work "unreadable" is to signify that it is either dull and turgid or unintelligible. It may, of course, be both. The first meaning is the more popular, but the second has been given a wider diffusion fairly recently as a literary critical concept associated in particular with the work of Roland Barthes.

Criteria of readability in both senses clearly vary enormously according to such factors as the cultural background, age, and literary sophistication of the reader. Thus a "good" detective novel is taken to be highly readable by fans of the genre because it is experienced as not only intelligible but gripping as well. An Edmund Wilson, on the other hand, would concede it readability on only the first count. To its cultivated critics, a popular detective novel poses no problems of intelligibility, but it fails to offer the forms of stimulation they expect from works of fiction. Nevertheless, until comparatively recently all classes of readers would have agreed that whatever pleasure is to be found in a novel is contingent upon intelligibility.

In extending our battery of critical concepts with the opposition between *le lisible* and *le scriptible*, between readable and writable texts,[1]
Barthes raised the whole question of the conventional character of narrative which causes stories to appear not only natural but intelligible.
A text is writable to the extent that it does not exist as a work of narrative to be read in a traditional sense. It has rather the character of a
pre-text, of a work in which the reader is required to acknowledge and
participate in the writing process: "The writable text is a perpetual
present that no logical discourse ["parole conséquente"] can grasp
(since it would inevitably transform it into a past); the writable text is
ourselves in the act of writing, before the infinite play of the world
(the world as play) is traversed, cut up, arrested, fixed by some peculiar system (Ideology, Genre, Criticism) that reduces the plurality
of entries, the opening of networks, the infinity of languages."[2]

Readable texts, on the other hand, are the great mass of novels with
which we are all familiar, the classics as well as popular works of all
kinds. And in reality the best such works can offer is what Barthes
refers to as "a moderate plurality," like the Balzac story he analyzed
in *S/Z* in order to illustrate his method. Such works deliberately limit
the play of significance as a consequence of the familiar narrative conventions they deploy. At best they are merely polysemic, in Barthes's
opinion, never multivalent, since they incorporate structures that a
genuinely plural text lacks: "for the plural text there can be no narrative structure, story grammar or logic" (p. 12). If Balzac's *Sarra-
sine* turns out to be only "moderately plural" compared with certain
examples of postmodernist writing to which Barthes refers, however,
a traditional detective story is by implication as close as possible to
being entirely "singular." It is at the opposite pole from the writable
ideal of which Barthes dreams. As such it may be regarded as the
basic model of the readable text. And it is the conventions of its structuration as readable text that I should like to explore further. Which
features of detective narrative account for its apparently instant deci-
pherability by its huge audience? Obscurity in literature has received

1. "Readable" and "writable" strike me as more precise equivalents of "le lisible"
and "le scriptible" than Richard Miller's "readerly" and "writerly." See *S/Z*, trans.
Richard Miller (New York: Hill and Wang, 1974).
2. *S/Z* (Paris: Editions du Seuil, 1970), p. 11.

a great deal of critical attention in our time; accessibility, on the other hand, is generally taken for granted.

In the first place, it is important to keep in mind that a book is a cultural artifact which comes with implied instructions for its use. Thus for a long time now most children in the West have learned early in life that a storybook is a greater source of pleasure if it is consumed page by page with the eyes rather than orally and at random. They also learn that it has to be placed the right way up, its pages turned in a fixed order from beginning to end and read top to bottom, left to right, in an unbroken sequence. In other words, reading stories from a book is a learned activity just as much as reading words is. Moreover, it involves the submission of self to the norms of the culture, including the discipline of linearity and a gradualist approach to pleasure. As a result, a storybook is a cultural artifact that is also an instrument of acculturation not least because it represents life as a chronological unfolding, a progress that steadily thickens the past and reduces the future until it achieves the satisfaction of an end.

A literary genre provides even more precise instructions for its use. This means, of course, that as soon as a reader sees the green and white cover of the Penguin Crime Series or the yellow and black of the French *Série Noire* edition, he will adjust his expectations to his experience of the detective formula. As Fredric Jameson has noted, "Genres are essentially contracts between a writer and his readers; or rather, to use the term which Claudio Guillen has so usefully revived, they are literary *institutions,* which like other institutions of social life are based on tacit agreements or contracts. The thinking behind such a view of genres is based on the presupposition that all speech needs to be marked with certain indications and signals as to how it is properly to be used."[3]

An experienced reader infers the nature of the contract from the signs constituted by a cover, a title, an author, or the silhouette of a recurring character on the jacket. The names Doyle, Christie, or Simenon, especially when accompanied at the entrance to a text by those signifiers which identify a familiar fictional character—pipes, hats, hobbies, eccentricities of speech or gesture—guarantee the terms of the agreement. Such devices may also be seen as the equivalent of

3. "Magical Narrative: Romance as Genre," *New Literary History* 7 (1975):135.

the indicators that, in speech-act theory, furnish the frame of reference and thus enable an utterance to be understood by a listener.

Until the twentieth century it was universally assumed that all works of fiction implied such a relationship of complicity between author and reader—a relationship fundamental to a readable novel. And in the so-called golden age of the formal detective novel, between the two world wars, it was openly acknowledged in the formulation of the Detective Club Rules.[4] The statement of what was and what was not admissible in a genre on the level of content has probably never been carried further, at least since the end of neoclassicism. The existence of such a code is interesting from my point of view here because it makes explicit the fact that reading fiction has traditionally been a game played with an author according to a set of rules. The relationship between an author and his reader that obtains in detective stories is that of a problem setter to a problem solver, but in a less obvious way the same is true of all novels. The antithetical operations of authorial encoding and reader decoding occur in all our textual transactions. That is why the success of a given work with a reader depends in the first place on the reader's willingness not only to suspend disbelief but also to play the reading game according to the rules of the genre.

It is, of course, true to say that the most important rules of the detective genre do not figure among those formally codified because whereas the latter relate to the choice of criminal and methods of murder or detection, the implicit rules concern formal properties that have already become thoroughly naturalized and hence imperceptible as conventions. Thus the Detective Club Rules have nothing to say, for example, about the fundamental structuring principles of the genre embodied in the familiar question ''Whodunit?'' and in the equally familiar action sequence of investigation that accompanies that question. A detective story always proceeds from a fixed point of departure to a fixed destination. It moves both from mystery to solution and from crime to punishment or, if not to punishment, at least to arrest. It is a genre dominated by a combination of the two sequential, non-

---

4. See S. S. Van Dine, ''Twenty Rules for Writing Detective Stories,'' in *The Art of the Mystery Story*, ed. Howard Haycraft (New York: Simon and Schuster, 1946), pp. 189–93.

reversible codes Barthes isolated in *S/Z* in the form of a highly visible hermeneutic code and a strongly articulated proairetic code. The former concerns, of course, the sum of units whose function in a given text is to formulate a question and its answer, as well as the various events which prepare the question or delay the answer. The latter, on the other hand, refers to any succession of acts, evoked in a novel and modeled on empirical actions, that constitute themselves into a nameable sequence, such as a murder, a journey, the eating of a meal, or the taking of a bath.

What the concept of the hermeneutic code in particular makes clear is how a reader's desire to know is stimulated by the author in such a way that it functions as a "structuring force." The corpse encountered in the opening paragraphs of many a mystery story poses a question that for the reader transforms the activity of reading the novel into the search for an answer. The desire to know turns the reader into an alert tracker whose virgin forest is the text through which he makes his way gathering and discarding apparent clues.

A detective novel is the most readable of texts, first, because we recognize the terms of its intelligibility even before we begin to read and, second, because it prefigures at the outset the form of its denouement by virtue of the highly visible question mark hung over its opening. At the same time, between the two poles of a question asked and answered, a long sequence of logically interconnected human actions is unfolded that succeed one another in time. And such sequences of actions constitute the armature of a readable text, especially where there is so little difficulty in recognizing them. If, as Barthes has suggested, "to read is to struggle to name,"[5] because of the author's helpfulness and the genre's conventions the reader of detective novels has relatively few problems. The most familiar sequences presented for naming are immediately identifiable as the discovery of crime, an investigation, an interrogation, an identification, an escape, a pursuit, an unmasking, and an arrest, though not necessarily in that order.

The action sequence that encompasses all the others in a detective novel, however, is the one which opens with the mystery of a crime and ends with its solution. In other words, it is an action sequence whose two terms coincide with the opening question and final answer

5. *S/Z*, p. 98.

of the hermeneutic code. If the denouement of a detective novel is looked forward to with such intensity, therefore, it is because it marks the end both of one of the most familiar action sequences and of the anxiety provoked by the threat of mystery.

The movement from concealment to disclosure which characterizes the genre also implies that individual works suddenly constitute themselves into wholes at their denouement. Whereas to the prospective eye of the reader the mystery of the initial crime opens on to further incidents that compound mystery, to the retrospective eye of the same reader all incidents are designed to appear suddenly as essential elements in a larger pattern. In the light of the concluding revelations, the apparently fragmented picture is revealed in its wholeness. Almost all novels demand a form of "retrospective repatterning"[6] as a reader advances through a text constructing and reconstructing hypotheses concerning a work's meanings, but nowhere does it occur with such formulaic regularity as in a detective story.

From the fighting of a war in the *Iliad* and the long journey home of the *Odyssey,* traditional narrative works pose problems to which they offer more or less delayed resolutions. And popular genres such as the detective story provide signals at the beginning which permit the recognition of the type of problem to be solved. From the cadaver in evening dress slumped over the spilt Madeira of the formal tradition to the corpse flung from a moving automobile in the hard-boiled school, the problem is the most easily recognizable and urgent of all, namely, a committed crime. And it is a problem that invariably generates a series of fixed functions in Propp's original sense,[7] whose sequence, if not as rigid as for Propp's folk fairy tales, is nevertheless far from random. The developed detective formula embodies the following sequence: the initial situation that is about to be or has just been disrupted, the discovery of the crime that disrupts, the appeal to and arrival of the detective, the pursuit of the unknown criminal via a series of investigations, searches, and interrogations that usually include attempts to divert or interrupt the detective in his pursuit, the

6. The term is Menakhem Perry's. See "Literary Dynamics: How the Order of a Text Creates Its Meanings," *Poetics Today* 1, no. 1–2 (1979):58–61.

7. "an act of character, defined from the point of view of its significance for the course of the action," Propp, p. 21.

progressive elimination of suspects, and the final unmasking and arrest of the criminal.

Moreover, to pursue Propp's model further, it is apparent to experienced readers of the genre that the above sequence of actions is distributed among a conventionally limited number of roles, of which the criminal and the detective are the most fundamental. They, too, stand in relation to each other as a problem maker to a problem solver and thus repeat inside the novel the relationship that exists between author and reader. The former scatters clues, the latter gathers them into viable hypotheses and finds himself aided or thwarted in his search by victims and witnesses, helpers and blockers, decoys and prizes. In practice, apart from the criminal or villain and the detective or hero, the other two essential roles of the detective story are the victim and the suspect or suspects, the latter role almost invariably occurring in the plural whereas that of criminal, detective, and victim may or may not do so.

Such easily recognizable roles derive from the type of problem posed and the action sequence required for its solution. They depend in other words on the dominance of the hermeneutic and the proairetic codes, which are also responsible for another important feature of a readable text, namely, the logico-temporal order imposed on the narrated events. A detective story probably more than any other genre is committed to the principle of noncontradiction and nonreversibility. As is the case with almost all novels until comparatively recently, detective stories have been read in the faith that, however tenuous it may sometimes appear, there is a system of multiple connections between all the isolatable parts of a written text, that everything which occurs is a necessary element in an ordered whole. The task of reading consists largely of the effort to perceive the connections involved in order to reconstitute the whole. Consequently, one of the clearest signs that we are in the presence of a readable text is that within it "everything fits together" ("tout se tient").[8] And in a detective novel author and reader alike are satisfied only if everything appears to fit together with a machinelike perfection. The tedium experienced by critical readers at the minutiae often reported in the course of the traditional concluding recognition scene is to be contrasted with the satisfaction appar-

8. *S/Z*, p. 162.

ently felt by fans of the genre when they are shown by an act of detective prestidigitation how everything falls into place: "The readable [novel] . . . is governed by the principle of noncontradiction, but by multiplying such solidarities, by underlining as often as possible the *compatibility* of the circumstances concerned, by joining the events narrated by a sort of logical 'glue,' the writing pushes this principle to the point of obsession" (p. 162). Dashiel Hammett's *The Maltese Falcon* offers a typical example of the way in which such an obsession in the reader is fed by a writer who first hides and then reveals with a rush at the end the "solidarities" to which Barthes refers.

Hammett's novel opens innocuously with the arrival of the glamorous and mysterious Miss Wonderly, with her routine problem, in Sam Spade's office. But before the end of the second chapter there is an explosion of mystery through two murders, one of Spade's partner, Lew Archer, and the other of the unknown Floyd Thursby. In a way characteristic of both Hammett and Chandler, after a quiet beginning mystery proliferates in more or less violent forms, especially through the surfacing of exotically grotesque or sinister figures and through a series of wild peripeteias that include by the end a further murder, temporary disappearances, an attempted stickup, a drugging, a wild-goose chase, and an entrapment. There is a gradual process of naming both mysterious characters—Brigid O'Shaughnessy; the Middle Eastern homosexual, Joel Cairo; the Fat Man; Casper Gutman; and the boy killer, Wilmer—and motivations, including especially the nature of the quest that brought the odd crew together in San Francisco. But the major task of explanation is left for the last two chapters of the novel.

The Fat Man especially is given the role there of recuperating all the outstanding isolated incidents and extant clues connected with the murders of Floyd Thursby and the ship's captain, Jacobi. His story uncovers the hidden logico-temporal order of events initially presented in a more random sequence. It is worth quoting one of the Fat Man's lengthy monologues to illustrate the care with which the past is gathered in so as to make it yield up all remaining mystery. Having received a detailed account of Thursby's murder, Spade goes on to inquire about the killing of Jacobi.

> After a shrewd look at Spade, Gutman smiled. "Just as you say, sir," he said. "Well, Cairo, as you know, got in touch with me—I sent for him—after he left police headquarters the night—or morning—he was up

here. We recognized the mutual advantage of pooling forces." He directed his smile at the Levantine. "Mr. Cairo is a man of nice judgment. The *Paloma* was his thought. He saw the notice of its arrival in the papers that morning and remembered that he had heard in Hongkong that Jacobi and Miss O'Shaughnessy had been seen together. That was when he had been trying to find her there, and he thought at first that she had left on the *Paloma,* though later he learned that she hadn't. Well, sir, when he saw the notice of arrival in the paper he guessed just what had happened: she had given the bird to Jacobi to bring here for her. Jacobi did not know what it was, of course. Miss O'Shaughnessy is too discreet for that." He beamed at the girl, rocked his chair twice, and went on: "Mr. Cairo and Wilmer and I went to call on Captain Jacobi and were fortunate to arrive while Miss O'Shaughnessy was there. In many ways it was a difficult conference but finally, by midnight we had persuaded Miss O'Shaughnessy to come to terms, or so we thought. We then left the boat and set out for my hotel, where I was to pay Miss O'Shaughnessy and receive the bird. Well, sir, we mere men should have known better than to suppose ourselves capable of coping with her. *En route,* she and Captain Jacobi and the falcon slipped completely through our fingers." He laughed merrily. "By Gad sir, it was neatly done."[9]

The purpose of the passage is to bridge the logico-temporal gap opened up by the earlier surprise appearance of the unknown and dying Captain Jacobi in Spade's office. The reason the Fat Man's explanation is characterized by a wealth of circumstantial details is that it responds to the desire, referred to above, to reestablish those "solidarities" apparently broken by the rupture of the chronology. The narration of Cairo's activities in particular, with its complex tense structure and dependent clauses—"He . . . remembered that he had heard in Hongkong that Jacobi and Miss O'Shaughnessy had been seen together"—confirms how obsessive is the desire to recover the past in its precise linearity. A detailed accounting is involved that places incidents precisely in time and space, plots the movements of characters in relation to each other, explains motives, and links clues to their causes. The passage is a characteristic example of the logico-temporal chain, whose fundamental form is "*because* that happened, *then* this followed." The suspension of sense provoked by the surprise appearance of Jacobi is thereby satisfactorily resolved.

9. *The Maltese Falcon*, pp. 172–73.

The reader of a detective novel finds it intelligible because he carries in his head the model of which the work in hand is an example. This includes the expectation that the novel to be read is structured by a familiar question and embodies a familiar action sequence, that it contains familiar roles and a familiar view of logico-temporal unfolding of the kind in which everything is seen to fit together in the end. For a detective novel to be easily intelligible, the author must also orient the reader immediately concerning the point of view to be adopted, the locus of the story to be told, and the initial situation or point of entry into the narrative matter. The opening paragraph of Dashiel Hammett's *The Thin Man* may serve to illustrate the above.

> "I was leaning against the bar in a speakeasy on Fifty-second Street, waiting for Nora to finish her Christmas shopping, when a girl got up from the table where she had been sitting with three other people and came over to me. She was small and blonde, and whether you looked at her face or at her body in powder-blue sports clothes, the result was satisfactory. "Aren't you Nick Charles?" she asked. I said: "Yes."[10]

Jonathan Culler has noted that the basic convention of traditional prose fiction is "an expectation that the novel will produce a world."[11] In this opening Hammett shows how economically this may be done by suggesting a scene situated in an implied place in contemporary time that confirms our sense of the possible *(le vraisemblable)*. The mention of a bar, a speakeasy, and Fifty-second Street is enough to call up metonymically the referent of New York City in the years of prohibition. As for the point of entry into this narrative of investigation, Hammett discloses in the next few lines that the problem to be solved will concern an already missing father.

Above all, however, Hammett's narrative art here is designed to allay as rapidly as possible the anxiety experienced by any reader who opens an unfamiliar text and has not yet had time to get his bearings. And the most helpful thing an author can do at the outset is to locate the source of the enunciation in a highly visible narrator. Detective stories rarely allow doubt as to who is speaking to persist beyond the opening paragraph. "Nick Charles" is a structural necessity before he

10. *The Thin Man* (1934; reprint ed., New York: Dell, 1966), p. 5.
11. *Structuralist Poetics: Structuralism, Linguistics and the Study of Literature* (Ithaca: Cornell University Press, 1975), p. 189.

is a detective hero, if the novel's plurality is to be reduced to a level compatible with easy intelligibility. "Nick Charles" is a device that sustains the fiction of an originating "I" antecedent to the text, and explains the text's existence in the same way that fictional editors in eighteenth-century novels gave a form of authenticity to memoirs and collections of letters. It is, moreover, typical of the hard-boiled genre that the narrator is immediately given a name, shown, shown seeing, and heard narrating what he sees.

Kafka, of course, revealed the significance of a name by substituting an initial for it. A name in a realist novel is usually a guarantor of social identity, a clue to race, ethnicity, or class, and therefore points to a place occupied in a given society. As well as naming his narrator/ hero, Hammett also shows him by detailing a set of characteristics, including a stance and a particular locale—"I was leaning against the bar"—and an attitude of tough male knowingness. But most important of all he chooses a voice that is identifiable by an idiom, and he does so in order to fix the point of view in a recognizable type. Moreover, like the vast majority of detective stories, *The Thin Man* is monologic, so that the easily identifiable voice of the narrator remains constant throughout. From the beginning a single authoritative discourse tells and reveals all, although it does allow tributary discourses, in the form of either direct or indirect speech, to flow for a time within it. In this as in much else *The Moonstone,* with its variety of narrative voices, is only apparently an exception. Not only is there a different voice for each well-defined part of Collins's novel, each voice is distinguished with great care precisely in order to locate the various sections in a "character," that is, in a recognizable social or human type. In this respect, as both Collins and Hammett are aware, the more memorable and even idiosyncratic the narrator, the more readable the novel is likely to be.

What also emerges from even such a brief passage as Hammett's is the way in which it is organized in terms of instantly recognizable elements of narrative discourse that are the equivalents in prose fiction of the parts of speech in a sentence. If reading a novel is a process of continuous reassessment, part of that process involves acknowledging the functions of the conventional "parts of fiction" constituted by narrative summary, description of scene, representation of character, analysis of mental states, dialogue, and dramatic action. Moreover, uncovering order and sense in a text is facilitated if the different parts of fictional narrative are clearly distinguished from each other by conventional marks.

Such signposting occurs in all forms of prose from a letter to a three-decker novel and chiefly takes the form of a variety of graphic signs that mark the written page at greater or lesser intervals. The function of all such devices—from punctuation and capitalization on the level of the sentence to indentation on the level of the paragraph and partly blank pages on the level of the chapter—is the establishment of identifiable units of discourse that can be integrated into still higher units. But such conventional rhetorical units are not to be confused with the parts of fiction referred to above. The function of the former is, in fact, to enable a reader to differentiate among the latter, so that he adjusts appropriately to the transition when an author shifts out of commentary into description of scene or out of dialogue into reported speech.

Further, in a traditional novel relations between such parts of fiction are determined by a tacit understanding of proportion and hierarchy. Because the novel has typically involved conflicts between identifiable personalities in a defined place, it has given rise to a set of expectations concerning the space to be occupied by and the relative importance of the elements of fictional discourse mentioned. In this respect, a novel may be compared to a traditional Renaissance painting composed of a series of receding planes. In the same way that the spatial organization of a picture enables us to distinguish easily the most distant plane of sky and landscape from the middle ground of a city square and a foreground of human interaction concentrated in two or three principal figures, so in a novel scene, character and analysis are traditionally subordinated to a similar end of human interaction. Even within the limits of the detective novel genre, there are variations to the permissible proportions among the different elements of fictional discourse, the reader of formal detective fiction usually showing a greater tolerance for that which is not action than the reader of a hardboiled story. Nevertheless, it is generally true that the more a detective novel allows its "foreground" of investigative action to be overwhelmed by "background," the less popular it will be. The persistent foregrounding of background material and, as with the later James, the exhaustive narration of barely perceptible action give rise to disturbing pluralities that make reading problematic.

Up to this point in my discussion of readability I have concentrated on the syntagmatic axis of narrative—on the way in which it is structured by the combined hermeneutic and proairetic codes, so that it forms itself into a logico-temporal whole—and on rhetorical devices employed to facilitate the reader's task by ordering and signposting the abundance of verbal material to be processed. It is perhaps just as important to realize that popular literature is also characterized by strong paradigmatic patterning of a kind we are perhaps most familiar with in competitive team games. The color coding that distinguishes the home team from the visitors in a game is often reproduced in a hardly more sophisticated form in popular novels as the attributes of the dramatis personae. In a melodrama the hero is no more to be mistaken for the villain than are the White Sox for the Red Sox.

Ian Fleming's spy thrillers are good examples of works in which a series of sharp binary oppositions simplify radically the potential complexity of a represented world. In an early structuralist attempt to explain the vogue of the James Bond novels, Umberto Eco defines them as "narrating machines."[12] Since Eco adopted the then standard structuralist approach of analyzing the Bond texts in the absence of a reader, he is not concerned with the problem of readability as such but with the way in which a Fleming novel is constructed out of isolatable units that are combined according to "strict rules of combination." Nevertheless, he shows how, by manipulating sharply differentiated binary oppositions, Ian Fleming was able to elicit strong identification or hostility from the reader.

The first six oppositions that Eco isolates are:

   a. Bond–M
   b. Bond–Villain
   c. Villain–Woman

---

12. "The Narrative Structure in Fleming," in *The Bond Affair*, ed. O. del Buono and Umberto Eco, p. 38.

d. Woman–Bond
e. Free World–Soviet Union
f. Great Britain–Countries not Anglo-Saxon (p. 39).

Even Eco's complete list is not exhaustive—he does not mention the fundamental Beauty–Ugliness, Human–Monstrous, for example—but the starkness of the oppositions he does locate in the texts suggests the Manichaean obviousness of the vision projected. It has the simplicity of a universe divided into an immediately recognizable "them" versus a well-defined "us," into white versus nonwhite, capitalism versus communism. Fleming's example reminds us that a hero is often no more than a man who wears a uniform of one color, a villain a man whose choice of color is different. In the United States, at least, "the Reds" are indifferently ideological enemies or a rival baseball team.

It is generally recognized that the pleasure of watching sports is greatly enhanced if we root for one of the teams involved. And it is a principle widely exploited in popular literature by means of its strong identifications. In this respect the pains taken by Ian Fleming to emphasize both the terrible consequences of the defeat of the hero and the sharpness with which the key roles are defined in opposition to each other are characteristic. The crime/problem raised at the beginning of Fleming's novels has an unusual obviousness only because of its scale. And the scale of the villainy in its turn demands an unusual hideousness in the villains. It is not enough for the criminal rivals to be Chinese or Russian, they have to be monsters or "Chigroes," with hooks for hands.

Fleming's novels in this respect also provide a good example of a feature common to most popular literature that also contributes to making reading simple, namely, redundancy of verbal material. This is especially true on the paradigmatic axis, where redundancy appears as the equivalent of "solidarity" on the syntagmatic axis. In the case of the character descriptions from Collins and Chandler quoted earlier, for example, there is a high degree of repetition and insistence that expresses itself particularly by means of synonym and metaphor. As in the Bond novels such material is typically organized into sharply contrasting patterns with the result that an abundance of verbal material in fact communicates relatively little information. For the purposes of comprehension of the text, therefore, only a limited amount has to be assimilated and stored by a reader.

At the same time there is also a well-known circularity in the typical strategy of realist fiction that details the physical characteristics of a character as signifiers of moral propensities and then goes on both to name those propensities directly and to show them acted out in a scene. Such an effect is not usually perceived as tautological, of course, but rather as a different form of solidarity among the elements of a narrative than the one discussed above. It is a guarantor of coherence and relatedness, of cause and effect. While it is true that the principle of nonrepetition is central to a traditional novel, therefore, what is meant is nonrepetition of the same combination of words and not of different ones saying more or less the same thing.

Alain Robbe-Grillet's description of a tomato first disturbed early readers of *The Erasers* not simply because what was ostensibly the same tomato did not always stay the same but also because it kept on reappearing as the more or less similar combination of words in a similar order. Moreover, it appeared to be a signifier without an obvious signified.[13] Had Robbe-Grillet employed the conventional narrative tautology of repeating the already known by means of synonyms or had his tomato functioned as a leitmotiv in the building of suspense— or for signifying atmosphere and mental state—it would have caused no reading difficulties. Consequently, saying the same thing often but with different words has in the end the effect not only of making a novel eminently readable but also of projecting the image of a world that is itself readable. Book and world are characterized by a similar order and coherence.

If he can read at all, anyone who is able to understand a game can read a James Bond novel in the same way that he can read a fairy story. Ian Fleming tells his reader immediately in the straightforward language of action fiction what the crime/problem is, where and under what circumstances it occurred, whose point of view is being adopted, and who among the characters should be the focus of the reader's sympathy and hate. As in a fairy tale, there is the loss of original har-

13. Stephen Heath writes of "the repression of the signified." *The Nouveau Roman*, p. 116.

mony because of a move made by an enemy, a period of pain and searching by Bond that involves a series of further moves and countermoves, the defeat of the enemy, and a return to harmony at the end with a heightened sense of pleasure. Thus the apprenticeship most of us serve as children in the art of first listening to and then reading fairy stories makes the transfer to Bond in adolescence simple enough. But the apprenticeship that begins in infancy is essential because it means that even before we begin to read we learn how to read stories.

We can read a James Bond novel with such ease, therefore, because we know how to handle a book and because we have a developed literary competence from a long experience of story telling. We have, so to speak, already read Fleming's works even before we come across them because they are the embodiments of fictional structures with which we are familiar from childhood on. *Goldilocks and the Three Bears* is certainly one of the first stories told to children throughout the English-speaking world, yet it possesses most of the basic elements encountered in popular fiction for all ages and therefore illustrates those qualities which make a text readable. It is also of particular relevance here because its pleasures are those of a crime story in a containing detective story.[14]

Goldilocks and the Three Bears is easy to read first of all because it names all its characters and sets up its fundamental structural opposition in the title. Having already answered the question, Who?, it goes on in its opening paragraph to answer the questions, When and Where? by naming a time and a place—"Once upon a time there were three bears. There were Daddy Bear, Mummy Bear and Baby Bear and they all lived together in a house in a wood." There follows an evocation of the initial situation as original family harmony—the ideal threesome at breakfast—their departure from home, and the appearance of the character who will play the role of criminal, Goldilocks. Reader interest is excited almost immediately because the ostensible heroine—the one who is most like us—is also the villain because she is engaged in the forbidden activity of entering someone else's house in their absence. And the initial crime is compounded in a way that deliberately heightens suspense by the patterned commission, involv-

---

14. One might also note that *Peter Rabbit*, too, is a crime story written from the point of view of a sympathetic criminal and shares many characteristics with *Goldilocks*.

ing trebling, of the further taboo-breaking crimes of sitting in other people's chairs, eating their food, and worst of all, usurping the place of another child in his bed. To the extent that she enters, breaks, eats, and takes, Goldilocks succumbs to a temptation familiar to all children, namely, that of undisciplined curiosity, possessiveness, and greed. Consequently, the action sequence that the tale embodies corresponds to the well-known naming of crime and punishment; a crime committed is followed by a search that ends with the discovery and disciplining of the criminal.

Further, *Goldilocks and the Three Bears* is structured around a series of binary oppositions similar to those isolated by Eco in the Bond novels, but of a kind easily identified by children: human–animal, blondness–brownness (or blackness), smooth hair–rough fur, smallness–bigness, child–adult, mother–father, good behavior–bad behavior, inviolate home–home violated. Yet, if anything, the fairy tale is aesthetically and morally more complex than the Bond thrillers because it is divided into two parts. The first part adopts the point of view of the criminal; the second part switches the point of view to the victims turned detectives. Furthermore, both parts of the story arouse the suspense of fear, first, in the action of breaking and entering and, second, in the step-by-step process of detection that leads to the sleeping girl in Baby Bear's bed. The suspense-heightening factor in the latter part is, of course, the fact that the reader is aware of what is both an approaching shock and an approaching threat, whereas the bears and Goldilocks are not.

While the story never ceases to be fully readable, however, the shift of point of view blurs some of the oppositions that are inherent in its structure. At different moments it elicits sympathy for the victims of crime and for the criminal; the tale's "they" is made to seem like "us" and vice versa. Thus, although the bears may appear at first sight to be gruff and threatening, they are the wronged party and they do have feelings, especially Baby Bear. Goldilocks, on the other hand, may be blonde, cute, and human, but she is also naughty. *Goldilocks and the Three Bears,* in fact, comes closer than most popular works to introducing the important idea of a third term that somehow mediates between the poles of hero and villain. Therefore, the traditional ending is the appropriate one inasmuch as it embodies a lesson in imaginative sympathy for differentness—what the French call *altérité*—that is mostly absent from the Bond novels. In the end justice is done. Goldilocks is discovered and deserves her scare but that is all she deserves. In short, anyone who finds the popular tale intelligible will have little difficulty with Fleming's thrillers. In both cases the authors succeed in minimizing all the obstacles to reader pleasure that are potentially inherent in narrative structures.

Finally, the example of *Goldilocks and the Three Bears* is useful as a reminder that formulaic popular literature is so readable because the limited number of story types it contains are already familiar to the average reader. Both folk fairy tales and detective novels confirm that the reading of fiction invariably has something of the character of a rereading. The most readable novel is, in fact, not only one which derives from a familiar model but also one we have previously read. Consequently, it is no accident if, with the possible exception of children, readers of detective novels show a higher degree of loyalty to certain authors than any other class of readers. Such fans return as often as possible to their Christies, their Simenons, or their Freelings, and they do so in order to encounter more of the same.

If reading detective novels is always a rereading, however, it is a rereading in which a limited number of structural constants are combined with an indefinite number of decorative variables in order to make the familiar new. As in the equally formulaic minor genre of joke telling, the audience's pleasure depends both on being familiar with the structure of the whole and on not knowing the specific outcome. The final solution of a crime, like the punch line of a joke, is recognized as the predictable formal term whose actual content is appreciated most when it comes as a surprise.

5

The Erotics of Narrative

In the preceding chapters I have been concerned with the narrative art
of the detective story and have placed particular emphasis on the two
axes formed on the one hand by the anecdote and on the other by
those various verbal intensities that impede its progress. Along the
first of the two axes, the author opens by focusing the reader's attention with a strong beginning in the form of a committed crime. And
that strong beginning—which may or may not be reinforced at intervals in the story by means of the repetition of crime—characteristically constitutes either the opening move in a familiar action sequence
(Barthes's proairetic code) or the announcement of a mystery
(Barthes's hermeneutic code). In most works of the genre, however,
represented events are frequently combined into units of both
sequences.

The second of the two axes consists of interpolated material that
delays progress toward the end of crime and the promise of punishment as well as toward the solution to mystery and an unmasking. An
underlying premise of the preceding chapters has therefore been that
the existence of the two axes results in a tension in the text which is
experienced by the reader as suspense.

What is surprising and what needs to be examined more closely is
the fact that as readers we seem to enjoy that experience. The distress
we normally feel at desire aroused and left unsatisfied is somehow
transmuted by narrative into an intensifier of our pleasure. Although
we may read a detective story compulsively in order to reach a con-
clusion/solution, we paradoxically enjoy the obstacles scattered by an
author in our path, both for their own sake and because they prolong
the state of tensed expectation. Such suspense, as was noted earlier,

depends on the recognition of fear in one of two fundamental forms—that of threatened danger or of love unfulfilled—or on the existence of an unanswered question that may also have an element of fear of the unknown. Just why suspense in its various guises should be experienced as pleasurable, therefore, will inevitably take us outside literary criticism as narrowly conceived into areas of our psychic life that have been illuminated particularly by psychoanalysis. It is in any case time that a greater effort was made to resist the long-standing tendency of most studies of the genre to separate detective fiction from the affective life of its readers and from related cultural phenomena.

To begin with, given that the pleasure derived from exposure to risk in one of its many guises is central to an understanding of the appeal of the detective story, it is necessary to ask why and under what conditions such pleasure is possible. The phenomenon is, of course, familiar among young children, but it is clear from their example that fear is enjoyed only if it is experienced under certain controlled conditions. Thus a father may briefly throw a child into the air because the child is certain that his father's arms will be waiting to catch him. A father may also play the role of a bear because he is still recognized as Daddy doing it. In this case, however, it is sometimes necessary for the father to step out of his role in order to reassure. If, on the other hand, a stranger does the throwing or plays bear, the result is more likely to be a pure and painful fear rather than an agreeable excitement. A similar response characterizes exposure to threatening situations in the adult world.

For fear to constitute an element of pleasure, it has to be experienced under controlled conditions that set a limit to the risks involved, conditions that obtain, for example, in certain kinds of participatory or spectator sports and in the theater. Incidents that would cause considerable distress in the street do not usually do so on a playing field or in a play. On the other hand, there is no pleasure in exposure to the danger that a soldier faces in battle or a woman in rape. Fear under those circumstances is more likely to result in a condition of shock of a kind that we are probably most familiar with in nightmares, where a direct threat to our bodies often leads to sudden impotence, to the terrifying feeling of being "rooted to the spot." Yet in the imaginative transpositions of literature, a war and a rape may be represented in ways that compel our excited attention.

The pleasure of fear is therefore, first, pleasure in the exposure to an acceptable dosage of fear—a dosage that does not cause us to close our eyes or swoon and that will vary greatly for both individual psychological and cultural reasons—and, second, the pleasure of an acceptable dosage of fear that is immediately followed by the return from fear. The idea of a given level of tolerance to fear suggests that the reason why fans of detective fiction return again and again to a favorite author is that they are certain to find in his works the dosage of fear they know they can enjoy. The movement from exposure to fear and a return from it is characteristic of most popular literature from fairy stories and tales of adventure to gothic novel, mystery story, melodrama, and spy thriller. In fact, its ubiquity implies not only that the morphology of narrative is fundamentally bicellular in nature but also that it is a movement we are responsive to from the earliest stages of our affective life. Beyond the threat of adventure and the return home from adventure of *Goldilocks* and *Peter Rabbit,* the bicellular morphology of narrative may be detected in the solitary game of disappearance and return. *Fort/Da,* played by a one-and-a-half-year-old boy and described by Freud in *Beyond the Pleasure Principle.*

Freud suggests three possible reasons why the boy should reenact in play the obviously painful experience of the departure of his mother, namely, for the pleasure of her return, for the sake of mastery, for revenge. But he assigns no final meaning. The anecdote is important in the present context because Freud invites "some system of aesthetics with an economical approach to its subject-matter" to consider painful artistic and play situations "which have a yield of pleasure as their final outcome."[1] If the game of *Fort / Da* represents narrative in its simplest form and is replayed in an infinite variety of imaginative permutations throughout the whole of our lives, it is clearly because of the yield of pleasure involved. Moreover, it confirms what has already been suggested, namely, that pleasure is based on the experience of contrast; the cultural achievement to which *Fort / Da* points is the understanding that pleasure is not pleasure without the prior experience of pain. Strictly speaking, the mechanism involved has an implied third term in the form of a preceding *Da.* The

1. *Standard Edition of the Complete Psychological Works of Sigmund Freud,* trans. and ed. James Strachey (London: Hogarth Press, 1935), p. 17.

whole structure of the experience of separation and reunion presupposes a union that antedates both—*Da / Fort / Da.* There is no loss of pleasure where there has been no previous experience of it and no joy in its recovery when it has not been lost. The infant player of the game, like the reader of a story, has made the calculation that the temporary renunciation of instinctual gratification will in the end lead to a greater reward.

Even before it becomes imaginatively incorporated into our narratives, in fact, *Da / Fort / Da* announces itself as the fundamental mechanism of our sensuous life at all levels. The effort to control the loss of a desired presence through play and to learn to enjoy the pleasure / tension of a postponed return of that presence is the beginning of the joys of sex before it is an introduction into the pleasure of narrative. Further, this mechanism is conceivably first learned at the oral phase of human development in the relations established between a mouth and a breast. It may be repeated at the anal stage through the withholding and production of the stool. And it achieves its fullest development by means of the postponement of orgasm in the genital phase. In all cases, however, it is important to realize that the space between the two terms is the space of culture, of the imaginative detours of play.

Confirmation of what I have referred to as the bicellular morphology of narrative may be found in the models invented by both Russian Formalists and French Structuralists. The hidden structural identity Propp uncovered in his corpus of Russian folk tales was, of course, founded on the isolation of common sequences of actions that he called "functions" and of which he isolated thirty-one. Subsequent modifications of his scheme by such structuralists as Greimas, Bremond, and Todorov have all tended toward simplifying it with a view to applying it to other genres. And in a simplified form involving a movement from an initial situation of well-being through loss, pursuit, combat, recovery, and return, the structural affinity of even Propp's original model with *Da / Fort / Da* is clear. In an enigmatic phrase, Barthes once asked the question, "Isn't every story basically the Oedipus story?"[2] It is likely that what he meant was that all narratives represent situations equivalent to the working through of the oedipal

---

2. *Le Plaisir du texte*, p. 75.

experience. In other words, all tales are tales of thwarted desire in which an obstacle comparable to the incest taboo obliges a character to take a circuitous path to fulfillment.

Moreover, if the original Freudian *Fort / Da* involves two characters, a child / lover and an apparently fickle loving mother who disappears and reappears unpredictably, the more elaborate narrative of the family romance always involves three characters. In Freud's nineteenth-century scientific retelling of the Oedipus story, to the lover and the loved one there is added the figure of the hated father, whose existence explains the fickleness of the loved one. The Oedipus story is a tale of violence as well as sex, and it makes the hated rival responsible for the middle term in the sequence *Da / Fort / Da*. The loss represented by *Fort* is, in fact, a theft, like that abduction carried out by the villain at the beginning of a fairy story. If, therefore, fairy stories like the Oedipus myth so often have the dual character of crime stories and romance, it is because both are rooted in our affective life practically from the beginning. Aggression, like eroticism, begins in the cradle. And in the imaginative reenactment of our pursuit of pleasure, it turns out that a tale of aggression has as much appeal as a tale of eroticism. In the long run, if we cannot have both at once we seem to find as much satisfaction in the overcoming of a rival as in the reunion with a loved one. The lesson of popular fiction is that the goal of a coupling is no more common than the destruction of an enemy as a source of pleasure. Violent adventure, crime, and detective stories have traditionally been at least as numerous as popular romances. From the point of view of their power to arouse, therefore, the representation of crime overcome is an alternative to sex, not a substitute. In the former case, since an act of violence launches the story, the reader's pleasure is in violence avenged at the story's end; in the latter case, the reader is satisfied only when the lack of a loved one has been made good.

The critical work that builds on both psychoanalysis and structuralism in order to address directly the question of the pleasure to be derived from narrative is, of course, *Le Plaisir du texte*. It is of particular interest to any study of popular literature because, in the endeavor to establish qualitative distinctions in the sphere of pleasure, it raises in a new way the fundamental problem of the erotic structure of narrative. Furthermore, precisely because it has the character of a manifesto of a new postmodernist sensibility and is dismissive of popular narrative forms, it indirectly reaffirms the importance of those qualities that the vast majority of readers have expected fiction to possess.

Barthes's classificatory scheme of *texte de désir, texte de plaisir,* and *texte de jouissance*[3] employs a patently sexual terminology in order to distinguish among intensities of sensations from the excitement of arousal (*désir*) to orgasm (*jouissance*). The lowest category in Barthes's hierarchy of texts offers not so much a scene of sex or violence as its imminence—"its expectation, preparation, rise"[4]—and is represented by a popular work of erotica or a detective story. The second category, characterized by the excess already discussed and by "euphoria, fulfillment, comfort and a sense of plenitude steeped in culture" (p. 34), is the highest level to which the traditional classics in the genre may attain. The third category, the *texte de jouissance,* comprises distinctly postmodernist texts, *nouveaux nouveaux romans,* where the anecdote is entirely submerged in the play of self-reflexive discourse and where language itself is materialized, experienced not as "a language" but as "language," that is to say, as substance. Such texts are recognizable because they produce in a reader a feeling of "shock, disequilibrium, loss" (p. 34).

The problem with the scheme is that Barthes's preferrred third category of texts signals the end of narrative as universally practiced down to our time. If *jouissance* means "definitive discontinuity," then there is no loss, no departure, and no return, because there is in the text no representation. The only "hero" is the perpetually disoriented reader adrift on the sea of language—"à la dérive." In short, continuous polyvalence and undecidability signify the end of *Da / Fort / Da* and Oedipus as the fundamental model of narrative, and along with them the detective story. Thus, if in the theory of *jouissance* Barthes champions a new erotics of reading, it is eroticism with a distinctly contemporary flavor because it is not end-oriented. Whereas narrative has traditionally been constructed according to principles similar to those viewed by Freud as characterizing adult sexuality, a *texte de jouissance* repudiates such principles. It stands

3. See chap. 3, above.
4. *Le Plaisir du texte*, p. 92.

in relation to a *texte de plaisir* as in Freud's theory sexual perversions do to the genital aim of the mature sexual norm.

In the second of the *Three Essays on the Theory of Sexuality* Freud contrasts infantile sexual life, in which "its individual component instincts are upon the whole disconnected and independent of one another in their search for pleasure,"[5] with that of the normal adult, "in which the component instincts . . . form a firm organization directed towards a sexual aim attached to some extraneous sexual object" (p. 65). And Freud goes on to speak of "organization and subordination to the reproductive function." As the key terms "organization" and "subordination" make clear, this view of sexuality is both directional and hierarchical in its structure and is, therefore, subject to the same strictures that Barthes applies to the sentence and *a fortiori* to the form of narrative which is the sentence writ large, namely, the novel. In Freud's normative theory sexuality takes the form of a grammatically correct sentence in which the relationship of control among the parts is always clear.

The fundamental difference between a *texte de désir* and a *texte de jouissance* is in the locus and nature of the pleasure they promote in a reader. Whereas the former might be compared to a form of sex without fore-pleasure, the latter in spite of its defining term dissipates the end-pleasure of genital orgasm by diffusing intensities throughout a text. A *texte de désir* concentrates single-mindedly on the goal of discharge, which is always postponed until the denouement; a *texte de jouissance* promotes the polymorphous perversity of the written word. Only Barthes's intermediary category, the *texte de plaisir*, can be said to conform to the traditional norm of adult heterosexual practice of the kind promoted by Freud. In a section of his third essay entitled "Dangers of Fore-pleasure," Freud makes that clear by reformulating what is, in effect, age-old civilized practice in both the erotic and literary spheres. There is, in Freud's view, "danger," "if at any point in the preparatory sexual processes the fore-pleasure turns out to be too great and the element of tension too small. The motive for proceeding further with the sexual process then disappears, the whole path is cut short, and the preparatory act in question takes the place of the normal sexual aim" (p. 77). Both in the civilized arts of love and in classic

5. (New York: Basic Books, 1962), p. 63.

narrative texts fore-pleasure precedes and is designed to enhance end-pleasure at the same time that the latter sharpens the former by the element of tension with which it invests its activities. In both spheres the suspense is in the fear that a promise may not be kept, that aroused desire will not in the end be satisfied through an appropriate act of discharge, i.e., in a denouement of (re)possession or of victory.

Barthes was clearly right to declare that the average formulaic work in the detective genre is no more than a *texte de désir*. However, it is proper to emphasize that the most durable detective stories, such as those discussed above, are also characterized by a form of excess that is always rooted in some way in the play of auto-reflexive language. Whether it takes the form of "realist" descriptions of scenes, "characters," objects, and places, of wit or a self-conscious garrulousness, of an agreeable stylishness or the energy of the vernacular, there is involved an intermittent thickening of the verbal texture. In brief, the best novels in the genre are like all the novels we most admire. That is to say, they are *textes de plaisir* which focus the reader's interest alternately on local excitements among words and on the progress of sequences of actions that embody a threat or a promise. Such texts are subject to principles of "organization" and "subordination" of the kind Freud refers to, but they fill the space between loss and recovery with richly various play.

D. W. Winnicott's description of a baby playing the game of *Fort / Da* with a spoon suggests beautifully both the mechanism and the intensity of the pleasure involved.

> Now he shoves it under the blotting pad and enjoys the game of losing and finding it again, or he notices the bowl on the table and starts scooping imaginary food out of the bowl, imaginatively eating his broth. The experience is a rich one. It corresponds to the mystery of the middle of the body, the time between when the food is lost by being swallowed, and when the residue is rediscovered at the lower end in the faeces and urine.[6]

The analogies I have made here between the structures of our erotic life and narrative—analogies implied but not explicitly worked out in Barthes's elusive work—confirm that novels in general and especially popular novels are used by readers in the interest of their pleasure.

6. *The Child, the Family, and the Outside World* (Harmondsworth, England: Penguin Books, 1964), p. 77.

Like those who go to the theater or watch movies and TV melodrama, the readers of popular literature are pleasure seekers. They read not in order to learn something but to feel something, not to be improved but to be moved. It therefore follows that reading fiction is not in some way *sui generis* but only one activity among many that might have been chosen to reach a similar end. Since, when we read, we allow our body to be played and played upon by a text, it follows that a novel is one among a number of familiar activities we engage in at different times and places in the cause of our pleasure. And what all these activities have in common is the single unitary physiological system on which they operate. That is why the metaphor of the rollercoaster suggests so well the excitement aroused by an average investigative pursuit novel. In both cases one may have the sensation that "one's heart is in one's mouth," that "one's hair is standing on end," that "cold shivers are running up and down one's spine," as popular speech has it, or that one must close one's eyes and is on the point of fainting from fright.

In short, both the roller coaster and the detective novel are machines for producing thrills—of the cooler kind in problem novels and of the more or less hot kind in traditional thrillers. A reader, like a rider, submits himself willingly to the prepared experiences of a closed-circuit system that promises to return him to the safety of his point of origin after having exposed him to a series of breathtaking dips and curves. The swish-back track of the roller coaster is the equivalent of the peripeteia of melodrama, with the important difference that the rider himself and not a character in a story is exposed to risk. In both cases, however, the sensations involved are experienced in a body, whether that of the rider or the reader. The analogy between popular literature and a roller coaster also helps us to realize that the pleasures we commonly engage in may themselves be divided into three distinct categories. There are those pleasures that we seek out by putting our bodies in the way of them directly, such as making love, eating, or playing a variety of participatory sports from tennis to skydiving; in such pleasures the element of risk is either practically nonexistent or very real. Second, there are the pleasures that we experience indirectly by watching others performing in live situations, such as certain spectator sports, where the risks are more or less limited but the consequences real and permanent. And third, there are those pleasures which we witness as imaginative constructions, where the risks may be unlimited but the consequences are also unreal and impermanent—the character we admired may be dead but the actor who played the part will get up again once the curtain falls.

Whether they be participatory or nonparticipatory, however, the three categories of pleasure-promoting activities all have in common the capacity to produce an agreeable state of excitement in the body. Furthermore, in most cases the excitement is associated with an element of fear or anxiety.[7] Even when they are noncompetitive, solitary activities, running and swimming commonly involve a challenge to the self—goals are set that are designed to prove one's power or fitness in such a way that the fear of failure is introduced. In all competitive sports, on the other hand, the fear of failure is a much more obvious factor. Thus, although it is true to say people run and swim among other things for the pleasure of feeling their whole body turned into an erotogenic zone through contact with wind and water, a higher oxygen intake, and an increased hearbeat, an awareness of risk commonly enhances such pleasure. In fact, some of the most popular of our contemporary participatory sports, such as skiing, sailing, and surfing, both stimulate the whole surface of the skin through the wind pressure involved and generate the agreeable tension associated with consciousness of risk.

No less an authority on literary suspense than Agatha Christie described surfing in a way that implies an analogy with narrative. There was, she declared, nothing like surfing: "Nothing like that rushing through the water at what seems to you a speed of two hundred miles an hour; all the way in from the far distant raft, until you arrived, gently slowing down, on the beach, and foundered among the soft flowing waves. It is one of the most perfect physical pleasures that I have known."[8] The two sentences, in fact, constitute an embryonic story that begins in a place of security—the raft—exposes the protagonist to the power of the wave and the sensation of great speed, and

7. Graham Greene has even gone so far as to suggest that "the basis of fear is in sex—the fear that we may not be able to bring it off. It spreads from there." Quoted from an interview in "Arts and Leisure," *New York Times* (March 9, 1980), p. 15.

8. *Agatha Christie: An Autobiography* (New York: Ballantine, 1977), p. 357.

returns her finally to the safe haven of the shore—"the soft flowing waves." Both the description of a downhill ski run[9] and a secret agent's mission would have a similar structure.

Such ways of organizing experience in order to stimulate and to satisfy are learned early in life, as D. W. Winnicott has made clear:

> Children, when playing, may get excited in a general way, and periodically the excitement can become localized and therefore obviously sexual, or urinary, or greedy, or something else based on the capacity of tissues for excitement. Excitement calls for climax. The obvious way out for a child is the game with climax, in which excitement leads to something, 'a chopper to chop off your head', a forfeit, a prize, someone is caught or killed, someone has won, and so on. [p. 152]

The various means, both direct and indirect, participatory and nonparticipatory, which adults employ in the pursuit of climax are not dissimilar. And narrative literature of all kinds is certainly one of the most reliable of such means. Moreover, it follows that the appeal of the detective story on the level of the anecdote is not in the end but in the process, in what it does to us as we read it rather than in the nature of the secret it withholds for the denouement. The reason why the classic psychoanalytic view of the genre's appeal is too narrow and simplistic, in fact, is that it ignores the reading process and the pleasure-producing structure of narrative. It assumes that the reader always reads a sexual meaning through the displacements and substitutions of the genre's violent imagery, that the mystery he pursues is always that of the primal scene. For Geraldine Pederson-Krag as for Charles Rycroft,[10] the transcendental signified of all detective stories is the secret of sexual intercourse.

The intent of the foregoing discussion, however, is to suggest that if detective stories share an affective structure both with erotic and competitive activities, with sex, sport, and war, it is not because in all these spheres we seek the revelation of parental lovemaking. Although sexual pleasure may be regarded as the touchstone by which

9. According to Conan Doyle's biographer, John Dickson Carr, Doyle introduced skiing to Switzerland and pronounced it "the nearest thing to flying." *The Life of Sir Arthur Conan Doyle* (New York: Harper and Row, 1949), p. 81.

10. "Detective Stories and the Primal Scene," *Psychoanalytic Quarterly* 18 (1949):207–14, and "The Analysis of a Detective Story," *Imagination and Reality* (New York: International Universities Press, 1968).

we measure all our pleasures, it is nevertheless true that we enjoy in our bodies a whole range of activities that should be regarded as substitutions for sex only in a metaphorical sense. The goal in our pursuit of pleasure is often not sex but excitation by another means. In the opposition between Eros and Thanatos, for example, the tendency to privilege the former in psychoanalytic criticism is overwhelming. Yet the popularity of the detective story suggests not that the latter is in some sense a substitute for the former, its perverted equivalent, but that both impulses are physiologically unified. Thus a detective novel may excite on the level of its manifest content of violence without any necessary allusion to a latent sexual signified.

Winnicott's comments on the way young children cope with the problem of excitation point to interesting parallels in adult life. He finds that among the mechanisms children devise is "employment of some sort of reliable climax, either eating or drinking or masturbation, or excited urination or defecation, or a temper tantrum, or a fight" (p. 156). Detective stories are for adults a sublimated form of "reliable climax" in which aggression is less a substitute than an alternative to sex. In this respect they resemble the stylized, rule-governed combat of competitive sport.

The testimony of a "squash widow," quoted by the London *Observer,* makes the point succinctly: "Arnold prefers to play younger men who are good at the game, but not as good as him since he hates to lose. Squash is the one time when he gets emotional and the main reason why he hasn't got time to have affairs. Competing with men is obviously more rewarding than dating girls."[11] And what is true of squash is equally true of a great many activities in which men choose to engage, from the hunting down of criminals, in life and in fiction, to gambling and chess. The pleasure is in each case similar to that derived from the reading of detective novels. Taken together all such activities confirm the idea of the unified character of our sensuous life that in the context of a meditation upon hunting was asserted by Thoreau: "all sensuality is one, though it takes many forms; all purity is one. It is the same whether a man eat, or drink, or cohabit, or sleep sensually. They are but one appetite."[12]

11. "Squash," *The Observer* (February 10, 1980), p. 45.

12. *Walden and Civil Disobedience: Authoritative Texts, Backgrounds, Reviews and Essays in Criticism,* ed. Owen Thomas (New York: Norton, 1966), p. 147.

PART II:
IDEOLOGY

6

Literature and Ideology

In the first part of this work I looked at the detective formula as an artifact designed to engage the attention and promote the pleasure of the reader, and I concentrated on its aesthetic properties and rhetorical strategies. Throughout, an implied premise of the discussion was that although at its outer limits the genre overlaps with the gothic novel and science fiction, on the one hand, and the novel of manners, on the other, mainstream detective fiction respects the conventions of the realist tradition. That is to say, it situates its actions in contemporary social reality, limits the type of crime and the methods of detection to what passes for rationally plausible, and chooses as its characters easily identifiable human or social types. Further, detective stories present themselves to their readers as substitute worlds or mirrors that reflect directly the reality beyond. All traces of their processes of production as texts are effaced in the interest of the illusion. Consequently, the reader of a detective story normally negotiates the modes of structuration of the verbal material without acknowledging their textual presence. Provided the rhetorical conventions are familiar to the point of transparency, the only other aspect of a work that may interfere with the easy processing of a text is represented material that is in unresolved contradiction with the reader's preconceptions as to how the world works. Missing from the discussion of readability in the previous section, in fact, is any reference to verisimilitude—what the French call *le vraisemblable*.

This concept assumed a new importance in France in the 1960s as part of the effort to understand how we accept a literary representation of reality as plausible, as in conformity with our own preconceptions.[1]

1. See *Communications* 2 (1968), and Gérard Genette, "Vraisemblance et Motivations," in *Figures II* (Paris: Seuil, 1969).

No novel is likely to be considered readable in either of the two senses discussed above if, apart from everything else, it appears to contradict our learned expectations concerning life's operations—unless, of course, the author anticipates the reader's objections and defines the work beforehand as a work of fantasy. Stephen Heath finds that a readable text is one "which repeats the generalized text of the social real institutionalized as Natural"; it is a discourse "that copies the discourse assumed as representative of Reality by the society (it is the *vraisemblable* of the society)."[2]

Stephen Heath touches here on the view that we learn fixed forms of social seeing and that one of the primary pedagogical instruments for transmitting such fixed forms is literature, particularly drama and the novel, and those derivatives from various kinds of literature to be found in the contemporary mass media. As defined by Heath, the concept of verisimilitude is used with a view to analyzing the role of conventions in the making of literary artifacts at all levels. The contemporary preoccupation with verisimilitude, in fact, forms part of that modern critical enterprise, deriving from phenomenology as well as from Marxism, which constantly reduces the domain of "the natural" by refusing to take any human activity at face value, beginning with perception. An interest in *le vraisemblable* as a collective conceptual system concretized in literary works, in its different historical forms, and in the modalities of its insertion into texts and of its transmission is therefore part of a renewed effort to come to terms with the question of ideology in general. *Le vraisemblable* is the most visible form taken by ideology in the mimetic tradition of literature. Before looking at the ideological systems embodied in that branch of the mimetic tradition we call detective stories, however, it will perhaps be helpful to suggest the meaning I am attaching to the endlessly discussed concept of ideology itself, more than a century and a half after the invention of the neologism.

The story of the origin of the concept in the circle of Destutt de Tracy and Cabanis and the change in its meaning effected in the early writings of Marx is by now familiar. It is, of course, significant that the term originated in the empirical tradition of the French Enlightenment only to be appropriated by the developing current of Young

2. Heath, *The Nouveau Roman*, p. 225.

Hegelian critical thought as a weapon against Hegelianism. It ceased in the process to mean a theoretical science committed to the study of the sources of ideas and came instead to signify the imaginary representation of concrete life situations. Its by now familiar premise in the new materialist German thought was that "life is not determined by consciousness but consciousness by life."[3] With the formulation of the fundamental Marxian distinction between infrastructure and superstructure, attention was focused on those mechanisms of the superstructure by means of which the reality of the historically conditioned material life processes reemerged transformed into unrecognizable ideas and systems of beliefs. Thus, in *The German Ideology* Marx and Engels sum up their critical purpose as follows: "we do not set out from what men say, imagine, conceive, nor from men as narrated, thought of, imagined, conceived, in order to arrive at men in the flesh. We set out from real, active men, and on the basis of their real life-process we demonstrate the development of ideological reflexes and echoes of this life process." (p. 47).

Marx himself was, of course, no mechanical determinist. Yet major refinements of his topographical model of an ideological superstructure resting on and determined by an economic infrastructure of the productive forces in association with the relations of production had to wait until the twentieth century. As far as literary studies are concerned, these refinements have been chiefly associated with the work of Gramsci, Althusser, Foucault, and Barthes.

By returning to a distinction, which had been crucial to Hegel and was updated by Marx, between political society and civil society, Gramsci introduced the important concept of hegemony to illuminate the way in which what he called the state agencies of repression (including particularly the bureaucracy, the army, and the police) function in a different sphere and in a different mode from those agencies of civil society that are the bearers of ideology (the church, the schools, the trade unions).[4] In Gramsci's analysis it is on account of the agencies of civil society, in fact, that the culture of the ruling class establishes domination over what is thought in a society. The conse-

3. Karl Marx and Friedrich Engels, *The German Ideology* (New York: International Publishers, 1978), p. 47.

4. *The Prison Notebooks: Selections*, trans. and ed. Quintin Hoare and Geoffrey Nowell Smith (New York: International Publishers, 1971).

quence is that the bourgeois state functions for the most part with the consent of the governed, resorting only relatively rarely to its agencies of repression to maintain its class rule.

The distinction made between the agencies of political society and those of civil society was further developed by Althusser in his important essay "Ideology and Ideological State Apparatuses." The question Althusser sets out to answer is how it is that the reproduction of the conditions of production in a given state is effected along with the reproduction of the relations of production. And he quickly passes from a discussion of the reproduction of the means of production—machinery and raw materials and the reproduction of labor power (via wages)—in order to emphasize the crucial role of ideology in the process of reproducing a disciplined workforce. After Gramsci, he finds that the superstructure may be broken down into what he calls the repressive state apparatus in the singular (the government, the administration, the army, the police, the courts, the prisons, etc.) and the plurality of ideological state apparatuses, such as the religious system, the educational system, the family, the legal and political system, including the party system, the trade unions, culture (literature, the arts, sports, etc.), and communications (press, radio, and television).

Althusser extends Gramsci's thought to the extent that he also seeks to know why we engage in ideological representation, and he discovers the answer not in the work of a caste of priests or despots practicing systematic mystification, nor, as with the young Hegelians and the early Marx, in the mechanism of alienation that returns men's activities to them objectified in unrecognizable and threatening forms, but in the nature of what is actually represented in ideology: "it is not their real conditions of existence, their real world, that 'men' 'represent to themselves' in ideology, but above all it is their relation to those conditions of existence which is represented by them there. . . . It is this relation that contains the 'cause' which has to explain the imaginary distortion of the ideological representation of the real world."[5] And he goes on to conclude later in the same essay that although ideology may be a form of false consciousness, as it has been

5. *Lenin and Philosophy and Other Essays* (New York and London: Monthly Review Press, 1971), pp. 164–65.

traditionally understood, we are nevertheless always "in ideology." Whether they live under bourgeois capitalism or Maoism, in effect, "individuals" are always "in a determinate (religious, ethical, etc.) representation of the world whose imaginary distortion depends on their imaginary relation to their conditions of existence" (p. 166). In short, "man is an ideological animal by nature" (p. 71).

In different ways both Michel Foucault and Roland Barthes have attached a similar meaning to ideology in exploring those ideological state apparatuses that are made up, on the one hand, of the human sciences and the institutions they support (asylums, clinics, prisons) and, on the other hand, of literature and everyday cultural systems. Foucault, of course, has redefined the term "discourse" in order to focus on the comprehensive value systems concretized in a dominant body of knowledge in an age. Barthes, on the other hand, first became known to a wider public through his analyses of the operations of "myth" in contemporary French culture, a term that in his usage recalls a phrase from *The German Ideology*, "those phantoms formed in the human brain" (p. 47). Barthes's most popular work, *Mythologies*, is useful for my present purpose because it shows how an ideological dimension may be discerned in a variety of apparently innocent representations, activities, and tastes. "Myth" implies a form of unreflective thought that permits political reality and its socioeconomic base to be dehistoricized. Through "myth" a value system becomes omnipresent and determinative and, if acknowledged at all, is looked upon as part of the permanent and necessary order of things. The sinister aspect of the process was suggested to Barthes by an analogy drawn from linguistics. The popular French "myths" that he analyzed, from the quasi-moral value attached to steak and red wine to the apparent naturalness of African soldiers saluting the tricolor flag, exhibit the presence of a denotative code that bears on its back an undeclared connotative code; a secondary mythical system is supported by a primary nonevaluative language system. And as *The Degree Zero of Writing* demonstrated at approximately the same time, something similar occurs wherever ordinary language is taken up and modified through the institution of literature; *écriture*, the middle term between (collective) *language* and (individual) *style* in Barthes's first book, is in effect class style.

In brief, all the above thinkers would concur with the idea that has by now become a commonplace, namely, that it is by means of the world of words that we imagine the world of things. Moreover, if we are always "in ideology," as Althusser put it, then a study of a popular genre, as of other manifestations of popular culture, is one of the ways we can better understand what it is we are in. The detective story belonged originally to that ideological state apparatus Althusser called culture, but since the rise of the mass media of film and television it is also associated with the overlapping ideological state apparatus of communications. Wherever we choose to locate it, however, what is certain is that nowhere more than in its popular literary genres are "the myths" of a culture more visible, in both Roland Barthes's and Richard Slotkin's sense.[6]

Before such "myths" are examined more closely, however, it is important to consider the connections between Western detective fiction in general and "the discourse of the Law" that was developed in the late eighteenth and early nineteenth centuries.

Like madness and medicine, crime and crime detection are cultural phenomena and therefore have a history. A crime always occurs in a community. It is by definition an antisocial act committed by one member of a human group against the group as a whole or another member of the group. As long as he remained alone on his island, Robinson Crusoe could commit no crimes, although he could continue to sin. Consequently, a crime implies the violation of a community code of conduct and demands a response in terms of the code. It always depends on a legal definition, and the law, as both Gramsci and Althusser make clear, is a key element of the superstructure in ensur-

---

6. Barthes's use of the term *myth* is somewhat narrower than that which has currency among English-speaking literary critics, largely on the basis of Anglo-American myth criticism. The differences as well as the common ground are apparent from Richard Slotkin's definition of the word in his important study of the myth of the hunter in American literature: "Myth, as I have defined it, is a narrative formulation of a culture's world view and self-concept, which draws both on the historical experience of that culture and on sources of feeling, fear, and aspiration (individual and universal / archetypal) deep in the human subconscious and which can be shown to function in that culture as a prescription for historical action and for value judgment." *Regeneration through Violence: The Mythology of the American Frontier, 1600–1860* (Middletown: Wesleyan University Press, 1973), p. 294.

ing the reproduction of the existing power relations in a society. As a result, in representing crime and its punishment, whether evoked or merely anticipated, detective novels invariably project the image of a given social order and the implied value system that helps sustain it. By naming a place and by evoking, however, glancingly, the socio-economic order that prevails within it, they confirm, in fact, that there can be no transgression without a code, no individual criminal act without a community that condemns it.

What is particularly notable about detective stories, however, is that they only exceptionally raise questions concerning the code; the law itself is accepted as a given. As a result, from a contemporary Marxist perspective the detective story may be understood as a branch of that ideological state apparatus called culture. It is, moreover, a branch whose particular mission involves the celebration of the repressive state apparatus or at least of that important element of it formed by the police. Detective fiction is part of "the discourse of the Law" that for Foucault was indispensable in the creation of the new "disciplinary society," which emerged in Europe in the post-Revolutionary decades.

The importance of modern critical thought in this respect—phenomenological and structuralist as well as Marxist—resides in the insight that while we seem to be taking only innocent pleasure in our popular readings, we are always at the same time inserted into a cultural value system. That is to say, whenever we learn to read, we learn not only how to decipher rows of words but also to accept at least in part the authority of the book. And the book reproduces the authority of the social order itself in its apparent coherence and naturalness. The dimension that is missing from formulaic works in the detective genre is, in fact, any recognition that the law itself, with its definitions of crimes and its agencies of law enforcement and punishment, is problematic.

Detective stories remind us that nothing brings ideological positions more sharply into focus than a crime, because a crime, in literature as in life, is for almost everyone a question that demands an answer. It always has the status of a symptom that raises the matter of cause and motivation, since the idea of a criminal *acte gratuit* is a scandal for both the heart and mind. Thus, in his short historical account of theories of crime, *Crime and Ideology,* Leo Radzinowicz shows how readily crime divides the liberal sheep from the conservative goats. He sums up the liberal theory of the social causation of crime in the following terms: "Society carries within itself, in some sense, the seeds of all the crimes which are going to be committed, together with facilities necessary for their development."[7] And he contrasts this liberal tradition with the conservative belief in individual causation or the concept of "criminal man," that is, with the view that a criminal is born and not made. Yet detective stories proper almost always ignore questions about the cause of crime or the legitimacy of the legal procedures such stories represent. In a detective story, unlike certain early nineteenth-century crime novels, in fact, the law itself is never put on trial.

In this respect detective fiction displays at a generic level that capacity for remaining mum at crucial points, which for Pierre Macherey characterizes all works of literature in some way or other. If a literary work can never know all of what it says, it can also never know all that it does not say, either. Consequently, the chief task of criticism comes to reside precisely in articulating the silences and the limits that a given work embodies: "The mirror is expressive just as much in what it does not reflect as in what it does. The true object of criticism is the absence of certain reflections or expressions. The mirror is from certain points of view a blind mirror but it nevertheless still remains a mirror in its blindness" (p. 151).

The fictional *mise en forme* of a found ideology, therefore, illuminates much of what went unstated concerning the new social order that emerged in the early nineteenth century. Whether consciously or not, the detective genre effectively remained silent about important aspects of crime by establishing narrow boundaries for its action from the beginning. A chronological model that encompasses the whole sequence of a criminal act and its expiation would need to distinguish the following phases: the preparation for crime, the crime itself, the investigation of the crime, the arrest of the criminal, the trial of the criminal and his punishment, which may mean his execution. But a detective story always effectively begins after a crime has been committed and at least for a time hides its criminal—in the formal detective story he is hidden right down to the denouement. On most occa-

7. *Crime and Ideology* (New York: Columbia University Press, 1966), p. 35.

sions, it also omits the trial—the closing scene in the library or its equivalent is usually sufficient to establish the truth of guilt. Finally and most significantly, the detective story invariably eliminates the concluding spectacle of punishment, except in a form associated particularly with the hard-boiled story, where punishment may be administered as in a shoot-out or a fistfight. In short, not only are the circumstances and motivation of the crime largely elided, along with the inner life of the criminal, but also on most occasions the spectacle of the momentous machinery of the law down to its apparatus of death and its hooded executioners.

The feat accomplished by the originators of the genre was to make the investigation itself dramatic and thus to avoid the representation of public punishment, which was associated with the practice of the *ancien régime* and was crucial to the sensationalism of popular broadsheet literature. From Poe on, the detective story confronted the atrocity of the crime with the gentleness of reason. Like the punitive practice of the nineteenth century itself, it strove "to put as much distance as possible between the 'serene' search for truth and the violence that cannot be entirely effaced from punishment."[8] Of the three ritual practices of the law, which are investigation, trial, and punishment, therefore, the nineteenth-century detective story usually retains only the first. Thus it reflects the reformed legal system of its time to the extent that it, too, reversed a previous state of affairs by making the investigation public and hiding punishment and execution. As Foucault has noted with reference to the detective genre, "we have moved from the exposition of the facts or the confession to the slow process of discovery; from the execution to the investigation; from the physical confrontation to the intellectual struggle between criminal and investigator."[9]

In brief, the developed form of the genre is to be seen as one expression of what Michel Foucault has called the new "sobriety in punishment." By the end of the nineteenth century at the latest, such sobriety had led to the radical revision of penal codes throughout the Western world, the institution of the prison sentence as the most common form of punishment for serious offenses, and an end to punish-

---

8. Michel Foucault, *Discipline and Punish* (New York: Vintage Books, 1979), p. 56.
9. Ibid., p. 69.

ment itself as a public spectacle. Yet central to Michel Foucault's thesis in *Discipline and Punish* is the idea that the price of the new mildness was constant surveillance. Thus his metaphor for the system of control established in the new age is Bentham's Panopticon. Instead of the dungeon that hides its prisoners in dark cells, the utilitarian's prison places its cells in elevated tiers that are always open to visual inspection from the tower at its center. At the core of the new penal system was an unseen seer.

Furthermore, what is true of the penal system is true of the organization of society at large. If the rise of the human sciences in the late eighteenth and early nineteenth centuries was indispensable for the establishment of the "disciplinary society"—a society in which order is imposed largely without coercion through the application of knowledge to human behavior—the human sciences were also crucial to the institution of the new police. The goal of that "police state," first erected with some semblance of its modern form under the regimes of the Revolution and the Empire, was control through surveillance. Ideally, society was to be made open to visual inspection down to its darkest recesses, so that dissent might be stifled, crime depoliticized, and the criminal underworld organized as a relatively harmless enclave within the established order. What was needed was an interlocking system founded on comprehensive surveillance and bureaucratic reporting with the prison at its center. Crime itself would be continuously monitored by a police whose typical instruments were the informer and the file index.[10] The new science of criminal investigation was, in fact, based on bureaucratic techniques of description and location that were supported by a developing technology, including eventually statistical analysis, forensic medicine, and the discovery of blood types, photography, telegraphy, more rapid modes of communication, fingerprinting, and the science of ballistics. Thus, by the

10. The influential reformer and author of *A Treatise on the Police of the Metropolis* (London, 1806), Patrick Colquhoun, promoted the idea of a "register" of all known offenders that would record among other things the history of their connections and their haunts. See W. L. Melville Lee, *A History of Police in England* (Montclair, New Jersey: Patterson Smith, 1971), p. 220. J. J. Tobias has called Colquhoun "an indefatigable counter and comparer," *Crime and Industrial Society in the Nineteenth Century* (New York: Schocken, 1967), p. 14.

time of Doyle, the Great Detective of fiction had himself the essential qualities of the unseen seer, who stands at the center of the social Panopticon and employs his "science" to make all things visible on behalf of the forces of order. It is no wonder if, under the new dispensation, investigation was found to generate drama enough. It represents in its way the exercise of lucid power over an identified enemy of society. The detective story promotes the "heroization" of the agent of surveillance in his struggle against threats from within.

Works in the genre always take a stand in defense of the established societal order, then, even when, as in certain hard-boiled novels, they uncover corruption among prominent citizens and public officials. And the cause of such generic "conservatism" is to be found in the first place at the level of the structure of the action. Like all popular literary genres—and this is confirmed by archetypal criticism as well as by structuralism—detective stories combine what might be called deep ideological constants with surface ideological variables. The former exist as indispensable structural elements of a deliberately delimited action and as the roles deriving from the action; the latter take the form of attributes of the dramatis personae, the character and milieu of crime, police methods, etc. The former are universal genre characteristics; the latter vary greatly from one cultural tradition to another and even from one author to another.

The deep ideological constant of the genre, therefore, is built into the action of investigation. The classic structuring question is always "Whodunit" and, secondarily, how will justice be done. In the beginning of a detective story is a crime that implies both a villain and a victim of villainy, but the action itself always focuses on the acts of a hero who is summoned in order to pursue and punish the villain and, wherever possible, to rescue the victim and restore the status quo ante as well. Whether the emphasis is placed on the problem of solving the puzzle of the crime or on the difficulty of the pursuit, on ratiocination or on the virile prowess demanded by a protracted search, the action of heroic investigation is unvarying. The point of view adopted is always that of the detective, which is to say, of the police, however much of an amateur the investigator may appear to be. In a detective story the moral legitimacy of the detective's role is never in doubt. Where in a social crime novel like *Caleb Williams* or *Les Misérables* the manhunt is made deeply problematic, in a detective story it is always legitimated, often by insisting on the peculiar horror of the crime committed.

Furthermore, the detective's role is such that he is always perceived as an exceptional individual whose powers are enlisted by the representative victims of a given community in a war with an enemy. As a result, it is clear that the detective story is a form of traditional heroic "discourse" in modern guise. It celebrates traditional heroic virtues and expresses many of the attitudes associated with an ideology of hero worship. Given that fact, the genre is potentially anathema to such ideological adversaries of heroic male action as certain religious leaders, libertarians, utopians, social collectivists, and radical feminists, whose purpose is to forge a new sensibility and new forms of human association.[11] There is, on the other hand, no structural impediment preventing a detective novel from choosing as its investigator an agent of either the KGB or the CIA because, once the principle of heroic male action against an enemy is conceded, such identifications occur at the level of surface ideological variables.

At that level, therefore, the genre is ideologically reversible, as the quasi-universality of its appeal suggests. The fixity of the investigative action that is the generic *sine qua non* gives rise to a limited number of roles which may be distributed among characters most of whose attributes are no more inherent in those roles than are the red and white uniforms in the functions of players in a team game or the black and white color in the power of the pieces in a game of chess. Consequently, a hero may be male or female, young or old, lean and tough or corpulent and benevolent, European or Asian, liberal or com-

11. Richard Slotkin describes as follows the traditional opposition between the mythology of the hunter and that of the shaman emphasized by Joseph Campbell in *Creative Mythology*: "The former provides the cosmology and ethic for a religion of world heroes, dominators, rulers, exploiters; the latter is the mythology of the saint and seer, the mystic adventurer in consciousness, who experiences and suffers the universe, mastering it through sympathy rather than power." *Regeneration through Violence*, p. 559. Note also Umberto Eco's comment that "Fleming is conservative as, basically, the fable, any fable, is conservative: it is the static inherent dogmatic conservatism of fairytales and myths, which transmit an elementary wisdom, constructed and communicated by a simple play of light and shade." "The Narrative Structure in Ian Fleming," p. 61.

munist. Heroism, it seems, may take the most unlikely of forms while remaining true to its essence. Moreover, the same is true of villainy.

When, at the denouement of a formal detective novel, the criminal is made to stand forth, he may be shown to have any possible combination of physiognomy, race, class, profession, and sex. The character types assuming the villain's role are as different as those who play detective. They may be defined as solitary psychotics, murderers for gain, the mobsters of organized crime, jealous husbands, double agents, or fanatical foreign ideologues. And it is precisely the genre's flexibility in these matters that accounts in part for its continuing popularity. The presence of crime remains constant along with the role of an investigating hero in pursuit of a criminal, but almost everything else is subject to change. As a result, the formula adapts itself easily to the changing objects of popular anxiety.

Nevertheless, what is perhaps even more remarkable is the persistence of certain recognizable national cultural traditions within the large corpus of detective fiction. The way in which successful writers from different traditions represent the fight against crime turns out to be an unusually fertile source of information about national "myths." Given that detective fiction owes it longevity to its power of grafting contemporary fears on to an endlessly repeated formula, it brings into focus the continuity of a social *vraisemblable* as well as the persistence of touchstones for both heroic and villainous behavior. That this is the case will appear most obviously where the national cultures share a common language and a common literary heritage. We are fortunate in having the two divergent strains of the British and American detective novel at hand as a remarkable example of the radically different meanings a formulaic genre can be made to contain at the level of its surface ideological variables. If for fundamental structural reasons the genre constitutes a "discourse" that limits the kind of issues that may be raised within it, nevertheless within those limits a detective novel may be made to accommodate a relatively wide variety of cultural norms.

It does not follow, of course, that all British writers will necessarily conform to the single model of the formal detective story, as the careers of James Hadley Chase and Peter Cheyney attest. Similarly, the success of American writers from S. S. Van Dine and Ellery Queen to Rex Stout confirms that there is no congenital limit preventing an American from writing detective novels in a recognizably British mode. Yet it is no accident if the work of all the writers just mentioned is essentially derivative and amounts to little more than the commercially successful exploitation of a vogue invented elsewhere.

The fact is that after Poe—who was writing at a time when there was still, in effect, a single Anglo-American literary tradition—by far the most memorable detective story writing in America is in the hard-boiled tradition, whereas in England the tradition of Collins and Doyle has remained the most vital. The emergence of hard-boiled detective fiction in the United States in the 1920s and 1930s can now be clearly acknowledged for what it was and what its most self-conscious practitioners already recognized it to be at the time, namely, the expression of the will to establish an anti-British countertradition in the genre. Hammett and Chandler in particular knowingly Americanized the detective story in response to the pressures of American life, tastes, and values.

Yet it should not be assumed that they created such an ideology whole. As Macherey has affirmed, "The writer is only apparently the author of the ideology contained in his work; in fact, that ideology was formed independently of him. One finds it in his books as he himself found it in life. The originality of Tolstoy's work will have to be sought elsewhere than in an ideology which did not need him in order to exist. Writers do not exist for the purpose of manufacturing ideologies" (p. 137). They do exist, however, for the purpose of making ideologies visible and they achieve this through the very activity of writing them into the forms of their fiction. To summarize Macherey further, the point is, finally, that ideologies are not embodied in literary works passively but they come to appear there objectified in all their fullness and contradiction; their significance is simultaneously asserted and defined through a perception of their limits. A realist novel is a mirror only to the extent that it is " 'a machine, which makes things stand out in relief a long way from themselves.' The mirror gives things a new dimension; it deepens them by means of other things which are not quite the same. It extends the world but it also grasps it, inflates it, tears it apart" (pp. 155–56).

A cursory reading of examples of the British and American traditionsin detective fiction is enough to reveal how thoroughly "visible" the national cultural ideologies and their class origins become. Where the prevailing moral ethos of the English formal tradition had by the 1920s become irony in gentility, that of the new Americans was a tough-minded cynicism. Where the English portrayed individual criminal acts against the background of a stable and harmonious society, the American writers showed crime as endemic and all-pervasive. The representation of mainly upper-middle-class life in semirural or elegant London settings gave way to a far broader social spectrum and a mixed urban backdrop. The realistic mode of native American naturalism and muckraking succeeded the satirical mode of the novel of manners.

The importance of both Hammett's and Chandler's appropriation and reconstruction of a model resides also in their redefinition of crime and its place in American life. In inventing a new language, a new investigator, and what might be called a new landscape for crime, these authors made the detective story communicate American myths that were largely alien to their British precursors. It is on such surface ideological variables that I shall concentrate in what follows, with particular attention to the important shifts in literary language as well as in the detective hero and in the landscape of crime. How the works in the detective genre of an author not writing in English embody a different fund of national myths will be suggested through an analysis of the fiction of Simenon. It will, I hope, be apparent that the most popular detective fiction everywhere represents an ideal form of policing insofar as it is in conformity with the most cherished behavioral norms of a given society. Wherever it appears, detective fiction always forms part of "the discourse of the Law," but what might be called the style of such discourse varies in interesting ways.

7

The Language of Detection

Hammett and Chandler have, of course, the reputation of being realists in crime for the reasons outlined by Chandler himself in his celebrated essay: "Hammett gave murder back to the kind of people who commit it for reasons, not just to provide a corpse; and with the means at hand, not hand-wrought dueling pistols, curare and tropical fish. He put these people down on paper as they were, and he made them talk and think in the language they customarily used for these purposes."[1]

The new realism that Chandler defines here is itself in the American grain because it operates on two fronts simultaneously, that of style as well as content. It is a continuation of the nineteenth-century campaign against the nightingale and the skylark as well as against the use of the King's English as the standard literary medium. In affirming Hammett's departure from the model of the detective story current in his time, Chandler shows that his own quarrel was with both the substance and style of the classic detective novel but not with the formula as such.

What he has to say about Hammett is, therefore, accurate but misleading. It is certainly true that Hammett did show how detective fiction might be made serious again. The reason why, however, is not that he represented life more accurately than did Agatha Christie but that he adapted to the genre a new and more exciting set of literary conventions better suited to the taste of the time and the place. Like all literary realisms, Hammett's and Chandler's is a matter of stylization. Nothing, as Roland Barthes demonstrated some time ago, is more obviously a matter of stylistic conventions than the so-called

---

1. "The Simple Art of Murder," in *The Simple Art of Murder*, ed. James Nelson (New York: W. W. Norton, 1968), p. 530.

naturalism of Zola and Maupassant. Like the realism of Mark Twain and Hemingway, that of the hard-boiled detective novel is an expression of ideological commitment, an *écriture*. Consequently, it has the status of a distorting mirror for Americans in search of self-definition, a cause for both self-congratulation and self-hate. And in the case of Hammett and Chandler as well as of Twain and Hemingway, the most important of the new conventions adopted, insofar as it conditioned everything else, was the choice of a stylistic level for their narratives that substituted an American vernacular for the standard British idiom.

The Soviet linguist V. N. Voloshinov has shed light on the process involved. In his Marxist critical study of theories of language in his time, *Marxism and the Philosophy of Language,* Voloshinov redefines the basic reality of language as "verbal interaction." By that he means all verbal communication is in some sense performative or dialogic in nature, including communications between a writer and a reader: "But dialogue can also be understood in a broader sense, meaning not only face-to-face, vocalized verbal communication between persons but also communication of any type whatsoever. A book, i.e., *a verbal performance in print,* is also an element of verbal communication." From the point of view of the present essay, the principle involved is important because it leads to the conclusion that "a verbal performance of this kind also inevitably orients itself with respect to previous performances in the same sphere, both those by the same author and those by other authors. It inevitably takes its point of departure from some particular state of affairs involving a scientific problem or a literary style. Thus the printed verbal performance engages, as it were, in ideological colloquy of large scale: it responds to something, objects to something, affirms something, anticipates possible responses and objections, seeks support, and so on."[2] Such is obviously the case with the American hard-boiled detective novel

2. Translated by Ladislav Matejka and I. R. Titunik (New York and London: Seminar Press, 1973), pp. 94–95. Macherey formulates a similar idea in the terminology of structuralism: "The literary work never appears alone. It is always determined by the existence of other works, which may belong to other sectors of literary production. There is no first book nor independent book nor wholly innocent book. Novelty and originality in literature as in other things are always defined in relational terms. Thus a book is always the place of an exchange. Its autonomy and its coherence are purchased at the cost of difference, which may also on occasion be a diminution." *Pour une théorie de la production littéraire*, p. 122.

and nowhere more obviously than in the search for an appropriate idiom.

It is, of course, a commonplace that like the Italians in a different historical context, American writers have always been preoccupied by the "questione delle lingua," because the language a people uses raises questions of national identity at the deepest level. The story of the Americans' relation to their language is familiar. In literature especially, the search for a native American idiom is among other things an expression of the traditional American ambivalence felt for British life, culture, and institutions. It was originally rooted in the historical circumstance of having inherited a mother tongue from a rejected fatherland, a circumstance that seemed to require the undertaking of a cultural and linguistic rebellion similar to the one that had already been completed in the political sphere.

If consciousness functions only by means of the material medium of language, as Marx already implied,[3] the difficulty of developing a different form of consciousness begins with the obstacle of an alien idiom. If we are to believe Voloshinov, in fact, as far as the individual is concerned the task is impossible to the extent that the existence of communal language always precedes the coming to consciousness. Language is a semiotic system without which there is no inner speech any more than there is outer speech: "consciousness can arise and become a viable fact only in the material embodiment of signs. . . . Consciousness takes shape and being in the interest of signs created by an organized group in the process of social interaction. The individual consciousness is nurtured on signs: it derives its growth from them: it reflects their logic and laws." Moreover, given further that "the domain of ideology coincides with the domain of signs" (pp. 10–14), the problem for the individual of escaping from the ideology of a given language system seems insoluble. Yet Voloshinov also provides the concept which suggests that for self-conscious groups within a wider language community, at least, there is a way out. The concept involved is that of "the social multiaccentuality of the ideological sign." What Voloshinov means by the term "multiaccentuality" is that in practice all the natural languages of complex societies are likely to possess a variety of more or less conflicting speech levels.

3. *The German Ideology*, pp. 50–51.

New modes of consciousness may therefore be fabricated on the contrastive systems within the broad system: "Class does not coincide with the sign community, i.e., with the community that is the totality of users of the set of signs for ideological communication. Thus various different classes will use one and the same language. As a result, differently oriented accents intersect in every ideological sign. Sign becomes an arena of the class struggle" (p. 23). Further, where for historical reasons new nations develop sharing a common tongue with older nations, the language itself may become an arena for a national cultural struggle. In the case of the rival claims made on English by the British and the Americans, it is clear that the national struggle has from the beginning been combined with a class struggle.

The task of inventing a new American man, undertaken during the revolutionary and early republican eras, therefore, had to begin with a language that, if it could not itself be new, should at least be perceptibly different from the original British model. The reason why American authors from Mark Twain on were peculiarly preoccupied with the task of fashioning an American vernacular adapted to serious literary ends was consciously ideological. They were responding to the widely felt need to make the language of a class-conscious monarchy suitable for the use of a democratic people living under a republic. Within the British verbal Empire, they sought to stake out an anti-British verbal territory. The creation of a recognizably American form of literary English was, therefore, tantamount to an assertion of cultural emancipation and independent national identity. Thus it is not surprising that in the Anglo-American fictional tradition the Americans are the ones more consistently preoccupied with the problem of "style," because what is involved is not simply the inscription of individuality but an *écriture,* that is to say a national style that is at the same time a class style. And what is true for the history of the American novel in general is confirmed by the detective novel.

The self-consciousness of the pursuit of an appropriate American idiom has been explored by, among others, Richard Bridgman,[4] and his study confirms Chandler's own awareness that the represented

---

4. *The Colloquial Style in America* (New York: Oxford University Press, 1966). See also Richard Poirier, *A World Elsewhere: The Place of Style in American Literature* (New York: Oxford University Press, 1966).

speech of fiction is always different from actual spoken language. Chandler makes clear in the essay quoted above how for Hammett as for everyone else a vernacular literary style is always a question of art:

> He had style, but his audience didn't know it, because it was in a language not supposed to be capable of such refinements. They thought they were getting a good meaty melodrama written in the kind of lingo they imagined they wrote themselves. It was, in a sense, but it was much more. All language begins with speech, and the speech of common men at that, but when it develops to the point of becoming a literary medium it only looks like speech. Hammett's style at its worst was as formalized as a page of *Marius the Epicurean;* at its best it could say almost anything. [p. 530]

Chandler's point is that it is nonsense to assume that adult American males have ever actually talked like Sam Spade or Philip Marlowe any more than American country boys once sounded like Huckleberry Finn. In both cases the languages employed were created by their authors for literary purposes. In a Twain or Chandler novel the reader is faced with a fabricated vernacular that is a form of idealized speech. The voices of Philip Marlowe and Huckleberry Finn are more American than American life itself. The stylistic level chosen to represent their speech is important for its connotative power apart from anything it might denote. Its real significance is mythic because it was invented to express by itself class and regional values that aspire to the status of cherished national values. As Stephen Heath has put it, "The choice of an *écriture* is the choice of a set of values, a way of seeing, an act of socio-historical solidarity."[5] Thus Mark Twain's *écriture* is the class style of middle-class, small-town, midwestern America, the literary idiom of the heartland. It is a class style that Hammett and Chandler were to update as something more urban and fast-paced.

A comparison of the opening passages of three first novels by Agatha Christie, Dashiell Hammett, and Raymond Chandler respectively suggests the gap consciously opened up by the American writers:

> The intense interest aroused in the public by what was known at the time as "The Styles Case" has now somewhat subsided. Nevertheless, in view of the world-wide notoriety which attended it, I have been asked, both by my friend Poirot and the family themselves, to write an account of the

5. *The Nouveau Roman*, p. 208.

whole story. This, we trust, will effectually silence the sensational rumours which still persist.

I will therefore briefly set down the circumstances which led to my being connected with the affair.[6]

I first heard Personville called Poisonville by a red-haired mucker named Hickey Dewey in the Big Ship at Butte. He also called a shirt a shoit. I didn't think anything of what he had done to the city's name. Later I heard men who could manage their r's give it the same pronunciation. I still didn't see anything in it but the meaningless sort of humor that used to make richardsnary the thieves' word for dictionary. A few years later I went to Personville and learned better.[7]

It was about eleven o'clock in the morning, mid-October, with the sun not shining and a look of hard wet rain in the clearness of the foothills. I was wearing my powder-blue suit, with dark blue shirt, tie and display handkerchief, black brogues, black wool socks with dark blue clocks on them. I was neat, clean, shaved and sober, and I didn't care who knew it. I was everything the well-dressed private detective ought to be. I was calling on four million dollars.[8]

The style chosen by Agatha Christie as the idiom of her narrator is that of a formal written prose characterized by its roundness and a fondness for the parenthetical phrase. The cumbersome but well-constructed sentences with their predictable adjectives—"intense interest," "world-wide notoriety," "sensational rumours"—and their British adverbs—"somewhat subsided," "effectively silenced"—connote social conformity, circumspection, and sobriety. They also suggest the self-confidence of a class that took its own vernacular for the norm of correct English speech and that therefore found it necessary to put the speech of farm laborers, shopkeepers, and cockneys into quotation marks.

Further, the style Agatha Christie produces for her first-person narrator, one that is not very different from her own authorial style, combines a taste for understatement with a leisurely formality. As such it supplies the appropriate voice for a character who goes on to intro-

6. *The Mysterious Affair at Styles* (1926; reprint ed., New York: Bantam Books, 1961), p. 1.

7. *Red Harvest The Novels of Dashiell Hammett* (1929; reprint ed., New York: Knopf, 1965), p. 3.

8. *The Big Sleep* (1939; reprint ed., New York: Ballantine Books, 1971), p. 1.

duce himself as a member of the World War I British officer class called upon to handle with delicacy a scandalous business.[9] The voice of Hastings is well suited to exemplify the tone of golden age British detective fiction in general. By the same token, it is also appropriate that Hastings turns out to be an officer returned from the Great War. The ethos of *The Mysterious Affair at Styles* might well be characterized as Welcome Back to All That.

Agatha Christie's choice of the polished version of polite middle-class English speech for the ideolect of her narrator was obviously made in full consciousness of the audience she was writing for. Moreover, it is characteristic of the formal detective genre that it does not incorporate any other level of speech into itself apart, occasionally, from the country or cockney speech of odd lower-class characters. Unlike that literary tradition which from Villon to Fielding, Dickens, and Victor Hugo admitted an element of underworld speech into its representation of criminal milieus for the sake of its inventiveness and irreverent energy, the formal detective story insists on good taste to the point of suppressing the threat of the underworld down to its slang. Agatha Christie's practice on the level of language confirms Voloshinov's theory that "the ruling class strives to impart a supra-class, eternal character to the ideological sign, to extinguish or drive inward the struggle between social value judgments which occurs in it, to make the sign uniaccentual" (p. 23).

The example of the British author's first novel also suggests that the choice of a voice also implies the delineation of a character type. In the absence of evidence to the contrary, the assumption a reader makes is that to sound like Hastings is to be a Hastings. And the truth of that circumstance is verified negatively by a novel like *The Murder of Roger Ackroyd*, which ironically exploits such an assumption. In order to conceal the fact that her narrator is himself the murderer, Christie offers as a guarantee of his reliability and honor the class speech of Watson / Hastings.

---

9. If it were not for the fact that Agatha Christie was deliberately representing a type, the passage could be offered as an example of Chandler's charge that written English style is inferior to American because of its tolerance for the cliché: "Consider the appalling, because apparently unconscious, use of clichés by as good a writer as Somerset Maugham in *The Summing Up*, the deadly repetition of pet words until they almost make you scream." MacShane, ed., *The Notebooks*, p. 20.

Further, the opening paragraph of Agatha Christie's first novel is also typical because it is deliberately constructed on the irony of claiming to deny the sensational in order to excite an interest in it. As such, it serves as a reminder that the formal detective novel is founded on the central irony of the surprise of crime, which expresses itself in three characteristic forms soon to become a predictable formula. To the endlessly repeated irony of the most unlikely suspect, the formal detective novel added those of the most unlikely detective and the most unlikely place. A foppish lord, a vain and overweight Belgian, and an elderly gentlewoman are only the most familiar of twentieth-century English examples of eccentric detectives. There is a similar eccentricity in siting crime in circumstances of order and beauty, from rural communities to Oxford colleges and gentlemen's clubs, rather than in the chaotic cities. The force of such ironies is to establish an ambience of play.

In this connection, the purpose of the circumlocutionary beginning here is to establish distance. Agatha Christie is still working in the tradition of Poe, Collins, and Doyle to the extent that she writes not a novel of spoken action in the mode of Hammett and Chandler but a form of memoir novel supposedly set down by a narrator / witness after the fact. The Holmes stories typically take the form of case-books, written in tranquillity by Dr. Watson. This strategy explains in part the cooler temperature of the formal detective novel when compared with the thriller.

In spite of the wit in the opening paragraph of *Red Harvest*, on the other hand, there is nothing playful about Hammett's novel. If a sentence were needed to introduce the tone of the new wave in detective fiction, it would be hard to improve on Hammett's first two lines: "I first heard Personville called Poisonville by a red-haired mucker named Hickey Dewey in the Big Ship at Butte."

The paragraph is a typically strong opening characterized by richness of verbal texture in the vein of the antipicturesque. It not only identifies memorably a place and points ahead to a dilemma, it introduces an unforgettable voice. Yet the reason it attracts immediate attention is rhetorical. The fact that Hammett forces the reader to pay attention to his medium suggests immediately that we are in the presence of a *texte de plaisir*. That first sentence is remarkable because of its staccato rhythms, its alliterative energy, and its internal rhymes as well as by the way in which it plays suggestively with evocative, no-nonsense American names. The whole paragraph recalls a direct, conversational American speech that is both funny and tough. Finally, with a movement characteristic of the hard-boiled tradition, it moves toward a climax which is understated but sinister. In other words, although Hammett makes references to contemporary American speech in this passage, the stylistic subtlety is of a kind associated with written prose.

In *The Big Sleep* Chandler follows the example of Hammett's first novel in closing the gap between narrator and detective common in the British tradition. His private eye reports directly, telling it both "like it is" and how it happens, combining the highly rated American skills of the newspaper reporter and the sports commentator. In the tradition of the hard-boiled detective story the technique of the first-person detective narrator is valuable because it permits a perfect match between language and behavior, speech and ethics. After Mark Twain, Lardner, and Hemingway, as well as Hammett, Chandler constructed his own form of action writing that relies for its richness on adapting spoken American.

In the first paragraph of his first novel, Chandler provides a flashier example of the antipicturesque than does Hammett. The passage introduces the characteristic note of toughness with its opening negative— "with the sun not shining." But in this particular passage the toughness is suggested largely through speech characterized by casualness and elliptical colloquialisms— "about eleven o'clock," "mid-October."

As with Hammett, however, the apparent casualness of represented speech hides a mastery of tone and rhythm. The four sentences following the opening evocation of a scene are typical of the rhetorical complexity to be found in Chandler's prose. All four are characterized by a structural similarity with rhythmic variation. They all open with the same "I was" and are followed by descriptions. As a result, at the same time that they communicate the information which defines a place, a task, and a point of view, because of a parallelism in structure the four sentences also prepare a surprise for the reader. Whereas the first three sentences are longer and involve a progression in describing details of personal appearance, the last sentence is short and describes an occurrence. It is the swift and unexpected climax of a slow buildup. The effect obtained is that of the punch line.

The whole passage is typical of the way in which Chandler's rhetorical control is designed to serve a functional end. The structure of the opening paragraph not only enables him to deliver the attention-grabbing last line—a lesser writer like Spillane would have to throw in a corpse—it also permits him to introduce an ethos and a type. If the "I's" are all up front here, it is in order to establish "the character" who will go by the name of Philip Marlowe. Chandler invents the speech in order to create the brash assurance of a self-advertising type with a sense of irony and an unapologetic city-bred, West Coast taste in manner and clothes. If in life speech is the most profoundly revelatory of all kinds of human behavior, in literature it creates such behavior. In a novel, speech makes the man who is offered up for the reader's evaluation.[10]

What we find in the language of the two American writers is, then, the implied preference for directness over formality, lower-class speech over upper, popular over high culture, American forthrightness over English gentility. The language chosen is a mode of address, a style of self-presentation, and an affirmation of American manliness. Through the medium of written speech both Hammett and Chandler provide clear examples of what Voloshinov has called "behavioral ideology," that is to say, ideology not as systematized in "art, ethics, law" but as perceptible in "the whole aggregate of life experiences and the outward expressions directly connected with it. Behavioral ideology is that atmosphere of unsystematized and unfixed inner and outer speech which endows every instance of behavior and action and our every conscious state with meaning" (p. 91).

At the same time the refashioning of American literary language was also crucial in the production of a new kind of action writing, an action writing that attempted to go as far as verbally possible in making the reader experience the pace and violence of the events narrated.

10. The literary self-consciousness of Chandler's written style is made clear by the reaction of recent audiences to movie versions of his work. The continuing vogue of Humphrey Bogart's private eye derives in no small measure from the camp taste that enjoys a form of dialogue and behavioral style that is experienced as dated and as too good to be true. Part of the pleasure is in seeing through cinematic formulas whose conventionality is evident to the spectator. It is not that American reality, including popular speech, has changed so much, but that the conventions adopted for representing it have. Philip Marlowe and Sam Spade look like period portraits that are as extravagant in their American way as is Sherlock Holmes in his English way.

As I noted earlier, however, the hard-boiled story strains verisimilitude by representing such events as the first-person commentary of a character who is simultaneously involved in the violent action. The reason the hard-boiled writers accepted such a risk was that it was a way of bringing the reader closer to the action as well as of justifying in print the colloquial American voice. The illusion created is of a point of view so close to the action that it is not so much from the ringside as from within the ring itself. A shoot-out scene in a dark apartment from Hammett's "The Whosis Kid" is typical.

> The Kid, whatever he was up to, made no sound.
> The dark woman began to sob beside me. Throat noises that could guide bullets.
> I lumped her with my eyes and cursed the lot—not aloud, but from the heart.
> My eyes smarted. Moisture filmed them. I blinked it away, losing sight of the watch for precious instants. The butt of my gun was slimy with my hand's sweat. I was thoroughly uncomfortable, inside and out.
> Gunpowder burned at my face.
> A screaming maniac of a woman was crawling all over me.
> My bullet hit nothing lower than the ceiling.
> I flung, maybe kicked, the woman off, and snaked backward. She moaned somewhere to one side. I couldn't see the Kid—couldn't hear him. The watch was visible further away. A rustling.
> The watch vanished.
> I fired at it.
> Two points of light near the door gave out fire and thunder.
> My gun-barrel as close to the floor as I could hold it, I fired between those points. Twice.
> Twin flames struck at me again.[11]

Perhaps the most striking feature of the passage is its graphic disposition on the page. It is made up of short sentences that are either isolated as if they were paragraphs or combined in twos and threes to make paragraphs that themselves never exceed roughly three lines. In defiance of the traditional norms of prose fiction, the spaces around words are exploited for the purpose of emphasis. A similar purpose is also served by a syntactical simplicity that takes the form of short dec-

---

11. *The Continental Op*, ed. Steven Marcus (New York: Vintage, 1975), pp. 234–35.

larative sentences, verbless sentences, and sentences of isolated words, all of which contribute to suggest the idea of speed and tension. A comparable technique of ellipsis also operates on the semantic level, where the action sequence is narrated as a series of sharp perceptions experienced in the body of a participant observer. A sensation of burning is noted without the report of a gunshot, the destination of the bullet from the Continental Op's gun is recorded, but there is no reference to his having fired it. Finally, there is the characteristic fondness for verbs that connote conflict ("flung," "kicked," "snaked backward"), tough colloquialisms ("lumped her," "maybe kicked"), and a reaching for neologisms or metaphors that make sensation new ("filmed" for cover with a film, "burned at" for burned, and "snaked backward").

Such inventiveness on the level of metaphor could produce the variety of ways of expressing gunfire to be found in *Red Harvest.*

> . . . a dozen guns emptied themselves . . .
> . . . a bullet kissed a hole in the door frame . . .
> . . . an automobile came down the street toward me, moving fast, leaking gunfire from the rear . . .
> . . . the machine-gun settled down to business, grinding out metal like the busy little death factory it was . . .
> . . . bullets bit chunks out of the car's curtains . . .
> . . . slugs were cutting at us from a wooden building . . .
> . . . a gun said something, the same thing four times, roaring like a 16-inch rifle under the iron roof . . . [12]

However, it is not only in its metaphors but in its total sign system of graphics, syntax, choice of words, and colloquialisms that the writing of the hard-boiled genre responded to the desire to make prose suitable for the representation of twentieth-century American action, for brawling and shooting, for automobiles, automatics, and machine guns. Traditional prose was redesigned to promote in a reader the disorientation and shock that accompany violent action. After this kind of writing there was probably nowhere else to go in the direction of the representation of violence than into the action comic strip, a peculiarly American medium that devised a highly original narrative

12. Quoted by William F. Nolan in *Dashiell Hammett: A Casebook,* p. 49.

graphic style and reduced language to the rudimentary level of stylized ejaculations expressive of power and pain.

In *The Colloquial Style in America* Richard Bridgman estimates that what he calls, "the process of establishing a literary imitation of colloquial speech and then polishing it" (p. 9) took until the 1920s to complete. Hemingway's first published book, *Three Stories and Poems*, appeared in 1923, six years before Dashiell Hammett's, and in Bridgman's view it was only with Hemingway that a satisfactory synthesis was finally achieved. In deference to American democratic principles, the effect was, in any case, not simply to remove the quotation marks in the texts from nonstandard speech. It was also to confer the dignity of print on what sounded like the language of ordinary people.

Richard Bridgman also asserts that "the motor force of a native style in the United States" was the triple one of "romantic individualism, nationalistic pride, and practical necessity" (p. 41). Whether or not these three contributing causes were equally valid in the nineteenth century, it seems certain that in the twentieth a further force was the spirit of populist antielitism.

The point to note here is that in order to fulfill such drives, the literary language invented does not have to be American; it has only to sound, or better still, to read like American. And it could achieve this by reading differently from standard British English. In general, as the above passage from Hammett suggests, for a written language to read like American meant choosing concrete words rather than abstract, and colloquial ones rather than their learned equivalents. It also meant preferring the simpler declarative sentences and repetitive rhetorical devices of conversation over the syntactically complex sentences and formal ornament of traditional literary prose. The style alone should suffice to remind the reader that "the abstract watchwords of a yeoman republic were . . . honesty, manliness, simplicity" (p. 42). The goal was a written word responsive to the belief still expressed in the 1920s by Sherwood Anderson that the truth lay among "farmers, working men, business men, painters."[13] It is on comparable ideological grounds that both Hammett and Chandler find in the tough talk of

13. Quoted by Bridgman, p. 154.

their private eyes the last refuge of truth in America—unlike Lardner, in whose work colloquial speech is as often as not a mask for moral sleaziness.

The examples of Hammett and Chandler are a reminder of the bridge that exists in all fiction between style as verbal choice and style as behavior. As far as the American authors are concerned, the precedent for such first-person narrators, who were both Western loudmouths and heroic men of action, extends far back into the nineteenth century. In "Big Bear of Arkansas" Thomas B. Thorpe's backwoodsman, Jim Doggett, is part clown, part hero, whose "class and condition are reflected in dress, boisterous manners, and dialect."[14] Similarly, in Chandler's novels the texture and tone of the written words create the character of the private eye and not vice versa. Philip Marlowe's spirit of independence is in the language Chandler chooses to express him before it is made explicit through commentary and incident. Chandler's fondness for stylish prose makes his stylish hero. Conversely, what Chandler's novels also reveal is that to equip a sympathetic and popular American hero with a colloquial style was to end up with the quintessentially American stylistic feature of the wisecrack and its figurative equivalent, the ostentatious simile.

Chandler not only constructs fictions that contain a great many arresting one-liners, therefore, he is also influenced by the form of the wisecrack in the construction of paragraphs and chapters as well as in the evocation of character, decor, and attitudes. What animates Chandler's narrative at all levels is the stylist's impulse to shape everything he writes in preparation for the delivery of a punch line. Such, for instance, is the case with the opening paragraph of *The Big Sleep* already quoted and with the denouement of the same work. That the archcriminal turns out in the end to be the perverted baby doll who falls into Marlowe's arms on the fourth page of the novel has about it the swift and unanswerable finality of the best punch lines and, in the context, warrants the sustained darkness of the mood with which the novel ends. Apart from anything else, Chandler's fondness for the form of the detective novel could be explained by a characteristic plot structure which ends with the shock of revelation.

14. *Regeneration through Violence*, p. 479.

In its own right, the wisecrack is the maxim of the American working classes. As with the maxim of the European aristocratic tradition, the wisecrack combines at its level the quintessence of style with the body of wisdom. Like the maxim it is pointed and ellipitical, but unlike the maxim, since its point of view is from the bottom up, it relies for its power on a cynical irreverence often made memorable by the shock of the vernacular. And it was above all Chandler who first realized the expressive possibilities of that most American of oral folk forms and allowed it to influence the structure, style, and choice of hero of a novel.

Further, it is in general true that no other writer of detective fiction has been so preoccupied with questions of vocabulary and idiom to the point of collecting examples of working men's and underworld slang.[15] And it is important to note that he came to such a slang as an outsider, a litterateur, who was drawn by the vitality and suggestiveness of the verbal material and who was aware that slang on the printed page is no longer slang. Its use by an author derives from a preoccupation with the poetic function of language in Roman Jakobson's sense, that is, with language that consciously foregrounds itself as verbal presence. It is perhaps not surprising, therefore, that Chandler comes close to the paradoxical conclusion that, in order to write American, it is better not to speak it unselfconsciously as a native: "All the best American writing has been done by men who are, or at some time were, cosmopolitans. They found here a certain freedom of expression, a certain richness of vocabulary, a certain wideness of interest. But they had to have European taste to use the material."[16]

The result in Chandler's case was that whereas he dropped the conventional ironies of the British detective tradition, he invented a new and original one, namely, the surprise of art. It is an irony that Chandler himself must have particularly enjoyed, since it permitted the resurfacing of the former British public school boy and Edwardian man of letters in the guise of an author of *Black Mask* magazine. Chandler's debt to California in his new role is considerable. It not only

15. MacShane, ed., *The Notebooks*, pp. 53–63.
16. Ibid., p. 22.

furnished him with a worthy object for his disgust,[17] it also provided the linguistic elements out of which he might construct a style to express disgust memorably. Disgust for life, as we know from Flaubert and from aestheticism in general, can inspire a passion for form. And in Chandler's novels of California life there is the same antithetical relationship between the brilliance of the style and the tawdriness of the matter that exists in *Madame Bovary*.[18]

17. "I've lived half my life in California and made what use of it I could, but I could leave it forever without a pang." Quoted by MacShane, *The Life of Raymond Chandler*, p. 76.

18. "If a man writes as well as I do (let's face it honestly) he creates a schism between the melodramatic exaggeration of his story and the way he writes about it." Quoted by MacShane, *The Life*, p. 149.

8

The Detective Hero

Unlike delinquents, detectives have not always been with us. Though all human societies have defined certain acts as contrary to law and have imposed punishments on those who committed them, the function of seeking out the perpetrators of such acts has been performed by a variety of figures and sometimes hardly at all. In the Middle Ages a reliance on trial by ordeal, on the oath, and on extorted confessions in the determination of guilt required less exact standards of proof, in any case, so that detection as we know it was superfluous. Moreover, as was noted earlier, although crimes abound in Western literature from the beginning, they are mostly mythic crimes often involving blood feuds. From classical mythology to Renaissance theater, therefore, our literature has been chiefly interested in the revenger as detector and prosecutor of crimes committed against self and family; however, the historical reality of law enforcement has been both more complex and more mundane.

Under the *ancien régime* the maintenance of law and order was centered upon the monarchy. The king was chief magistrate as well as ruler, with the right to impose "the King's peace." In practice, this meant that given the absence of a standing army or of any centralized corps of officers of the peace, law enforcement was local and mutual, as is further implied by the institution of the Watch and Ward in the cities—the closing and manning of the city gates at night was a civic responsibility assumed by the inhabitants, a responsibility later extended to a Marching Watch. Similarly, the pursuit of malefactors was a duty of all, the sheriff having the right to muster able-bodied men in a *posse comitatus*. Down to the seventeenth century the citizenry was, in effect, its own police; it had the responsibility to possess weapons at home (Assize of Arms) and to participate in the Hue and Cry, which under the Tudors was still "the only practical agency for the pursuit and capture of delinquents."[1] By the eighteenth century, however, the system of petty constables acting under the direction of the justices of the peace was firmly in place.

Yet by the eighteenth century also both literature and history reflect the fact that law enforcement by no means enjoyed the support of the population at large. There came to exist what has been called "a battle-ground around the crime," such that the agents of law enforcement themselves could be regarded, at least in certain sections of society, as a greater evil than the delinquents they prosecuted.

In a recent book on British detective fiction, Ian Ousby has described "the presentation of the detective himself."[2] Yet in spite of his relatively narrow focus, he does not examine very closely the important question of how it was possible for the pursuer of delinquents to appear most commonly as the villain in the popular literature of the eighteenth century and as the hero in works appearing a few decades into the following century. The process of "heroization" of the detective that we associate with Poe and Doyle clearly involves a profound transformation of attitudes, when one remembers that some of the most representative popular heroes of the eighteenth century, both in England and on the continent, were bandits and highway robbers such as Jack Sheppard, Claude Duval, Dick Turpin, Cartouche, and Schinderhannes.

In eighteenth-century England, as in eighteenth-century France, it is clear that a good deal of opprobrium was attached by the popular mind to the law itself as well as to the makers of the law and its enforcers. In England its patently class character appeared most obviously in gaming laws that prohibited smallholders from hunting even on their own land. But its statutes relating to the rights of property owners in general were extended in a variety of ways in order to make the enclosure movement possible. Not only were most members of Parliament and the House of Lords landowning squires and aristocrats, in fact, justices of the peace were also drawn from the same

1. W. L. Melville Lee, *A History of Police in England*, p. 104.
2. *Bloodhounds of Heaven: The Detective in English Fiction from Godwin to Doyle* (Cambridge: Harvard University Press, 1976), p. viii.

class.[3] At the same time the extreme severity of the legal code enhanced a widespread sense of social injustice that explains the perception of certain legendary highwaymen as "social bandits" in the sense
Eric Hobsbawn has given to that term.[4]

The stature of the legendary highwaymen like Jack Sheppard and
Dick Turpin, who were celebrated in broadsheet and ballad, is due in
part to the fact that their victims belonged chiefly to a class of wealthy
exploiters. At the same time, their notoriety was also clearly enhanced
by that theater of cruelty which was the public execution. Along with
the severity of sentences for many minor crimes, the high visibility of
punishment induced hostility in the mob toward the punishers as often
as to the punished. Incompetent hangmen, who took too long to exe-
cute their suffering victims, and those surgeons who collected the
hangman's corpses for their anatomy lessons both aroused resentment
at the unwarranted cruelty of the law.[5]

Finally, before the advent of the Bow Street Runners in the latter
part of the eighteenth century, the two instruments of law enforcement
that were the watch and the amateur "thief-takers" also excited widespread contempt. The incompetence of the poorly paid watch and its
relative helplessness in the face of rising urban crime were notorious.
And the "thief-takers" were, in effect, bounty hunters, who moreover
were paid not simply for arrests but for convictions. Consequently,
the system was open to the worst kinds of abuse, as Henry Fielding
noted in explaining the unpopularity of those engaged in pursuing offenders: "The person of the informer is more odious than that of the
felon himself; and the thief-taker is in danger of worse treatment from
the populace than the thief."[6] Obviously, under the circumstances the
most effective thief takers were themselves thieves, as the spectacular
career of Jonathan Wild, the self-styled "Thief-taker General of Great
Britain and Ireland," makes clear. His success as a thief-taker de-
pended on a criminal organization that profited in the first place from

3. See, e.g., Douglas Hay, "Property, Authority and the Criminal Law," in *Albion's
Fatal Tree: Crime and Society in Eighteenth-Century England*, ed. Douglas Hay (New
York: Pantheon Books, 1975), pp. 17–63.

4. See above, chap. 1, n. 4.

5. See Peter Linebaugh, "The Tyburn Riot against the Surgeons," in *Albion's Fatal
Tree*, pp. 65–117.

6. Quoted by Ousby, *Bloodhounds of Heaven*, p. 10.

theft. In *The Life of Mr. Jonathan Wild* Henry Fielding explains its operations: "Wild had now brought his gang to great regularity: he was obeyed and feared by them all. He had likewise established an office, where all men who were robbed, paying the value only (or a little more) of their goods, might have them again."[7] Thus, from Fielding and Gay to Brecht, Wild's career has helped maintain a literary tradition of skepticism about those who claim to live close to crime in order to enforce the rule of law.

In order to make possible the rise of the detective as heroic literary type in such figures as Dickens's Inspector Buckett in *Bleak House* and Collins's Sergeant Cuff, a profound change of attitude had to occur. This change of attitude was dependent not only on the creation of a new police but also on important developments in sociopolitical relationships. If no less a figure than Dickens, with his radical sympathies, gave the new methods of law enforcement in London such a good press, it was not simply because of the apparent success of Peele's metropolitan police but also for reasons both positive and negative that transcended the narrow question of law enforcement.

On the positive side, once the fear of Jacobin rebellion and the social unrest provoked in the opening decades of the century by economic depression, industrial change, and the corn laws had diminished, the reform movement became increasingly influential. The combined efforts of Enlightenment thinkers and turn-of-the-century reformers such as Beccaria, Bentham, Howard, Romilly, and Colquhoun led to a major revision of the legal and penal systems as well as to the reorganization of a professional police. As a result, not only did the police themselves appear relatively efficient and free from corruption, a more graduated system of punishments and a more discreet application of severer forms of punishment also reconciled greater numbers of people to the law and its agencies. Such spectacles as chain gangs, pillories, stocks, public whippings, and the procession to Tyburn disappeared, although the Newgate execution remained a sensational public event well into the nineteenth century and was witnessed by writers of such distinction as Dickens and Thackeray. At the same time, by the 1840s a greater diffusion of the nation's wealth into the middle and lower-middle classes resulted in a form of *embourgeoise-*

7. (London and New York: Dutton, 1932), p. 99.

ment that led to a more positive perception of the forces of order. Politically, also, the enlargement of the suffrage after 1832 involved a broader section of the population in the making of the laws they were compelled to obey. As a consequence, the most visible class features of the law tended to disappear.

On the negative side, if eighteenth-century England could still be regarded as a "policeless state," the impact of radical political ideas around the turn of the century and of a perceived crime wave—in which "political" crimes like violent street demonstrations, rick burnings, and machine breaking were often confused with civil crimes— prepared middle-class opinion for a new attitude toward the police. Historical events led to an acceptance of the idea that a corps of professionals might be required in order to protect political institutions and to exercise social control. Such a change in attitude did not occur quickly, however, because a native English hostility to an organized police force in the capital that would be directly responsible to the home secretary had to be overcome, since such a force was associated with the idea of an occupying army and with the centralized institutions of Revolutionary and Napoleonic France. From the point of view of the late twentieth century, it may perhaps come as a surprise that in the land of the "Bobby" and of Scotland Yard the idea of a strong police force was once looked upon as "expensive, tyrranical and foreign."[8] It is worth remembering, however, that the creation of the metropolitan police, composed of salaried professionals under an independent commissioner, was the work of Robert Peele's Tory government and was carried through in the face of radical opposition. The establishment of a detective department followed in 1842.

Economic, social, and political events of the late eighteenth and early nineteenth centuries prepared public opinion for the eventual establishment of a professional police in Britain. Yet in spite of Peele's determination to make the police respected and not feared by the populace,[9] their subsequent popularity could not have been foreseen in the 1830s. The source of such popularity, in fact, transcends the

8. Ousby, *Bloodhounds of Heaven*, p. 8.

9. Ben C. Roberts has noted, "It is difficult to overestimate the significance of a police force that relied not on the weapons of war to enforce its authority, but on winning popular support for its function." "On the Origins and Resolution of English Working-Class Protest," in *Violence in America*, p. 255.

goodwill and professionalism displayed, on the whole, by the metropolitan police themselves and depends on a complex series of historical events that have been summarized by the British historian Ben C. Roberts as follows:

> The period from 1783 to 1867 has been called an age of improvement. There can be no doubt that during this time the most remarkable changes occurred in Britain. Perhaps the most astonishing of all was the change from a conflict-ridden society in which mob violence was matched by the savage brutality of hangings and transportation for life to a society in which conflict was regulated by rules adopted voluntarily. The principal factors responsible for transmuting the tradition of violent behavior on the part of both the poorer classes and the authorities into a pattern of orderly procedure for the settlement of social and political conflicts were economic growth, political reform, moral suasion, and institutional developments. It is difficult to assign an exact weight to each of these factors; however, they combined to influence decisively the course of events. (p. 264).

The emergence of the new police in general and the "detective police" in particular were predicated on both the political and industrial revolutions. And among the most important consequences of the latter were the demographic explosion and the appearance of a mobile surplus population, the rapid growth of large urban centers and the loss of the kind of social control characteristic of stable small-town life, the consequent massive bureaucratization of social life and the new bureaucratic methods employed in the effort to regain the lost control of populations, and the increasing division of labor that follows technological development. The changes that occurred in New York City were even more dramatic in this respect than those that happened in the long established metropolises of London and Paris. Until roughly the mid-1820s, New York was still a relatively small city with a homogeneous population and an effective form of social control that made for a low crime rate. A system of constables supplemented by marshals who were appointed by the mayor did all the policing that was required. The change came in the 1830s and the 1840s. According to James F. Richardson, these were

> decades of rapid growth with sharp increases in immigration, heightened distinctions between class, ethnic and religious groups with consequent social strain, and a dizzying economic cycle of boom and bust. These social changes greatly complicated the city's police problem. No longer was the

city a homogeneous community with a common culture and shared system
of values and moral standards. Rather the city was becoming a mosaic of
subcommunities, separated from one another by barriers of class and culture and by attitudes and behavior derived from different traditions, or in
the case of many immigrants, by the destruction of tradition.[10]

With the important exception of the scale of foreign immigration,
similar forces were exacerbating the social tensions and the problem
of urban crime in Europe's major cities. Consequently, the pressure
for a London-style police force became generalized among the middle
and upper-middle classes in all large cities where one was not already
in place. In New York the traditional American hostility to the idea of
being policed by professionals seems to have been overcome, at least
among the better-off, by events such as the riots of 1834 and the loot-
ing after the fire of 1835. The change of attitude seems to have been
inspired not only by the higher incidence of crime but also because of
its higher visibility due to the expansion of the popular press. The
migration of tales of crime from ballad and broadsheet to newspaper
faits divers is in itself an interesting phenomenon of the new industrial
technology and the new wealth. And coupled with public disorders,
stories of robbery, rape, and murder—of which the murder of Mary
Cecilia Rogers in 1841 remains the best known because of Poe's tale
on the subject—finally led in 1844 to the new state law that set up a
"Day and Night Police" with wards and station houses and a chief of
police.[11]

That the respectable citizenry besieged by a variety of sensational
faits divers might under the circumstances come to look to the police
for protection is perhaps understandable. For the agents of law enforcement to be transformed into the heroes of popular literature, however, something more was needed. An eighteenth-century constable
could hardly be a hero any more than could a "thief-catcher"—what
Godwin called a "blood-hunter." In order to be heroic the type
needed a new name, a new task, new methods, and a new status. And
such a type was, in effect, anticipated in Colquhoun's plans for police
reform before it appeared in fiction. By proposing that "a scientific

10. *The New York Police: Colonial Times to 1901* (New York: Oxford University
Press, 1970), p. 25.
11. Ibid., pp. 36–37.

campaign against the enemies of society should be inaugurated, under the direction of experts,''[12] Colquhoun prepared the creation in the 1840s of the "detective police," whose expertise and methods became central to the new urban mythology by the end of the century.

By the 1830s and the 1840s the conditions that would make possible the "heroization" of a new kind of policeman were already in place in a number of Western societies. And literary reflections of those changed conditions appeared with Poe's tales in the 1840s and with the writings of Dickens, Collins, and Gaboriau in the 1850s and 1860s. The earlier *Memoirs* of Vidocq, on the other hand, continued to dramatize the adventures of what was, in fact, an eighteenth-century fictional type. The literary Vidocq is lent the persona of the shrewd but amiable rogue; like Jonathan Wild, he is the thief turned thief-taker and claims neither purity of motive nor a learned expertise.

Nevertheless, even where the heroics of the new police activity is concerned, there is an important bifurcation between the models furnished respectively by Poe and by Dickens. The former created the prototype of the aesthete as amateur detective, and the latter introduced the character of the seasoned police professional. At the moment of inception of scientifically based police work, the goal of Edgar Allan Poe was to emphasize the limits of science and logic wherever the tutored imagination was not engaged. Dickens's purpose, on the other hand, was clearly to reconcile English society to the tasks and methods of the new police.

An article written for his popular weekly journal, *Household Words*, in 1851, entitled "The Metropolitan Protectives," suggests very well the role of intermediary between police and public that Dickens took upon himself. The piece belongs to the tradition of the journalistic sketch and it evokes a night in a station house in order to reassure the respectable classes that the Great Fear associated with the Great Exhibition and the influx of undesirables into London from all over the world is groundless. It addresses itself to "nervous old ladies, dyspeptic half-pay officers, suspicious quidnuncs, plot-dreading diplomatists, and grudging rate-payers."[13] And it describes the events

12. Melville Lee, *A History of Police in England*, p. 221. New York City followed London's example in the 1860s.

13. *Charles Dickens' Uncollected Writings from Household Words: 1850–1859*, ed. Harry Stone (Bloomington: University of Indiana Press, 1968), p. 254.

of a night in the life of the station house in order to assert that the metropolitan police is more than adequate to the challenge: "If after our details of the patience, promptitude, order, vigilance, zeal, and judgment, which watch over the peace of the huge Babylon when she sleeps, the fears of the most apprehensive be not dispelled, we shall have quitted our pillow, and plied our pen in vain!" (p. 256). Inspector Buckett of *Bleak House* will be the fictional embodiment of the virtues referred to here.

Dickens's voice is important because it suggests how, along with such ideological state apparatuses as nonconformist religious movements, the various educational institutions, and the trade union movement itself, popular middle-class literature also functioned in nineteenth-century Britain as an important instrument in the "moralization" of the lower-middle and working classes. Dickens's social novels in particular have a moral dimension as well as a sociopolitical one. They suggest both how the institutions of the state need to reform in response to changing human needs and how individuals must improve themselves if they expect to find happiness in a reformed state. More specifically, a novel like *Bleak House* also implies not only that the new police are to be trusted by respectable citizens to see justice done but that to trust the new police is in itself already a sign of one's respectability. Dickens belongs to that tradition in nineteenth-century English liberal thought which sought to forge links between the working classes and the middle class in the cause of social harmony: "The middle class provided an exemplar of a pattern of life to which the skilled worker could with reasonable expectation aspire. The artisan with his apprentice-acquired skill and membership in a friendly society, cooperative society, and trade union had a secure place in the structure of society that placed him only a step below the counting-house clerk, the shopkeeper, and the small factory employer."[14] As a consequence of such a social climate it is possible to understand the "heroization" of the police in general and the detective in particular.

The important differences of character type between Poe's Dupin and Dickens's Buckett, however, imply from the beginning of the fictional "heroization" of the forces of order that the ideal detective may take a wide variety of forms. As was suggested above, the myth of

---

14. Roberts, "On the Origins," p. 262.

the hero is built into the structure of the detective formula itself, whereas the attributes of the characters who play the detective's role are diverse. If a novel ends up becoming a best-seller, however, we may be sure that such attributes were not chosen at random. Popular literature does not force its heroes on a passive population; it constructs them out of an Identikit of national myths, cultural norms, and class attitudes, as Richard Slotkin demonstrates so convincingly for the myth of the hunter in American tradition.

The Russian Formalists' view of a literary hero was, of course, that he was "a by-product of the narrative structure, and as such, a compositional rather than a psychological entity."[15] In his history of British detective heroes, on the other hand, Ian Ousby by implication adopts the conventional view that a popular story exists as a vehicle for the exhibition of a hero. That is, the character is regarded as antedating his adventures in the same way that in life a person exists before the given set of experiences he happens to undergo. Such an essentialist point of view is, of course, in itself the expression of an ideology, but more importantly in the present context it tends to inhibit an appreciation of the ideological presuppositions in the literature on which it focuses. The fact that a given "character" is perceived at a given time and place as an adequate motivation of the devices embodied in a literary work of art can be explained only on ideological grounds. For a literary hero to be seen as a suitable instrument for linking the action sequences of a given plot, not only does the myth of the hero first have to exist in a culture in some form or other, the kind of prowess deployed by the hero has also to be culturally approved.

The detective as higher public servant and as the protector of an innocent citizenry threatened by the criminal classes began to appear in the popular literature of the 1850s and 1860s. But it was not until the last decades of the century in the era of High Victorianism that he achieved full mythic stature. The appearance of Sherlock Holmes coincided with the cult of heroic male action so central in British life at the height of the British Empire. Thus, though the beginning of the process of mythification in English literature may be observed in Inspector Buckett and Sergeant Cuff, both Dickens's and Collins's de-

15. Erlich, *Russian Formalism*, p. 241.

tectives remain fallible police professionals from lower-class backgrounds. In spite of the preternatural shrewdness that sets them apart, they are secondary characters in their respective fictions, not the kind of popular supersleuth who functioned as the chosen instrument for joining crime to its solution in the age of jingoism.

Along with Dupin, Holmes illustrates Michel Foucault's point that "the man of the people was now too simple to be the protagonist of simple truths."[16] Doyle's work also confirms how as soon as the detective novel becomes itself through being centered on the exploits of a detective hero, it becomes preoccupied with style both in the literary sense discussed in the previous section and in the more popular sense of cutting a figure. The appeal exerted by Holmes is inherent in his urbane life-style and the swagger with which he exhibits the workings of his intellect. His attraction is not only that of power through reason but also of leisure and privilege, of upper-middle-class bachelor life, of heroic adventure punctuated by pipe smoking in gentlemen's chambers, meditation, and opera. Holmes never has to stoop to earn his living or appear at an office the way a clerk does. He is the polished, chivalrous hero of a culture whose ideal in all human endeavors is the well-heeled amateur, because the amateur at his best is not only brilliant and incisive, he is also relaxed and disinterested, a man of honor imbued with the spirit of *sprezzatura*. Holmes is public school gone scientific, a higher public servant who, initially at least, revealed a streak of romantic melancholy that was the period sign for a sage, a man who dominated and served his world but stood apart on the lonely pinnacle reserved for genius.

Thus, if after Sherlock Holmes the gentlemanly amateur of genius is the most distinctive heroic type of British detective fiction, it is because there existed a cult of stylishness characteristic of an upper-middle-class culture still dominated by an aristocratic ideal. And such a cult of stylishness associated the professional with a dull and bureaucratic single-mindedness. The reason why for a long time official police detectives do not appear as heroes in British detective stories is not that they were suspected for their political role, as in France, or for their susceptibility to corruption, as in the United States, but that they were non-U. Policemen were not gentlemen and therefore could

16. *Discipline and Punish*, p. 69.

not be heroes. Shakespeare's *Henry V* is a distant but important model that suggests how in the English heroic tradition roles are distributed along class lines—a lesson learned among others by those makers of World War II British action movies. Simple soldiers have a heroic role to play, like lesser commanders with Welsh or Scottish accents, but such roles are always supportive. The central heroic figure and embodiment of the national chivalric ideal is in Shakespeare's play an English king. Moreover, a further key element in the representation of a national self-image is the fact that, unlike his French foils, Henry combines manliness with chivalry. To the aura of kingship he joins the attributes of the valiant soldier and the tongue-tied but respectful wooer of women.

Similarly, in the very different world of nineteenth-century Britain, Holmes is a class hero before he is a national hero. He embodied the heroic qualities of an ascendant middle class that had learned to groom itself for an imperial role under the influence of a variety of ideological state apparatuses, including particularly the public schools, the press, and middle-brow literature. Compared with heroic soldier-adventures like Drake and Raleigh or explorers like Cook, Holmes may appear to be a somewhat idiosyncratic figure with romantic propensities; nevertheless, his investigative adventures were capable of matching the frontier heroics of the American West or the exploits of the heroes of the Empire itself, from Clive and Wolfe to Cecil Rhodes, General Gordon, and the young Churchill. Furthermore, although the constraints of the detective formula obliged Doyle to restrict his fictional detective's role, there is a significant overlap, if not in the careers of author and character, at least in the implied value systems that sustained those careers. Together with Kipling, in fact, Doyle was widely regarded as the representative middle-brow author of an age. His best-known biographer, John Dickson Carr, has no hesitation in claiming that in 1903 at the age of forty-three Conan Doyle was "one of the most famous men in the world and perhaps its most popular writer."[17]

It is difficult to imagine a public man who more completely embodied the values of his society and his times. In an age of scientism,

17. *The Life of Sir Arthur Conan Doyle* (New York, Evanston, and London: Harper and Row, 1949), p. 162.

Doyle was a scientist to the extent that he had a degree in medicine. In an age of sportsmanship, he was a soccer player and a cricketer of outstanding ability, a boxer, a skier, and an enthusiast of the new sport of motoring. In the age of the large Victorian family and the grand country house, he was a patriarch and the owner of a sizable estate. In an age that cultivated heroic action, he was an adventurer who had hunted whales in the Arctic and journeyed to West Africa. In an age of nationalism and of commitment to the imperial mission, he was a patriotic citizen who briefly joined Kitchener's army in the Sudan as an observer and who served in a field hospital during the Boer war. Moreover, his role as a molder of national opinion was taken very seriously both by himself and by the population at large. And he wrote among so much else a pamphlet on army reform, a semiofficial history of the South African war, and a work warning about the German submarine menace.

The value system that sustained all these activities derived in the first instance from his professional middle-class family that was descended from the Irish Catholic landed gentry on his father's side, and from ancestors claiming descent from feudal nobility on his mother's side. Thus we learn that the young Doyle acquired the code of chivalry from a mother who was fond of such pronouncements as "Fearless to the strong; humble to the weak"[18] and from works such as Scott's *Ivanhoe*. Later a commitment to the chivalric code that embodied the idea of service to king and country was complemented by a belief in the power of reason.[19] And Doyle seems to have clung to the latter belief all the more strongly as a result of his loss of the Catholic faith of his Irish family. Equally as important as the codes of chivalry and reason in guiding Doyle's conduct was finally the Emersonian doctrine of self-reliance, which was summed up in a letter by a friend as " 'Do' is a finer word than 'Believe,' and 'Action' is a far surer watchword than 'Faith'."[20] In spite of all one knows about Doyle and the Victorian world from which he came, including his authorship of historical novels of chivalry, it comes as a surprise to learn that when he died in 1930 he requested that the following words be carved on the headstone of his grave: "Steel true, blade straight."

18. Quoted by Carr, p. 7.
19. "Reason is the highest gift we've got; we must use it." Quoted by Carr, p. 31.
20. Quoted by Carr, p. 24.

The extraordinary hold of "myth" over conduct could hardly be better illustrated than in this choice of an epitaph twelve years after the end of the Great War and less than a decade before Guernica. The vehicle of the metaphor is the *arme blanche* of an aristocratic tradition that was already doomed by the introduction of gunpowder into warfare in the fifteenth century.

I have lingered over Conan Doyle's relationship to English society in his time because the evidence of his life reinforces so strikingly on the level of ideology what is already apparent from his practice of the detective genre. Even more significantly, however, Doyle's career also confirms the idea referred to above that popular literary heroes are culture chosen. Popular literature differs greatly from the more sophisticated kind, in fact, because it does deal with heroes in the traditional sense of the word and heroes do not appear to be such at all times and places. On the contrary, heroes often do not travel well and find themselves in need of updating every generation or so. Moreover, this fact largely accounts for the embarrassment we experience for our grandfathers' heroes and the rapidity with which the great majority of popular works date. From the late 1960s, it is for instance the dourer antiheroic heroics of John Le Carré and Len Deighton that seem in tune with contemporary British taste, an antiheroics whose most influential progenitor was clearly Graham Greene. But even in the 1920s the emergence of a very different type of fictional detective suggested that the heroism of those young upper-class Britons who went to war with Kipling or Sir Henry Newbolt in their heads, if not Horace, was dead.

One might speculate that the national experience of 1914–18 combined with the fact that Agatha Christie was a woman in order to give rise to an important shift of emphasis in the 1920s. With Hercule Poirot power has become wholly cerebral. His triumph is the triumph of subtlety and the sedentary life. Poirot does not indulge in Holmes's elaborate disguises, nor does he expose himself to the risks of penetrating the underworld of London's East End dives, its riverside, and opium dens, let alone hotfoot after his criminal adversaries or even on occasion tangle with them. It is in the nature of the development of the detective story that, because of the constraints built into its structure, novelty has to be pursued through multiplying superficial differences of style, character, and ambience. Thus, in practice, the search for differences on such a basis led to the creation of increasingly odd types down to the absurd but brilliant Poirot himself. Agatha Christie may have been inspired to make her detective Belgian by the presence of Belgian war refugees in her hometown of Torquay, but that is as far as the realism of her character extends. Poirot's "Belgianness" has the quality of a comic eccentricity like his vanity and his *gourmandise*. As his mock heroic name suggests, "Hercule Poirot" (Poireau = leek) is of the order of a Belgian joke—"Sherlock Holmes" had signified for Doyle "the click of an opening lock."[21] This trend issued subsequently in the consciously anachronistic figure of Dorothy L. Sayers's Lord Peter Wimsey, the aristocrat as detective whose Dr. Watson is a manservant. In such characters the genre approaches self-parody.

At the same time the result of seeking originality in the detective novel through the pursuit of difference was to promote an increasing oddness that led away from the detective novel of adventure to the detective novel of manners. The ideological consequences of this development are interesting. A feature of the traditional comedy of manners is its dependence on the well-defined social roles of a stable society. It plays off one against the other not so much humors as the familiar foibles of class or the mannerisms of condition. In the case of the formal British detective novel of the 1920s and 1930s, such characteristics of the comedy of manners come to be combined rather surprisingly with the heroic ideology built into the structure of investigation. The image projected therefore is of an English society in which social relations remain fixed in an Edwardian state and whose heroes are almost invariably eccentric establishment types. Unlike earlier crime novels from Godwin through Dickens, such detective novels always take the law and the institutions of law enforcement for granted, even if they sometimes gently mock their various official representatives.

This point has been well made by Agatha Christie herself:

> When I began writing detective stories I was not in any mood to criticize them or to think seriously about crime. The detective story was the story of the chase; it was also very much a story with a moral; in fact it was the old Everyman Morality Tale, the hunting down of Evil and the triumph of

21. Carr, p. 46.

Good. At that time, the time of the 1914 war, the doer of evil was not a hero: the *enemy* was wicked, the *hero* was good; it was as crude and as simple as that. We had not then begun to wallow in psychology. I was, like everyone else who wrote books or read them, *against* the criminal and *for* the innocent victim.[22]

Writing in the fifties and sixties, Agatha Christie still puts herself squarely on the side of the victim of crime. And having mentioned the interest in criminology that naturally tends to be developed in any author of detective stories, she goes on to indicate her own belief in what Radzinowicz has referred to as the conservative view of crime, of "criminal man": "There seems no doubt that there are those, like Richard III as Shakespeare shows him, who do indeed say, 'Evil be thou my Good.' They have chosen Evil, I think, much as Milton's Satan did" (p. 528). The causation of crime is individual, not social; it is the result of moral choice or psychic disorder, not of institutional malfunctions in a complex society. Under the circumstances, it is not surprising if Julian Symons finds that "the values put forward by the detective story from the time of Holmes to the beginning of World War II, and by the thriller and the spy story up to the advent of Eric Ambler are those of a class that felt it had everything to lose by social change."[23]

The ideal policing, about which the formal British detective novel fantasized, involved detectives who are not even recognizable as such but who have no difficulty in distinguishing guilt from innocence. They are social types who might be admitted without embarrassment into upper-middle-class drawing rooms, but their facade of benevolence and even dottiness conceals a hidden toughness that often functions in defense of class interests. Those *Black Mask* writers who in the 1920s began publishing a new type of detective story on this side of the Atlantic created an ideal policeman of a very different breed. The mainstream fiction from which the hard-boiled genre originally drew its inspiration was not comedy of manners but the American adventure tale, on the one hand, and American naturalism, on the other. The effect in both Hammett and Chandler was to Americanize crime

---

22. *Agatha Christie*, p. 527.
23. Symons, *Mortal Consequences*, p. 10.

and detection. They took a familiar genre and invested it with a cultural mythology wholly alien to the one found in the British model or in its unashamedly elitist American progenitor, Edgar Allan Poe. In taking to the streets not only was crime democratized in the fictional agent of law enforcement, the combat against it comes to be conducted in terms that hark back to the origins of the American literary tradition in the Indian war and captivity narratives of the early colonial era.

In this connection, it should come as no surprise that the new authors in the hard-boiled genre were not originally men of letters in the traditional sense but men of the people who wrote about milieus with which they were familiar. In fact, J.S. Shaw, the editor of *Black Mask* after 1926, preferred "writers who were themselves men of action"[24] in the tradition of Bret Harte, Mark Twain, and Jack London. Thus, if Doyle was in so many ways the epitome of that upper-middle-class Victorian and Edwardian manhood which is reflected in his fictional detective, Hammett was also a type of 1920s American Bohemian adventurer who had much in common with his private investigators. Hammett had received a "knock-about education." Before he became a *poète maudit* of the urban frontier, he was in turn a freight clerk, stevedore, timekeeper, yardman and laborer, and nail-machine operator as well as a Pinkerton agent and an ambulance corps man. Moreover, in his memory, at least, his mother's proverbial injunctions already took a hard-bitten form that contrasts sharply with those of the elder Mrs. Doyle: "Never go out in a boat without oars—and don't waste your time on a woman who can't cook."[25]

Along with the democratization of the detective genre and the appearance of a new kind of author, there also occurred under the influence of naturalism a reversal of the relationship that had traditionally confronted American innocence with European experience. The new realism of the hard-boiled school was a reaction not against British sophistication but against British innocence. The American detective novel took the muckrakers' theme of "the shame of the cities"[26] and gave the world a foretaste of the tough thrillers Hollywood was soon

24. Nolan, *Dashiell Hammett*, p. 41.
25. Quoted by Nolan, pp. 11–12.
26. *The Shame of the Cities* was, of course, the title of Lincoln Steffens's muckraking classic that appeared in volume form in 1904.

to let loose on much wider audiences. The revitalized genre offered not that "rural ignorance"[27] which Crèvecoeur had sought to promote but urban knowledge. And in the process a type of heroic investigator was defined whose style and ethics were developed in response to different historical conditions and within a different geographical space.

Nevertheless, it is heroism in a recognizable American mode insofar as it implies once again in a different generic context that scorn for "British regulars" and those who imitate them, and praise for "American irregulars," which are as old as the myths of the French and Indian wars. The style of heroism involved is one that requires the protagonist to know his savage enemy and fight him on his own terms in his own familiar haunts. In the hard-boiled detective genre there persists that conscious purpose of so many American popular writers from colonial times to create a representative American equal to American tasks, a hero who from the beginning "could be set off against the culture heroes of Europe and express the Americanized Englishman's view of himself, his new perception of his place in the wilderness and the world."[28]

The detective fiction of pure ratiocination, whose founding father was Poe, has never been genuinely popular. In order to appeal to a broader public, it needed the vital admixture of action or manners, violence or satire. A tale like *The Purloined Letter* is calculated to interest litterateurs because it has the most intellectual of heroes who sets out to verify a philosophical proposition. It establishes the precedent of an action confined to a conflict between pure minds; the only exchange between hero and villain is an exchange of words. A solution to the problem posed comes from the superior deductive powers and knowledge of the world of a mind isolated in its book-lined study. Dupin visits Minister D——'s house only in order to confirm what he already knows and to prove the superiority of his intellect by recovering the letter through a repetition of the original theft.

At the time of the first publication of *Black Mask* magazine, in

27. Commenting on Crèvecoeur, Leo Marx has referred to "all the later fictional writers who begin in the same way, impulsively dissociating themselves from the world of sophistication, Europe, ideas, learning, in a word, the *world*, and speaking in accents of rural ignorance." *The Machine in the Garden* (London, Oxford, New York: Oxford University Press, 1964), p. 109.

28. *Regeneration through Violence*, p. 189.

1920, the best-known detective story writer in the United States was S. S. Van Dine (Willard Huntington Wright), a writer who still harked back to the tradition of Poe as mediated by Doyle. The *Black Mask* school, on the other hand, was prepared by American pulp novels from as far back as the 1860s that had celebrated a variety of frontier heroes from Daniel Boone and Kit Carson to Buffalo Bill, Sam Houston, and General Custer. Its most important single source is, in fact, that myth of the hunter which, according to Richard Slotkin, ''in the hands of second- and third-rank literary intelligences, became an informing structure in the popular literature and thought of the United States.''[29] Moreover, with John R. Coryell's Nick Carter stories in the 1880s a precedent was even established for urban adventure. In the words of the historian of American literary taste, James D. Hart, ''Dime-novel stories of shootings in the Wild West had led to the subject of banditry, and tales of frontier lawlessness and in turn led to ones about the more sophisticated crime of Broadway and the Bowery. In 1886 Russell Coryell created the first of the Nick Carter stories and the dime novel plunged into a world of detectives and cardsharps, of opium-dens and abductions.''[30]

It is ironic that before he took to writing detective stories and became the most influential practitioner of the genre in the classic British mode, Conan Doyle had aspired to imitate Bret Harte's model and write adventure tales of frontier life. His first published story was entitled ''The Mystery of Sasassa Valley'' and appeared in 1879. But by the time of the Holmes stories, the element of adventure, at least in terms of exposure to hardship and physical violence, is more muted. Nevertheless, it should not be forgotten that the second part of *The Valley of Fear*, which was completed in the spring of 1914, returns to the United States for its background and anticipates the hard-boiled novel in its setting and in the level of violence represented. It also has a Pinkerton agent as its detective hero. But the major difference between Doyle and his hard-boiled successors is that he makes no serious attempt through the texture of his writing to define his American detective hero as a distinctly American type. The formal British detective novel followed Poe's example in choosing heroes who were in-

29. Ibid., p. 518.

30. *The Popular Book: A History of America's Literary Taste* (New York: Oxford University Press, 1950), p. 156.

tellectual, upper class, or simply eccentric. Thus, although the average readers of the genre might recognize such heroes as their champions in the fight against evil, they did not identify with them. The Continental Op, Sam Spade, and Philip Marlowe, on the other hand, are fitted out by their authors to resemble average American types, whose speech, life-style, taste, values, and income invite a far greater measure of identification from an American public.

The difference is first written into the physical descriptions of the new detectives, among which the sketch of Sam Spade's face at the beginning of *The Maltese Falcon* is particularly memorable: "Samuel Spade's jaw was long and bony, his chin a jutting V under the more flexible V of his mouth. His nostrils curved back to make another, smaller, V. His yellow-grey eyes were horizontal. The V motif was picked up again by thickish brows rising outward from twin creases above a hooked nose, and his pale brown hair grew down—from high flat temples—in a point on his forehead. He looked rather pleasantly like a blond Satan" (p. 3).

Hammett opens his novel with a jaw, a chin, and a mouth, in order to set before the reader a physique that expresses neither beauty nor ugliness but an angular man of experience who is also a common man, durability with an amiable face. It is, moreover, a face whose mythical connotations are sufficiently evident to have endured since 1931 and the beginnings of the comic strip as illustrated suspense story in Dick Tracy. As in all realist fiction, the physical appearance of Sam Spade is intended to be a visible manifestation of a hidden moral correlative that in this case is a foursquare toughness. Sam Spade may not look like much, but as the rest of the novel will confirm, he has the qualities needed to survive in a hard world and is as honest as his name.

The problem of naming is, in effect, also raised by implication in Hammett's paragraph, but it is raised in order to be dismissed. The inference to be drawn from such a description is that there is a simple, direct equivalence between words and the things they denote. Sam Spade is named by his author by means of words that themselves have the honesty of concrete things, and Spade will himself be used as an instrument of further honest naming. The stylistic message of such a passage is the recognizably American one that the world may be disclosed through the word, if the word divests itself of conventional literary associations and makes itself plain again in order to record no more than the senses perceive.

In the previous section I touched on the importance of the wisecrack as a fundamental stylistic feature in the composition of Chandler's novels. It is equally important in the creation of the private investigator as heroic type, because the making of a style both for Hammett and for Chandler also involved a definition of heroic behavior. The wisecrack is an example of behavioral ideology because it is an ideal form of the vernacular characterized by its tough-mindedness and its terseness, and it signifies an irrepressible set of folk attitudes wherever it is a distinguishing feature of a character's speech. The style in this case makes the man.

Moreover, he who makes wisecracks is a wise guy. That is to say, someone who is no respecter of authority, wealth, power, social standing, or institutions. A wise guy talks too much, asks too many questions, and answers back when an effort is made to put him in his place. The wisecracking hero is also typically a city-bred phenomenon, the antithesis of the slow-spoken, monosyllabic cowboy. And his wit is the weapon that enables him to expose people, situations, and institutions for what they are.

It is noteworthy that we have to go to the American vernacular for the word which best defines the quality of Spade's and Marlowe's wit, namely the "wisecrack." It is equally noteworthy that we have to refer to the same source in order to describe the faculty which the hardboiled private eye relies on, instead of deductive reasoning or scientific method, to solve his crimes, that is to say, the "hunch." The term has no equivalent in British English. The hunch is a form of male intuition; to trust the hunch over the operations of the rational intelligence is therefore to believe in native wit or the untutored powers of the nonrational self. The hunch derives from a combination of folk instinct and experience.

Unlike the classic well-educated British detective, then, the private eye relies on no esoteric learning or scientific expertise and admits to little formal education. On the contrary, he shares with American popular culture in general the Jacksonian distrust of intellectuals and experts. Thus, if when the type was first developed in the 1920s the private eye appeared "unconventional" in both the literary and behavioral sense, he nevertheless sprang from a well-established American popular tradition. He appeared "unconventional" only because he was a professional wise guy with bad manners and because in his cultivated naturalness he contrasted so strikingly with the British upper-class stereotype of the fictional detective. His "unconventionality" is profoundly and consciously American. In contrasting the detective of the British formal tradition with the American private eye, one is reminded that, in the nineteenth century, transatlantic stereotyping found symbols for the rival English-speaking cultures in the monocle and the spittoon.

Although from Hammett's Continental Op to Chandler's Marlowe the hard-boiled private eyes are fast with their mouth and rely on the educated hunch in their crime solving, perhaps their most memorable characteristic is physical endurance. Sam Spade's physique is significant above all because it equips him for fighting and for the dirty business of actually laying hands on his criminal adversaries. Moreover, he usually enjoys the work. In the words of the Hammett biographer, William F. Nolan, "the Op is an animalistic man of violence, pain-prone; a fight tones his system, fires his blood" (p. 44). Consequently, the fight sequences, often coupled with shoot-outs, are among the most predictable set pieces of the hard-boiled genre. Furthermore, the private eye establishes his claim to a heroic role in his capacity not only to inflict pain on an adversary but also to take pain and come back fighting with fists and guns or, failing that, with the mouth. Thus Nolan finds that the beating-up of the problematic hero of Hammett's *Glass Key* is "one of the most brutal sequences ever written" (p. 70), although by the standards of Mickey Spillane it is not especially so. But it is above all in the punishment sooner or later inflicted on his criminal enemies that the private eye most often expresses his physical power.

The arrest of a criminal, not to mention a brawl or a shoot-out, is usually avoided by the detective of the classic British tradition as beneath his class dignity. His job is done once guilt has been established. Punishment is assumed to follow, but it is left to the slow-moving, impersonal forces of the law to carry it out. The American private eye, on the other hand, often acts as his own judge and jury.[31]

---

31. See John G. Cawelti's section on Spillane, *Adventure, Mystery, and Romance*, pp. 183–91.

Thus, even in Hammett and Chandler, it is common to find that initial acts of criminal violence find fulfillment in savage counterviolence, although the gloating executions performed by Mickey Spillane's Mike Hammer are missing. The fate of Doctor Soberin at the end of *Kiss Me, Deadly* is characteristic of Spillane's stomach-churning effects.

> It caught him so far off base I had time to get halfway across to him before he dipped his hand in the drawer and I had his wrist before he could get the thing leveled. I let him keep the gun in his hand so I could bend it back and hear his fingers break and when he tried to yell I bottled the sound up by smashing my elbow into his mouth. The shattering teeth tore my arm and his mouth became a great hole welling blood. His fingers were broken stubs sticking at odd angles. I shoved him away from me, slashed the butt end of the rod across the side of his head and watched him drop into his chair.
>
> .   .   .   .   .
>
> I said, "Doc . . . " and he looked at me. No, not me, the gun. The big hole in the end of the gun.
> And while he was looking I let him see what came out of the gun.
> Doctor Soberin only had one eye left.[32]

The private eye is always a law unto himself, but with Hammett and Chandler there is an at least implicit commitment to a higher law when an assault on a criminal is represented. Mickey Spillane's private eye, on the other hand, often operates as a lynching party of one. That theater of punishment which had disappeared from public life in the nineteenth century and was also suppressed in the formal detective story reappears at the denouement of the hard-boiled genre, as was noted above. Moreover, in Spillane it reappears with the regularity of a protracted ritual in which a beating precedes the killing.

In his historical study of bandits Eric Hobsbawn makes the interesting observation that "moderation in killing and in violence belongs to the image of the social bandits." But he nevertheless goes on to point out that there are bandits "who not only practice terror and cruelty . . . but whose terror actually forms part of their public image . . . They are not so much men who right wrongs, but avengers, and exerters of power; their appeal is not that of agents of justice, but of men who prove that even the poor and the weak can be terrible." Like

32. (New York: Signet, 1952), pp. 172–73.

Mike Hammer, they belong to a class of "public monsters" (p. 50). It is probable that the gentlemanly code associated with the paradigm of social banditry that is Robin Hood has been consciously refined over the centuries in response to changing manners. That in any case under certain conditions of repression and humiliation such a code would appear an inadequate reaction is clear. Popular resentment may be transformed into a kind of rage against the world and lead to what Hobsbawn refers to as a "revolution of destruction" (p. 56). It is to the expression of such a rage that the hard-boiled genre tends in its least polished practitioners.

That the private eyes of the American detective story are not "social bandits" in a strict sense is clear. Nevertheless, it seems equally clear that in the representation of the urban forests of twentieth-century American life they play a similar mythic role to that of the Robin Hoods and highwaymen of earlier centuries. They are the righters of wrongs and the avengers of ordinary people in a world where power is represented as corrupt and official law enforcement the agent of corrupt power. Consequently, they represent a third position, which is neither that of the police nor of the criminals.[33] As such they are the people's champions, who stand on the margin of the law as representatives of a higher law.

In effect, to the extent that they stand between two cultures, that of respectable society, on the one hand, and the criminal underworld, on the other, their situation is equally as ambivalent as that of the Indian fighter and hunter of colonial times. Just as early seventeenth-century New England settlements could be safeguarded only through a knowledge of the wilderness and of its Indians, so in the modern American city the survival of civilized order is made to depend on the private eyes' familiarity with the haunts and the lore of the gangster. And just as the process of "Indianization" led to a marginal existence for the Indian fighter and hunter in frontier narratives, so too the private eye is represented as no longer at home among settled, property-owning citizens. The fact that in hard-boiled fictions the equivalent of the Indian fighter / hunter is also lent some of the attributes of the social bandit may be explained by the more patently class character of early

33. Nolan comments that the Continental Op "is a half-way house between the cops and the crooks" (p. 24).

twentieth-century American capitalist society and the corruptibility of its institutions.

The violence of the reaction of solitary investigators against those who are perceived as a threat is not usually a problem in Hammett or Chandler, however, for two reasons—although Chandler's racist innuendo does occasionally pose a problem at a time of heightened sensitivity to race relations. In the first place, both Hammett and Chandler choose with some care such traditional targets of popular anger as the immoral rich, exploitative industrialists, venal politicians, corrupt and brutal policemen, organized criminals, and petty hoodlums. In the second place, until Spillane, the violence of the private eye is relatively swift and reactive, when it occurs.

From Filson's Daniel Boone on, the myth of the American hunter has often embodied an ethic of self-restraint that tends to be derived from a feeling of awe for the wilderness, on the one hand, and from an original white American ambivalence concerning the hunt inherited from European myths of the "wicked hunter," on the other.[34] And such an ethic is visible in the constraints imposed by both Hammett and Chandler on the behavior of their fictional private eyes, although its connection with the traditional myth of the hunter goes undeclared. In Chandler's case the intermittent self-restraint embodied in Hammett's more purely nativist heroes seems to have been reinforced by a latent and improbable code of chivalry that recalls Conan Doyle's example.

The extent of the violence that may be legitimized against certain targets of popular anger under threatening conditions is suggested by the example of Mike Hammer. The sadistic evocation of violent acts perpetrated upon characters defined in the context as evil has been sufficiently remarked to require no emphasizing here. The important point to note about Mike Hammer, however, is that he is explicitly defined as the defender and avenger of down-home, red-blooded American values, not only against hoodlums but also against deviant foreign ideas and those evil enough to represent them.

---

34. "The hunter possesses a natural humility, a reverence for something greater than himself (God, nature) that checks the full expression of his will. He will kill only when and only so much as practical necessity requires." *Regeneration through Violence*, p. 552.

The chosen instrument of the private investigator's executions is almost invariably the gun. The mythic significance of the gun in American cultural life is, of course, a phenomenon that has generated a substantial literature.[35] Historically the role of the gun in the long process of establishing American nationhood was equally crucial in the times of the first settlers' struggle to survive against the wilderness, Indians, and competing European peoples, in the period of the Revolutionary War, and in the era of Western expansion. Given that the first English colonies in their remoteness from the motherland had to learn to defend themselves from the beginning, it is no exaggeration to say that the cult of self-reliance in America began with the concept of self-defense, and self-defense in its turn began with the knowledge of how to handle a gun. Furthermore, because of the gun's role in enabling a hastily organized militia to defeat the standing army of autocratic monarchy, it very early acquired an important ideological significance also. Unlike aristocratic Europe, where the use of firearms by the population at large has always been strictly controlled, in America historical and geographical circumstances dictated the weapon's wide dissemination. Consequently, the gun in our culture has become the totem of democracy. It is the great equalizer. Armed with a gun, Jack is as good as his master, the Yankee farmer the equal of a redcoat, and an ordinary citizen a match for a mobster. Its mythical value is summed up in the sentence, "God created men; Colonel Colt made them equal."[36] From such a vantage point, it is not difficult to understand why possession of a gun is regarded as a political right as important as the vote. It is a sign as well as a guarantor of political emancipation.

The private eye with his gun derives, then, from a tradition that is at least as old as the United States. The ethic embodied in his struggle against evil in his time is that the protection of self, family, and property, like fighting wars, begins at home. It is not surprising, therefore, if the ideal policing represented in the hard-boiled novel should be the work of urban frontiersmen who because of sociopolitical circumstances have some of the characteristics of social bandits. Private eyes are

35. See, e.g., Lee Kennett and James La Verne Anderson, *The Gun in America* (Westport, Conn., and London, 1975), pp. 315–23.
36. Quoted by Kennett and Anderson, p. 120.

recognizable as the champions of ordinary Americans because they are the embodiment of an idealized average Americanness both in their self-reliance and in the assertion of an egalitarianism of the gun. Thus, as many commentators have pointed out, hard-boiled investigators are avatars of an American mythic hero who is older than John Filson's Daniel Boone and James Fenimore Cooper's Leatherstocking and as new as the heroes of Hemingway, Faulkner, and James Dickey. Some of the consequences of the acceptance of the hunter as archetypal American hero have been drawn by Richard Slotkin. He notes that such acceptance has involved "adapting the hunter's anti-intellectualism, his pursuit of the material and the ephemeral, and his love of exploit and violence for the sake of their blood-stirring excitement—a love akin to the insatiable incontinence dreaded by Puritans" (p. 307). For the private eye as for the Indian scout, the hunter, the cowboy, and the soldier, the final test of self-worth and of the quality of an individual's manhood occurs in violent action.

The problem faced by both Hammett and Chandler, however, was how to combine adventure with naturalism, how to reconcile the tradition of heroic American individualism with a realistic representation of the seedy circumstances of a private detective's actual life in the cities of Dreiser and Lincoln Steffens. In the twentieth century "Grace under pressure" may still ring true beneath an African sky, in a Spanish arena, or even in upstate Michigan, but it hardly fits the circumstances of a small-time operator in a sordid business in the new urban wilderness.[37] Hammett's solution, like Chandler's after him, was to make a virtue of smallness and turn his private eye into what is, in

37. In this respect Chandler was fully aware of the gap between the hard-boiled fictional tradition and reality: "The real-life private eye is a sleazy little drudge from the Burns Agency, a strong-arm guy with no more personality than a blackjack. He has about as much moral stature as a stop and go sign." Quoted by MacShane, *The Life of Raymond Chandler*, p. 70. Vernon L. Parrington has described how a similar mythification of a shoddy reality had occurred in the case of Davy Crockett: "The real Davy was very far from romantic. . . . It was a slovenly world and Davy was pretty much of a sloven. Crude and unlovely in its familiar details, with its primitive courtships and shiftless removals, its brutal Indian campaign and fierce hunting sprees, its rough equality, its unscrupulous politics, its elections carried by sheer impudence and whiskey, the autobiography reveals the backwoods Anglo-Irishman as uncivilized animal . . . yet with a certain vigor of character. Wastefulness was in the frontier blood, and Davy was a true frontier wastrel." Quoted by Slotkin, *Regeneration through Violence*, p. 555.

effect, a populist hero. The portrait Hammett drew of his Continental Op in this respect set the precedent for the genre: "I see him . . . a little man going forward day after day through mud and blood and death and deceit—as callous and brutal and cynical as necessary—toward a dim goal, with nothing to push or pull him to it except he's been hired to reach it."[38]

However dour and weary it has become, this is a restatement of the heroic ethic under circumstances that are hard on heroism. By choosing the city of late nineteenth-century naturalism as a background for adventure, in fact, Hammett set himself an unusually difficult task. It is of the essence of classic adventure stories that they tell of victories achieved by heroes against great odds. Since Zola, on the other hand, naturalism has represented the struggles of relatively ordinary individuals overwhelmed by the weight of social and material forces. At the same time that he acknowledges the power of such forces, therefore, Hammett indicates the way in which small and always provisional victories might be achieved by ordinary people, as long as they are tough enough and do not expect too much. Moreover, in representing such victories Hammett is very specific in isolating the kinds of evils to be overcome and the qualities of the agent required to overcome them. In both the targets of his animosity and the heroic type he furnishes to attack them, Hammett expresses a broadly populist faith. If the politics of comedy of manners is conservatism, from Zola on the politics of naturalism has always been a form of radicalism. But whereas the nineteenth-century French writer championed utopian socialist collectivism, Hammett looks to populist individualism as twentieth-century America's last best hope.

The political implications of Hammett's work are apparent from the beginning. In his first novel, *Red Harvest*, the Continental Op combines the radical activities of muckraker and racket buster with his investigating. Thus, although he solves his murder swiftly, he stays on simply to clean up a corrupt small town run by its leading businessman in collaboration with the police. In effect, by equating worldly success with corruption in contemporary America, both Hammett and Chandler make modest circumstances an outward sign of moral rectitude. Philip Marlowe's "To hell with the rich. They make me

38. Quoted by Nolan, p. ix.

sick''[39] is calculated to appeal to a nation that had not yet emerged from economic depression and was still in search of scapegoats. It is a phrase that echoes the contemporary popular song, ''Nice people with nice manners have got no money at all.'' The private eyes of both authors are, then, genuinely popular heroes, because while they have remained small men by choice, as a point of honor, they also always manage in the end to have the last word against the class enemies of ordinary people—the rich, the powerful, and the official police. The apparent loser for once is the moral winner. The message is anti-Horatio Alger and as such gives a sharp focus to working and lower-middle-class ressentiment.

The traditional American value system from which the private eye is descended has been described by Richard Hofstader in *Anti-Intellectualism in American Life*. In evoking the phenomenon to which his title refers, the author claims that far-right attitudes are characterized by ''a categorical folkish dislike of the educated classes and of anything respectable, established, pedigreed, or cultivated.''[40] However, such attitudes are by no means exclusive to the political right in America. They also characterize the American populist tradition. And from the Continental Op down to Mike Hammer, the private eyes of the hard-boiled tradition embody some of what Hofstader refers to as ''the pervasive and aggressive egalitarianism of American life'' (p. 50). Even the most stylish of them, Philip Marlowe, speaks with the voice of populist antielitism and antiaestheticism. In *Farewell, My Lovely*, for example, Marlowe's reaction to the living room of the Harvard educated Lindsay Marriott is characteristic: ''There was plenty of nice soft furniture, a great many floor cushions, some with golden tassels and some just naked. It was a nice room, if you didn't get rough. There was a wide damask covered divan in a shadowy corner, like a casting couch. It was the kind of room where people sit with their feet in their laps and sip absinthe through lumps of sugar and talk with high affected voices and sometimes just squeak. It was a room where everything could happen except work'' (p. 46).[41] The

39. *The Big Sleep*, p. 59.

40. (New York: Vintage Books, 1963), p. 12.

41. (1940; reprint ed., London: Penguin, 1949), p. 46. Although in a formulaic genre one should not necessarily infer directly from his fiction what an author believes

inverted snobbery projected through the urban folk wit of Marlowe is an antidote to the upper-class kind implicit in the fictions of Christie and Sayers. Probably the most widespread native American hostility is hostility to the suspected snob.

The passage from *Farewell, My Lovely* also serves to remind us that the hard-boiled tradition was first associated chiefly with California. In Nolan's words, "The old and the new West blended in the image of the private detective" (p. 37). The ideological point of view is, therefore, not only from below up, it is also from the outside in. Whereas American political power, its social elite, and most prestigious institutions of higher learning have been concentrated on the Eastern seaboard, the private eye in his most memorable incarnations has been Western and apparently without a college education as well as lower class. The targets of his wit and anger, therefore, have a lot in common with those of a tradition going back beyond William Jennings Bryan and even Andrew Jackson in politics, and beyond the Southwestern humorists and Western tellers of adventure tales in literature. There is a similar hostility to large-scale industrialism, to modernity and modern ideas, to the Eastern establishment, to the college educated, and to all those institutions from the government in Washington to the local police that exert power over people and make living more complex. This late version of the long-standing revolt of the West against the East, of the "frontier" against "civilization," is associated in nineteenth-century literature, for example, with Bret Harte and Mark Twain.

The point of view of the typical private eye is, then, a concentrate of populist ideology in a broad sense. That at certain moments of crisis and national self-doubt such a point of view may reveal a potential for hysterical violence against scapegoats outside the American mainstream is revealed in the work of Mickey Spillane. Through his hero, Mike Hammer, Spillane turns the popular genre into the voice of a new cold-war populism at the same time that Senator McCarthy was

---

as a man in the world, Chandler does seem to have shared some of Marlowe's attitudes toward intellectuals. His comments on the writing of intellectuals is typical: "the language of intellectuals . . . is a loathsome language." Quoted by MacShane, *The Life*, p. 122.

its xenophobic and anti-intellectual D.A. It is not fortuitous if apart from individual Establishment figures, the senator's principal targets were such institutions as the State Department and the army. Had the issues not been so serious, in fact, an innocent contemporary might have been forgiven for assuming that those Senate committee hearings he witnessed on his TV screen were Hollywood social melodrama, and that the senator from Wisconsin with his Middle American male face and his heavy build had been chosen by a casting director to embody plainness and toughness. From the point of view of his supporters, in any case, McCarthy was perceived as the heroic embodiment of an aggressive individualism that represented ordinary Americans in the fight against corrupt institutions and those corrupt individuals who ran them.

The strength of the hostility felt by many Americans toward the institutions of government is, of course, as old as the Republic and as new as the 1980 presidential campaign. Thus, in commenting on the nineteenth-century American opposition to the idea of a standing army as well as of a centralized and uniformed police, James F. Richardson notes, ''the political theory of the American revolution stressed the struggle between liberty and power as the major problem of politics. Liberty was passive and static and constantly required preservation against dynamic power, which was always encroaching or attempting to encroach upon liberty.''[42]

The year 1929 illustrates the persistence of such a tradition because it witnessed both the publication of the first full-length hard-boiled novel, Dashiell Hammett's *Red Harvest,* and the inauguration, shortly before the stock market crash, of a president committed to the policies of American political conservatism. Thus, in his well-known work on the major currents in American political thought, *The American Political Tradition,* Richard Hofstader entitled his chapter on the first depression president ''Hoover and the Crisis of American Individualism.'' It is ironic that someone attempting a similar work on popular American writers could do worse than entitle a chapter on the major originator of the hard-boiled genre ''Hammett and the Reaffirmation of American Individualism.'' The irony is in the circumstance that the private eye began to flourish in popular literature at a time that coin-

42. *The New York Police*, p. 22.

cided with a major crisis of American individualism as the political philosophy of industrial capitalism. In the fiction, if no longer in life, the myth of heroic individualism persists. The Continental Op reaffirms his mastery over a city out of control in a way that the president signally failed to do for American society at large.

If the institutions of Big Government, Big Business, Big Labor, and Big Crime have been the most common targets of populist agitation, the distrust involved encompasses institutions of all kinds and extends far beyond the political oratory of public figures from Bryan to George Wallace into the writings of the nation's philosophers. Thus the Dreyfus affair in France was interpreted by no less a thinker than William James as a warning for the United States in the matter of institutions: "We 'intellectuals' in America must all work to keep our birthright of individualism, and freedom from these institutions (church, army, aristocracy, royalty). Every institution is a means of corruption—whatever good it may also do. Only in the free personal relation is full ideality to be found."[43]

Ample warrant for James's position was, of course, near at hand in those burgeoning industrial cities that are the beats of the fictional private investigators. In New York, for example, political patronage and graft seem to have been associated with city government at least since the election of the first professional politician, Fernando White, to City Hall in 1854. And by the 1890s the institution of the corrupt chief of police had been entrenched in such figures as Captain Alexander S. "Clubber" Williams and William Devery. Alfred Hodder wrote of the latter, "He presided like an Oriental caliph ungoverned by law or evidence, inspired by the witticism or the irritation of the moment."[44] A committee appointed in 1894 to investigate police practices was unequivocal in its findings: "The results were extremely embarrassing to the police, demonstrating a systematic and pervasive pattern of police corruption, brutality, election fraud, payoffs for appointments and promotions, political interference in transfers and assignments, police involvement in confidence frauds, and the police conception that they were above the law."[45]

43. Quoted by Hofstader, *Anti-Intellectualism in American Life*, p. 39.
44. Quoted by Richardson, *The New York Police*, p. 282.
45. Richardson, p. 240.

Such lessons from contemporary American life were not lost on the best of the hard-boiled novelists. As a result of their contacts with the powerful and with the representatives of such institutions as business, politics, the law, and the police, their private investigators uncover a similar pattern of corruption and brutality. Under the circumstances, as Chandler makes clear, the only refuge for "ideality" in his fiction is a man alone,[46] without possessions, ready to defend himself: "After a little while I felt a little better, but very little. I needed a drink, I needed a lot of life insurance, I needed a vacation, I needed a home in the country. What I had was a coat, a hat and a gun. I put them on and went out of the room."[47]

That in Hammett's case at least there was a genuine relationship in this respect between the way he lived and the private investigators of his fiction is confirmed by the truculence he displayed in 1951 on being subpoenaed for questioning in a conspiracy trial of four communists. He refused to answer questions and reported to Lillian Hellman that though he did not "like this kind of talk," he would rather give up his life than testify: "I would give it for what I think democracy is, and I don't let cops or judges tell me what democracy is."[48] Down to the reluctance to make political and social beliefs explicit, this is the voice of Sam Spade in his encounters with the official representatives of the law. It is also the voice of the man who, like Hobsbawn's social bandits, shows no respect for institutionalized authority but "makes himself respected."[49]

Thus, in a situation where, as often as not, the open contempt for the police was as great as the anger felt for parasitic criminals, the resort to the *private* investigator in life as in literature might well appear to be the only hope of seeing justice done. The original liberal distrust of standing armies and of the idea of a uniformed police— they were still denounced as "liveried lackeys" in the 1840s—was reinforced by the experience of American law enforcement in the late

46. The spareness of the private eye's life-style is, of course, reminiscent of "the utter simplicity of Gatsby's room," to which Richard Poirier has referred and which he interprets as an expression of "the environment of inner space" so central to the American literary imagination. *A World Elsewhere*, p. 30.

47. *Farewell, My Lovely*, p. 207.

48. Quoted by Nolan, *Dashiell Hammett*, p. 55.

49. *Bandits*, pp. 28–29.

nineteenth and early twentieth centuries. Under the circumstances Pinkerton's idea of establishing policing on a businessman/client relationship, in which he charged fees for his services, had an understandable appeal, even apart from the fact that in the absence of a federal bureau, Pinkerton's National Detective Agency also filled a need when it was founded in 1850. And it was Pinkerton's agency that invented the symbol for the fictional myth; its trademark was a wide-open eye coupled with the slogan "We Never Sleep." In the disciplinary society of the United States the ideal unseen seer of law enforcement was conceived to be an independent businessman, who in his most memorable fictional incarnations is strictly free-lance. He runs his own agency and is hired by a client to do a job.

Along with the widespread distrust of institutions of government at the local as well as at the federal level, the socioeconomic conditions of the twenties and thirties also help explain the rise of the private eye to the status of a dominant mythic hero, first of popular literature and later of Hollywood movies. The private eye could become the hero of a modern American populist culture because he embodied in an urban setting and in economic hard times that "omni-competence of the common man" which Richard Hofstader refers to as "the original populist dream."[50] Yet if the private eye is the embodiment of an ideal American ordinariness, it is ordinariness with a difference, because in an industrial age of maximum division of labor and of the big corporation, he combines independence with omnicompetence. In a world of wage earners and fixed working routines, of the rich, the poor, and the relatively poor, of the powerful and their victims, of suckers and con artists, Spade and Marlowe in their shabby offices remain aloof, ready to intervene occasionally in the cause of justice but outside the system. They lead the free-lance life that is unburdened by problems of domesticity and boring routine work and unencumbered by debts for services rendered them. Neither exploiters nor exploited, they insist on fair payment plus expenses for work done because their fee is the sign of their freedom and integrity. Money is always an issue in hard-boiled novels, as it rarely is in formal detective fiction, as an expression of the accepted folk wisdom that you can make an honest buck but not an honest million bucks—a point of view that is as

50. Hofstader, *Anti-Intellectualism*, p. 34.

American as the countermyth, associated with the self-made Hoover himself as well as with Horatio Alger, that wealth is the reward for talent and hard work.

Moreover, the private eyes' appeal as folk heroes, which is related to their condition of freedom in a world where the great majority recognize themselves to be under some form of bondage, is also shared with social bandits: "Banditry is freedom, but in a peasant society few can be free. Men are shackled by the double chains of lordship and labour, the one reinforcing the other."[51] Similarly, in the stage of industrial capitalism represented by the progressive era and the depression years, a great many Americans undoubtedly regarded their own much vaunted freedom as a strictly circumscribed thing.

Like the social bandit of broadsheet and ballad, therefore, the private investigator in the popular literature of the twenties and thirties reflects a phenomenon of social protest. In this respect he has something in common with figures like Bonnie and Clyde, who have a more obvious link to the tradition of social banditry. It was to an important degree the depression that could also make petty hoodlums appear to be folk heroes. Ordinary rural Americans were able to identify with Bonnie and Clyde because the targets of their banditry were those financial institutions and individuals from whom dirt farmers had to borrow money to raise their crops and to whom they were obliged to pay rent or yield their land. As a subject for ballads, Bonnie and Clyde are in a direct line of descent from the social bandits defined by Hobsbawn: "men who, when faced with some act of injustice or persecution, do not yield meekly to force or social superiority, but take the path of resistance and outlawry" (p. 29). Yet the private investigators of the hard-boiled genre are more authentic representatives of the phenomenon of social protest because in spite of their pessimism and, even, cynicism they also hold on to a lingering hope. In Chandler's familiar formulation, hope is embodied chiefly in the character of the detective hero: "In everything that can be called art there is a quality of redemption. It may be pure tragedy, if it is high tragedy, and it may be pity and irony, and it may be the raucous laughter of the strong man. Down these mean streets a man must go who is not himself mean, who is neither tarnished nor afraid. The de-

51. Hobsbawn, *Bandits*, p. 23.

tective in this kind of story must be such a man. He is the hero; he is
everything. He must be a complete man and a common man and yet
an unusual man.''[52] Hope for Chandler has taken refuge in the personal sense of honor of a man alone.

What Chandler does not say, however, is that the faith he places in
his common-man hero is an atavistic faith. Sam Spade and Philip
Marlowe display the knowledge of how to survive and remain free
with your integrity intact against superior odds and against all comers.
This kind of knowledge was possessed by a great many folk heroes of
the American popular tradition as well as by legendary social bandits.
Consequently, the reformulation of the old frontier dream of self-
sufficiency and independence in the inhospitable urban environment of
advanced industrial capitalism is a striking example of the persistence
of cultural myth under historical conditions that seem to deny its validity. If, in Richard Slotkin's complete statement of the American
myth of the hunter, the denouement embodies a form of spiritual renewal, following the pursuit of and victory over the wilderness
through its creatures, in the truncated version of the mythic narrative
structure to be found in the hard-boiled novel there is violence without
regeneration because the link with the true wilderness has been sev-
ered. The radicalism of the hard-boiled tradition is therefore a radicalism of nostalgia for a mythical past. If any political program is implied at all, it is one that looks forward to the restoration of a
traditional order of things, associated retrospectively with the innocent
young Republic and its frontier, a traditional order that was destroyed
with the advent of large-scale industrialization.[53]

In reality, the police detective is a typical example of the division
of labor in modern society, a trained specialist within the police department itself. Yet the literary detective of the classic detective novel
is always represented as something more than a narrow specialist because he treats the work of detection itself as a hobby. That is why
his amateur status is of such ideological significance. Well-heeled am-

52. ''The Simple Art of Murder,'' p. 533.

53. In this respect, too, there is continuity between the attitudes of the social bandit
and the private eye: ''Insofar as bandits have a 'programme', it is the defence or restoration of the traditional order of things 'as it should be. . . .' '' Hobsbawn, *Bandits* p.
21.

ateurs have never been much involved in the solving of real crimes in England or anywhere else. But with a lot of leisure on their hands, they have played a great many games. Consequently, crime solving for the Great Detective in the British tradition has itself had the status of a game that combines something of the physical excitement of the chase with the intellectual challenge of bridge.

Moreover, in contrast to the hard-boiled private eye, the fictional British detective almost always has an enthusiasm, further hobby, or durable personal relationship that he enjoys apart from the business of detection. Dupin's esoteric learning, Sergeant Cuff's passion for rose growing, Holmes's friendship with Watson, his enthusiasm for science, and his love of the violin and of opera, Poirot's relationship with Hastings and his interest in clothes and food, Wimsey's love affair with Harriet Vane and his taste for the finer things in life all imply a commitment to civilized living and to society beyond the dark sphere of crime. Such pursuits suggest a rootedness within a stable and harmonious social order that is threatened only temporarily by criminal acts.

By contrast, the private eye has no hobbies apart from drinking and women. Nor does he engage in any pleasures that are not in some sense destructive or self-destructive, from the hunting down of criminals to heavy smoking, heavy drinking, and occasionally at least, casual sex.[54] He has no wife to return to, no home or agreeable gentleman's chambers. Not only does he have no garden to cultivate, he has no fixed address. And the reason is that, like the outlaw, hunter, and Indian fighter, he lives on the margin of established society. But such is the price of the freedom which sets him apart from the ordinary men he in other ways resembles. In spite of the urban industrial context, he has much in common not only with the Indian scouts and the gun-slinging cowboys of frontier myth but also with the Haiduks from central European peasant cultures. Like the Haiduks of the traditional ballads, private eyes are propertyless, childless, and kinless men, "whose swords were their only sisters, whose rifles their wives. . . . Death was their equivalent of marriage."[55] If the original tools of civ-

---

54. Nolan notes that Hammett himself "was a compulsive gambler—cards and crap games—loved prize fights and hunted when he could afford to" (p. 55).

55. Hobsbawn, *Bandits*, p. 67.

ilization are the plow and the ax and the builders' implements, he whose only tool is the gun must always remain marginal to civilization. But in the detective genre only the American tradition has celebrated such marginality because of the longstanding ambivalence for that civilized order which the private eye, like the Indian fighter and hunter before him, regarded as his mission to protect. It is an ambivalence derived originally from the perception that the extension of white civilization into the wilderness would in time do away with the need for the frontiersman's heroic interventions, but it is compounded in the age of the private eye by overwhelming evidence that white civilization itself is perhaps not worth protecting after all. The private eye typically is a hero with nowhere to go and with a mission in which he does not fully believe.

The private investigator's code, as defined by both Hammett and Chandler, is an updated version of a traditional warrior code. As applied to the private investigator, it commits him to a life of duty and renunciation in between bouts of loose living. Consequently, he is an example not only of the division of labor but also of an extreme sex role differentiation associated with the division of labor. Like the original Dupin, classic detective heroes have typically been dons, scientists, enthusiasts, collectors, or men of taste and fashion, as well as sleuths. That is to say, they are associated with cultural and intellectual pursuits which were anathema to traditional American popular culture because they are theoretic rather than pragmatic, unworldly, and upper class. As a result, the detectives appear unmasculine. Where it was possible, therefore, to conceive of women detectives, at least within the terms of the classic British detective novel, until the 1960s it was impossible to do so in that American tradition which began with *Black Mask* magazine. To be hard-boiled and to have retained a heroic integrity was to be a man. The culture had generated no precedent for a tough-talking, worldly-wise woman, capable of defending herself in the roughest company, who also possessed the indispensable heroic qualities of physical attractiveness and virtue. A woman in the private eye's role would have been conceivable only as fallen or comic, as Belle Watling or Annie Oakley.

Thus the new ethos of hard-boiled detective fiction was not only anti-English and antielitist, it was also antifeminist. The equation that makes gentility equal femininity, and the civilized life a woman's estate, is a well-documented fact of American cultural life. What has perhaps not been sufficiently emphasized is the role of the vernacular style in confirming that equation. Those stylists who from Mark Twain to Hemingway, Faulkner, and Norman Mailer created the idiom of the American literary mainstream also conspired to ensure that the voice of American fiction should be an aggressively male voice. At least until Erica Jong there has been no vernacular for women outside quotation marks. Bad grammar, slang, and even a strong regional accent, like cussing, blaspheming, hard drinking, and tomcatting, were the prerogatives of men and boys, defensive reactions against the encroachments of civilizing womankind and the tyranny of hearth and home. A linguistic double standard operated, making such language in a female mouth the sign of a bumpkin or a fallen woman. In domocratic culture the implications of such a taboo are far-reaching. Unusually attractive women in popular literature tend to be either ladies or whores, nature's snobs or its sexually overripe dropouts.

Typically, therefore, although there is far more overt sexuality in the hard-boiled tradition than in the classic detective story, in most cases it goes unconsummated. In this respect the course taken by "romance" in *The Maltese Falcon* became a model for the genre. Sam Spade is susceptible to the physical presence of the beautiful, young Brigid O'Shaughnessy, is eventually propositioned by her, but after having established her complicity in crime he turns the tables in the end by spurning her offer. The denouement of Hammett's third novel is worth quoting, in fact, because the trap Sam Spade prepares for Brigid O'Shaughnessy has been so often imitated.

> She put her face up to his face. Her mouth was slightly open with lips a little thrust out. She whispered: "If you loved me you'd need nothing more on that side."
>
> Spade set the edges of his teeth together and said through them: "I won't play the sap for you."
>
> She put her mouth to his, slowly, her arms around him, and came into his arms. She was in his arms when the door-bell rang.
>
> Spade, left arm around Brigid O'Shaughnessy, opened the corridor-door. Lieutenant Dundy, Detective-sergeant Tom Polhaus, and two other detectives were there.
>
> Spade said: "Hello, Tom. Get them?"
>
> Polhaus said: "Got them."
>
> "Swell. Come in. Here's another one for you." [p. 195]

This type of denouement is by implication a test of male will. The private eye is temporarily excited by an attractive woman, finds himself betrayed, and ends up demonstrating his mastery over sexual temptation by rejecting, arresting, or in some cases killing her. This opportunity for a fantasy-fulfilling display of male invulnerability involves a teasing followed by a spurning of a woman. And once again it has a popular mythic precedent in the American hunter hero. In Hammett and Chandler in particular, although the private eye is consciously associated with the virility of a womanizing male, he is nevertheless basically celibate, not because celibacy is a functional necessity, as it is with the hunter seeking union not with womankind but with feminine nature itself, but because celibacy is a sign of his heroic status. It signifies that the private eye belongs to the caste of hunters of the fully developed myth and shares some of their noble destiny in spite of urban squalor: "Ideal chastity, however, is part of the acculturated American's ethic of solitude, as embodied by Leatherstocking. It enables the hero to submit to the Indian dark of the Wilderness without becoming debased by sexual amalgamation."[56]

In Mickey Spillane's novels the complex sado-erotic charge of the hunt itself, especially in the form of a woman-hunt, is particularly evident. In this respect the structure of Spillane's narratives often derive from the premise that sexual renunciation is rewarded with a yet intenser pleasure; the experience of intercourse is not to be compared with that of the kill. Where evil women are involved, his denouements typically take the form of a ritual act of rejection / possession through murder. In a macabre parody of sexual relations satisfying to Eros and Thanatos at the same time, Spillane plays with the imagery of the phallic pistol. The bullet entering a beautiful female body becomes a definitive assertion of male power. In the context it is a form of death-causing penetration that provokes the ultimate orgasmic swoon of a dying. On such occasions Spillane pushes the myth of the hunter to its limit, representing him as one "who deserts religious discipline for the grossly materialistic, sex-linked passion of the hunt."[57] Unlike the trophies of the mythic frontiersman, however, Mike Hammer's typically take the form not of Indian scalps or dead animals but

---

56. *Regeneration through Violence*, p. 531.
57. Ibid., p. 490.

of women's bodies. In sex as in war male prowess may be assessed in body counts.

In the attitude expressed toward women as in so much else, the British detective novel differs significantly from the hard-boiled kind. Doyle took to heart his mother's injunction, "Chivalry to women, of high or low degree."[58] And from Doyle on, the Great Detective of the classic tradition has been chivalrous in the treatment of women, assuming they are ladies until shown otherwise. Holmes's view of relations with the opposite sex is close to the classic one of the Victorian clubman. Wimsey and Poirot share similar opinions in marriage or outside it.

If the hard-boiled novel ends with the rejection of a woman and a retreat from intimate personal relations, the classic detective novel often couples the solution of a crime with an engagement or a wedding, although only exceptionally does this involve the Great Detective himself. From *The Moonstone* on, the British detective novel confirms its links with the comedy of manners by the relative frequency with which it ends by promising a wedding. Thus the union of Franklin Blake and Rachel Verinder is integral to Collins's vision of social harmony within a hierarchical society. And at the end of *The Sign of Four* Watson finds an appropriately genteel soul mate.

Although there are exceptions, women as a group and more especially gentlewomen are seen to be worthy of a man's love and respect in golden age detective fiction, which, given the preponderance of women authors, is not surprising. As throughout the British tradition, at least up to the age of the spy thriller, the criminal investigation involves a suspension of ordinary living that is nevertheless resumed with the investigation's conclusion. Once the crime has been solved, the house party can go on and young love find its mate. Since the elimination of the evil criminal marks the return to health and normality, it invites the ritualistic celebration of life that is, in fact, a literary wedding, whatever the Detective Club Rules might say about the inappropriateness of mixing romance with mystery. In the hard-boiled novel, on the other hand, the discovery that love, too, is perverted occurs as a final confirmation of quasi-universal corruption. The lesson that the American tradition in crime detection seems to embody is

58. Carr, *The Life*, p. 66.

that antifeminism in literature is an expression of social pessimism. The principle involved is that of the festering lily.

At the end of *The Big Sleep*, having traced the peculiarly ugly murder of Rusty Regan back to the young Carmen Sternwood, Philip Marlowe walks away reflecting on the squalor of life: "What did it matter where you lay once you were dead? In a dirty sump or in a marble tower on top of a high hill? You were dead, you were sleeping the big sleep, you were not bothered by things like that. Oil and water were the same as air and wind to you. You just slept the big sleep, not caring about the nastiness of how you died or where you fell. Me, I was part of the nastiness" (pp. 215–16).

This concluding passage is also a reminder that if the hard-boiled detective novel is the voice of a new urban populism, it is a populism without much optimism. Thus Philip Durham attributes the popularity of Hammett's private investigator to the fact that he "speaks for men who had lost faith in the values of their society during war, gangsterism and depression."[59] Significantly, when Chandler attempts to conclude on an upbeat note, as in the denouement of *Farewell, My Lovely*, he lapses into the sentimentality characteristic of his early English writings. Anne Riordan, an attractive young woman who is also "nice," apparently posed a problem for Chandler that he was unable to solve satisfactorily within the terms of the hard-boiled formula and its myths. A similar sentimentality attends the conception of the giant hoodlum, Moose Molloy, as a Gatsby figure, and of the little Velma he pursues as in the end motivated by compassion for her doting husband.

The staple attitude of the formula toward romance was expressed memorably by Hammett's Continental Op in the gory story entitled "The Gutting of Couffrigal": "You think I'm a man and you're a woman. That's wrong. I'm a manhunter and you're something that has been running in front of me."[60] Unlike the formal detective story, the hard-boiled genre does not so much lack romance in connection with its heroic investigator, it rejects it. The suspense of the manhunt is invariably resolved satisfactorily; the romantic suspense of the woman-hunt, on the other hand, rarely is. Women are typically rep-

59. Quoted by Nolan, *Dashiell Hammett*, p. 6.
60. Quoted by Nolan, *Dashiell Hammett*, p. 23.

resented as either too bad or too good, but in both cases the pleasures they stand for do not match those of the chase itself. The private investigator does not just flee women as a softening and / or civilizing distraction from his difficult task, he finds the excitement of the manhunt a superior alternative to sex.

Finally, it is noticeable that when the hard-boiled model is repatriated to the land of the classic detective novel in the form of the spy thriller, the private eye turns organization man but retains his self-destructive and antifeminist attitudes. James Bond learns his lesson in the first novel of the series, *Casino Royale*, where he falls in love only to discover that his beautiful Vesper is a double agent. The new jingoism of the cold war era legitimized a heroic type in Britain whose tastes and manners were still upper class but who was no longer an amateur and a gentleman. A readership conscious of a world divided into two armed camps was ready for a cool and disciplined professional killer with the exterior of a playboy. James Bond is public school to the extent that he is a strong-bodied, unreflecting team player with a deep institutional loyalty, but his hobbies are those of discriminating consumption—of food, wine, and women—as well as of the fashionable competitive game playing that is traditionally an alternative to hunting and combat as a test of male self-worth.

In short, James Bond is a late-fifties fantasy man who lives life as if it were an exciting and dangerous play against ruthless opponents, and who takes or leaves the women offered. In Fleming's updated characterization of the detective's role, Chandler's conception of honor in independence is reduced to an unquestionable commitment to duty. The private eye is turned into the deadly instrument of a secret government department. James Bond is represented as a man with a national mission who has the toughness of the private eye but not his virtues of independence and populist wit. In a newly Manichaean world he was the British version of the cold war gladiator in the same way that Mike Hammer was the American.

9

The Landscape of Detection

The important contribution made by descriptive passages both to the generation of suspense and to pleasurable digression has been discussed in previous chapters. That such passages also have in their context a clear ideological significance will come as a surprise to no one. At least since Ruskin diagnosed the "pathetic fallacy," it has been apparent to critics that the verbal evocation of place and of scene in particular always involved more than a mere naming. And the qualities writers have discovered in landscapes of all kinds have invariably provided valuable indices to more or less consciously held beliefs.

If this is true of the novel in general and especially the realist novel, where the space occupied by description is so large, it is also true of detective fiction. A crime always occurs and is solved in a place that, depending on the tradition in which an author is working, will be evoked with more or less precision. A detective setting about his task finds himself situated in a physical environment whose latent moral significance may be explicit or implicit, apparent from the beginning or uncovered only at a later date. In its broadest sense, then, the landscape which is represented as the backdrop to crime in a detective novel is as ideologically significant as stylistic level and the type of hero.

Furthermore, a reading of the landscape descriptions of detective fiction confirms what structuralist cultural critics have claimed for some time, namely, that writing is in an important sense a form of recycling of the previously written. Authors of detective stories endlessly repeat the vocabulary, tropes, and topoi not only of predecessors writing in the genre but also of the culture as a whole. They practice a form of exclusionary "discourse," i.e., one that is usually not aware of its own silences or of its continual repetition of the story of the same familiar world. And nowhere is the phenomenon more obvious than in the evocation of landscape. Detective fiction deals in the kind of mythic geography of our various cultures that has given rise to such stubborn concepts as "the mysterious Orient" and "the dark continent."[1]

From the beginning many of the most interesting works in the genre claim to be about places on the map as well as about the detection of crime. The Paris of Poe's tales, Collins's Yorkshire, and Doyle's London are fictional locations by means of which the threat and fascination of crime are made tangible for a reader. They are also the context that makes the crime comprehensible. In the detective novel, at least, you can judge a place by its relation to crime. In other words, if landscape in the sense I am giving it here is so central to stories involving crimes, it is because a relationship is affirmed between site and event. This relationship may be either conjunctive or disjunctive, sympathetic or ironic. Landscapes appear either as the source and extension of the crimes reported or as their antithesis. The background a writer chooses for his work and his perception of its relationship to the evil events narrated express a socially evaluating vision.

G. K. Chesterton defended the genre on the grounds that it was "the only form of popular literature in which is expressed some sense of the poetry of modern life." And he found the source of that poetry in the representation of the city, in the "realization of a great city itself as something wild and obvious."[2] Yet in the British tradition, at least, the detective novelist has more often than not preferred a rural or semirural setting for the locality of crime. In such a setting as much as in its class heroes the genre's fundamental traditionalism is expressed.

Nevertheless, Doyle, who was for so long the most influential model in the genre, suggested the possibilities of both kinds of backgrounds to crime by alternating between detection in the city and detection in the country. On the one hand, he borrowed the gothic motif of ancestral county seat, and on the other, he reinvented "London" for his purposes in the same way that Poe and Gaboriau use "Paris"

1. See, e.g., Edward W. Said's valuable recent work, *Orientalism* (New York: Vintage Books, 1979).

2. "A Defence of Detective Stories, "in G. K. Chesterton, *The Defendant* (London: Dent, 1901), p. 119.

as a source of suggestive imagery. His literary point of departure in the former respect was, of course, Dickens. And Doyle is very skillful at weaving Dickensian topoi and atmospheric effects into the texture of his stories. Thus, "The Man with the Twisted Lip," one of the best-known tales from his third volume of stories, opens with an evocation of the East End dockland before the description of that lower-depth world of the opium den with which Dickens had begun *The Mystery of Edwin Drood.*

> . . . by the light of a flickering oil-lamp above the door I found the latch and made my way into a long low room, thick and heavy with the brown opium smoke, and terraced with wooden berths, like the forecastle of an emigrant ship.
>
> Through the gloom one could dimly catch a glimpse of bodies lying in strange fantastic poses, bowed shoulders, bent knees, heads thrown back, and chins pointing upward, with here and there a dark, lack-lustre eye turned upon the newcomer. Out of the black shadows there glimmered little red circles of light, now bright, now faint, as the burning poison waxed and waned in the bowls of the metal pipes. The most lay silent, but some muttered to themselves, and others talked together in a strange, low, monotonous voice, their conversation coming in gushes, and then suddenly tailing off into silence.[3]

This is the city of the *poètes maudits* as well as of Dickens, the modern metropolis with its various and transient human population and its sympathy for vice. But one would have a great deal of trouble finding a comparable phantasmagoric realism in so-called golden age detective fiction.

Moreover, in *The Valley of Fear* Doyle went beyond the Dickensian example and evoked the cityscape of American naturalism. Perhaps the most interesting and paradoxical aspect of that work is, in fact, that it breaks down into two very different parts of which the first is set in rural Sussex and involves the traditional Holmesian mix, whereas the second places the adventures of a Pinkerton agent disguised as a hoodlum in industrial Pennsylvania. Probably nowhere else in the genre is there such an effort to combine in a single work the antithetical landscapes of the country house and the chaotic city. The loveliness of a site characterized by centuries of civilized order in

3. *The Complete Sherlock Holmes* (New York: Doubleday, n.d.), p. 231.

the first part is made to contrast with the raw squalor of industry in the second:

> We walked down the quaint village street with a row of pollarded elms on each side of it. Just beyond were two ancient stone pillars, weather-stained and lichen-blotched, bearing upon their summits a shapeless some-thing which had once been the ancient lion of Capus of Birlstone. A short walk along the winding drive with such sward and oaks around it as one only sees in rural England, then a sudden turn, and the long, low Jacobean house of dingy, liver-coloured brick lay before us, with an old-fashioned garden of cut yews on either side.[4]

> The country had been a place of terror; but the town was in its way even more depressing. Down that long valley there was at least a certain gloomy grandeur in the huge fires and the clouds of drifting smoke, while the strength and industry of man found fitting monuments in the hills which he had spilled by the side of his monstrous excavations. But the town showed a dead level of mean ugliness and squalor. The broad street was churned up by the traffic into a horrible rutted paste of muddy snow. The sidewalks were narrow and uneven. The numerous gas-lamps served only to show more clearly a long line of wooden houses, each with its veranda facing the street, unkempt and dirty.[5]

Moreover, the meanings attached to such settings here are tradi-tional in the genre. In the first part, the shadow of the gothic super-natural is cast by the ancestral home until all mystery is dispelled at the denouement. But in the second part the reign of terror enforced by a corrupt union brotherhood turns out to be only too real. The material of "the valley of fear" is that of Hammett, down to political graft, police corruption, beatings, murders, and bombings. In this part, therefore, the relationship between landscape and crime is sympa-thetic, whereas in the first it turns out to be ironic. Doyle was inspired to represent crime in the alien milieu of industrial Pennsylvania by stories told him about the Molly Maguires by William J. Burns of the detective agency. It is noteworthy that contemporary critics found the work too political, thus providing an example of the way in which a reading public exercises pressure on a popular writer to keep his work within well-defined limits.

4. Ibid., p. 787
5. Ibid., p. 819.

By the time of golden age detective fiction, that lesson had been thoroughly assimilated. The appeal of the country in opposition to the city is mythic in origin; its forms and order are easily mistaken for those of nature itself. Unlike the obviously man-made city, it may more easily appear to be untouched by history because the historical origins of its contours have been lost sight of. Therefore, the country comes to stand not only for nature but also for permanence in a world where so much else is threatened by undesirable change. As a result, the potentially political material of the modern city was largely eschewed and the setting of country house and picturesque village became the norm, with the attendant predictable irony of the surprise of crime. W. H. Auden defined such a setting as "the Great Good Place," adding, "the more Eden-like it is, the greater the contradiction of murder."[6] Against a background of order and harmonious social relationships in a hierarchical society, crime is the exception that proves the rule. It is the result of an individual act of iniquity motivated by some simple human passion such as jealousy or greed, and is usually without social significance because it is random. Crime under such conditions is a function of "human nature," a sign of the persistence of old Adam or of the diabolical principle eternally at work in the world.

Yet, in some of the best-known works of the British tradition the relationship between site and event is more complicated than that. The country houses of *The Moonstone, The Hound of the Baskervilles*, and of Dorothy L. Sayers's *Nine Taylors* find themselves threatened from without as well as from within in their rural communities. In British mythical geography the Yorkshire coast, Dartmoor, and the East Anglian fen country in winter constitute landscapes of encircling wildness. The peculiar potency of Dartmoor in the English imagination as a place of evil has been reinforced by the existence there of a top-security prison. But what Doyle exploits is the late romantic vision of moor and heathland as infertile, empty, and hence ungodly spaces. And the North Sea has traditionally been a metaphor for a similar landscape of desolation.

Thus, in the works just mentioned, the sphere of culture that is formed by the great house with or without the attendant church and

6. "The Guilty Vicarage," p. 151.

village finds itself enclosed within the sphere of a still savage nature. The element of the marvelous inherited from gothic and mystery story is situated in an external nature evoked to suggest the vulnerability not only of human life but also of benevolent and enlightened culture. Further, in *The Moonstone* particularly, the threat from without is reinforced through the invasion of English geographical space by the alien occult realm of India, an invasion that is also a disturbing presence in *Edwin Drood*.

The detective novel of the above type implies a complicity against civilized order between the natural savagery without and the criminals among us. In Chesterton's words: "By dealing with the unsleeping sentinels who guard the outposts of society, it [the romance of police activity] tends to remind us that we live in an armed camp, making war with a chaotic world, and that the criminals, the children of chaos, are nothing but the traitors within our gates."[7] The significance of the embattled great house in such a context is obvious. And it is characteristic that in Collins's and Doyle's novels there is a threat to the continuity of a noble family by means of an attempted usurpation, a threat that is thwarted in the denouement. The perpetuation of civilized society itself is dependent on the preservation of the humane moral order symbolized by the great house. Those who conspire against it are, therefore, to be hunted down and eliminated.

Her taste for such houses and the sleepy village is characteristic of Agatha Christie's fiction between the two worlds wars. And her novels are inhabited by that narrow range of social types associated with such a milieu, including the local gentry, doctor, vicar, lawyer, village "characters," and the manor house's weekend guests. In her case, however, even nature itself is benevolent, so that nothing disturbs the calm flow of rural life among the upper-middle classes except the criminal deeds themselves. If her settings are those of "the long weekend," therefore, such settings constitute for her fans part of the charm of her fictions. They are ideal locations for witty, self-absorbed play and the pleasure in difficult times of irresponsibility. Against the real background of a depressed agriculture, rural unemployment, slow economic recovery, slump, and the preparation for war, Agatha Christie projected the vision of a mythic England of cot-

7. Chesterton, *The Defendant*, pp. 122–23.

tage and manor house, churchyards and country lanes, where only solvable crimes posed a threat to age-old ways of life. *The Murder of Roger Ackroyd* appeared in 1926, the same year as the general strike, which is referred to in her autobiography only because she had to drive her husband, Archie Christie, to London after just three driving lessons.

Her autobiography also makes clear the fondness she still felt in the fifties and sixties for the late Victorian and Edwardian idyll, which in her case is particularly associated with her childhood home in Torquay. The period before World War I is seen as imbued with a lost innocence that is not simply personal to her. Her epigraph for the first part sets the tone: "O! ma chère Maison, mon nid, mon gîte / Le Passé l'habite . . . O! ma chère Maison." And she evokes there the solid middle-class life of the large in-town house with the reassuring presence of an extended family and servants, with teas in the nursery and games of fantasy in the enclosed garden. Later there would be travel to the continent and to British Egypt, country-house parties, riding, horse races, motor cars, golf, archery, croquet, lawn tennis, and even a ride in an airplane. In retrospect she recalls that "it was a happy lazy life" (p. 241).

In her fiction such an ambience of pleasure and play lives on, but its function is in part to enhance the surprise of crime at the same time that it cushions the shock of it. When, as in the formal detective story, the description of the body is either vague or nonexistent, a corpse in a library is a scandal for the mind only and not for the senses. A corpse in a library, unlike a cadaver in a tenement, contradicts our expectations and signifies the entry of violence into the holy place of culture. Its message once again is *Et in Arcadia ego*; it is the sign that threatens the return of barbarism to surroundings both civilized and reassuringly familiar. But it is conjured up only in order to be exorcized at the end. Agatha Christie's quietist traditionalism may serve, then, as a reminder that anglo-American conservatism for a long time took country life for a sociopolitical as well as an aesthetic norm. In the same way that English Tory gentry once regarded the settled rural community with its manor house, church, and village street as an ideal, in the United States the Jeffersonian vision of a nation of independent yeoman farmers gave a liberal and republican form to the Tory concept.

Against the background of a civilized order founded on the socio-economic relations of English rural life, crime in detective fiction appears as an aberration; it is the exception which proves the rule of moral order. Crime under such circumstances is eccentric, a random asymmetry in a context of harmony. And it derives from a few fundamental human motives that share a nomenclature with sins, such as greed, jealousy, envy, or even hate. Such motives are, in other words, givens, constants of human behavior, and therefore not to be traced back to the failure of a social system. Consequently, detective novels written in the mode of Agatha Christie are from this point of view comic morality plays designed to communicate a muted thrill on the way to identifying greed or jealousy behind the masks of respectability and kindliness.

If the typical topos of the formal detective story is that of the enemy within the isolated and privileged community of great house, village, island, or intercontinental express, hard-boiled adventure starts in the private eye's bare office or hotel room and moves out into the streets, bars, poolrooms, apartment houses, and millionaire's mansions of California. In the same way that Hammett adapted an urban American vernacular to the purpose of reinventing the detective novel, he also adopted the antipastoral cityscape as the appropriate background for violent crime. And his choice of milieu has to be seen as an expression of radical sympathies.

The reality that the hard-boiled story first reflected was, of course, the chaotic American city of the "Roaring Twenties," one of whose major themes, as Kennett and Anderson have noted, was "an obsession with threats to law and order and traditional values." Along with a reemergence of xenophobia, immigration curbs, and a "Red Scare," an unprecedented crime wave also occurred that caught the public imagination because it was "spectacularly innovative" in its tactics, weaponry, and mobility. Not only was there a big increase in firepower involving the use of automatics, sawed-off shotguns, and tommy guns, the automobile also gave criminals a speed of movement that made daylight raids a commonplace. The result was that "the eastern metropolis came to resemble the western cowtown, with its daylight holdups, gun battles in the streets, and cross-country pursuits."[8] Moreover, during the depression years of the thirties the incidence of crime further increased.

Novels like *Red Harvest* and *The Glass Key* are, therefore, direct reflections of contemporary American anxieties and manifestations of a national dream turned nightmare—an early version of *Red Harvest* was entitled "Nightmare Town." Hammett projects a vision of "the wild and obvious" city as a realm of the rich and the poor, of work, money, organized exploitation, corruption, death, and dying. As a result, at least until later novels like *The Maltese Falcon* and *The Thin Man*, there is often a visible political dimension to his fiction of a kind that recalls early nineteenth-century crime novels. Moreover, the relationship between crime and the landscape of urban America is portrayed as a sympathetic one. Violent acts are no longer aberrations or isolated events but, as the frequency of beatings and shoot-outs suggests, endemic. And the cityscape evoked at the beginning of *Red Harvest* already suggests why: "The city wasn't pretty. Most of its builders had gone in for gaudiness. Maybe they had been successful at first. Since then the smelters whose brick stacks stuck up tall against a gloomy mountain to the south had yellow-smoked everything into uniform dinginess. The result was an ugly city of forty thousand people, set in an ugly notch between two ugly mountains that had been all dirtied up by mining. Spread over this was a grimy sky that looked as if it had come out of the smelters' stacks" (p. 3).

Hammett's Poisonville resembles the cityscape of American naturalism, which is also that of "the valley of ashes" in *The Great Gatsby*. That is to say, it appears as the typical environment of an unregulated industrial capitalism, which acknowledges no limits to the pursuit of private wealth. Both detective hero and reader are, therefore, faced with the alienated product of human labor on the level of a total environment. Moreover, Hammett's example in this became a model for the hard-boiled genre, whether subsequent writers shared his radical tendencies or not. The cityscapes of his early writings are represented as perverted fiefdoms of the owners of capital and of those strong-arm men who support them and live off their greed. And the victims are ordinary citizens who have recourse neither to their polit-

8. *The Gun in America*, pp. 187–88.

ical leaders nor to the law because both politics and law enforcement are part of the corrupt system. If American literature is a literature of extremes, if it veers between the poles of utopian quest and a nightmarish realism, it is because in the twentieth century, at least, its implicit theme has so often been the shattering of the pastoral dream on the concrete surfaces of the urban wasteland. And in their own way both Hammett and Chandler have made important contributions to the dark myth of the unredeemable city.

The big house, that enduring symbol of social stability through hierarchical order in the British tradition, takes in Chandler the form of the Sternwood mansion (*The Big Sleep*) or the Grayle home (*Farewell, My Lovely*). That is to say, it is the outward manifestation of mere wealth without social responsibility or a prescribed social role. The ostentatious luxury of the decor serves chiefly to point up the ironic contrast with the moral corruption of the inhabitants. Consequently, unlike *The Moonstone,* both *The Big Sleep* and *Farewell, My Lovely* end not with the renewal of life but with death. No civilizing dynasty can issue from General Sternwood's perverted blood or from the effete Grayle.

The significance of the land in American national mythology is too well known to need repeating here; however, it should be noted that the sprawling industrial metropolis marks the end of the frontier just as much as the West Coast itself does. If Southern California is the homeland of the private eye, of the cynic in whom the dream survives only in the form of personal honor, it is because in its cities derelict streets and acres of parking lots spill out across land ideally intended for orange groves and lapped still by the magical Pacific. To the extent that in Crèvecoeur's version of the American dream the existence of the land held out the possibility of regeneration, the end of the land in the twentieth century must exclude that possibility. The reason why, apart from anything else, Los Angeles is the city American writers most love to hate, therefore, is that there the land ran out. When it was still a Spanish settlement, its situation ensured the ironic role it would finally play as the destination of an American myth.

In a passage from *Farewell, My Lovely* that echoes the end of *The Great Gatsby*, the dream is remembered chiefly through the sights and sounds of the Pacific Ocean itself: "After a while there was a faint smell of ocean. Not very much, but as if they had kept this much to remind people this had once been a clean open beach where the waves came in and creamed and the wind blew and you could smell something besides hot fat and cold sweat'' (p. 39). In the age before offshore oil rigs, the Pacific could still appear as the final remaining example of virgin territory, unmarked and apparently unmarkable. Such glimpses of primitive nature in Chandler's fiction are relatively rare, but they are important because they suggest the realm beyond from which the reigning squalor might be judged. In this passage Chandler makes his private eye sensitive to that "tonic of the wilderness," which was so important to Thoreau and so central to the American hunter myth.[9] In the cityscape of American literary naturalism, however, the wilderness is experienced only as an intolerable absence. The lack of something that is not man-made, something that may be perceived as greater than ourselves, makes impossible what Richard Slotkin has described as "the characteristic American gesture in the face of adversity," namely, "immersion in the native element, the wilderness, as the solution to all problems, the balm to all wounds of the soul, the restorative for failing fortunes" (p. 267). Unlike the savage nature of Collins, Doyle, and Sayers that mounts its threat against a human order, Chandler's Pacific Ocean represents no menace, therefore. On the contrary, the more the land itself is polluted and despoiled, the greater the significance of the ocean as the last refuge of a lost hope.

Finally, the hard-boiled social pessimism that Hammett and Chandler introduced into the sphere of a popular genre confirms native myth in another way. Their dark vision serves as a reminder that America, unlike those European nations from which it drew the great majority of its immigrants, has lacked a theory of society that regarded the city as its normal focus and center. If Washington, D. C., was established in a swamp, it is because those founding fathers who possessed the political intelligence required to devise an enduring form of republican government were nevertheless profoundly suspicious of that urban life in which political philosophy was originally nurtured. The view of the city as the cradle of civilized values and civilized living, which has been so prominent in European thought, for a long time found no sympathetic echo in a land that dreamed it-

9. *Regeneration through Violence*, p. 532.

self into existence as a virtuous agrarian republic. The frontier and pastoral myths have never been matched by an equally generous, countervailing urban myth. Even before industrialism, therefore, city life could be regarded not as the norm but as a fall from the norm, whereas even in England the attraction first of the royal court and later of the London town house with its social and artistic season have traditionally exercised a counterattraction to the pleasures of country life. English Augustan literature in particular celebrated the civilizing life of the metropolis. And its ideal of the city was suggested in a different medium by that eighteenth-century English favorite, Canaletto. As a consequence, unlike his urbane British counterpart, the private eye is always represented as the lonely and alienated guardian of the failed city, the hero of last resort in a milieu where all other institutions have broken down.

Typically, the only healthy social order Ross Macdonald's Lew Archer can conceive of is the illusory order of art: "I turned out the light and crossed the outer room and stood in front of Matisse's Blue Coast lithograph. I had a fierce nostalgia for that brilliant, orderly world which had never quite existed. A world where nobody lived or died, held in the eye of a never-sinking sun."[10] And Chandler invokes the image of another artist that has the quality of a self-portrait, in order to suggest the characteristics needed to live and survive in spite of urban chaos.

> They had Rembrandt on the calendar that year, a rather smeary self-portrait due to imperfectly registered color plates. It showed him holding a smeared palette with a dirty thumb and wearing a tam-o'-shanter which wasn't any too clean either. His other hand held a brush poised in the air, as if he might be going to do a little work after a while, if somebody made a down payment. His face was ageing, saggy, full of the disgust of life and the thickening effects of liquor. But it had a hard cheerfulness that I liked, and the eyes were as bright as drops of dew.[11]

This brightness survives in Chandler himself, alongside the disgust, as stylistic exuberance.

Moreover, Chandler's stylistic exuberance in combination with his pessimism places him in an American literary mainstream in spite of

---

10. *The Barbarous Coast* (New York: Bantam Books, 1957), p. 167.
11. *Farewell, My Lovely*, p. 39.

his British education. It is by now a commonplace of literary history that since Hawthorne and Melville a major feature of the American literary tradition has been its pessimistic view of certain central tendencies in American life. From the late Twain, Henry Adams, and Dreiser down to the lost generation, Fitzgerald and Nathaniel West, most major writers have been infected by a sharp sense of disappointment and frequently of nostalgia for an America that might have been. The loss of faith in the regenerative possibilities to be derived form immersion in nature, either directly or through the hunting down of nature's creatures and its primitive men, leaves the urban detective, like the heroes of so many classic American novels, with no place to go. In common with their high brow fellow writers, therefore, the best of the hard-boiled novelists illustrate Richard Poirier's thesis that from the mid-nineteenth century on American authors have been committed to the building of a "world elsewhere" and to exhibiting "an eccentricity of defiance." He interprets their achievement as powered by the effort to free their heroes by sheer force of style "from systems . . . from the presence of time, biology, economics."[12] And it is by virtue of the polished vernacular Chandler in particular devised for his hero that Marlowe achieves his most memorable personal triumphs over the city of chaos.

12. *A World Elsewhere*, p. 5.

10

The Case of Simenon

That popular fiction is a repository of national cultural values and national myths is evident from the examples of detective novels from the two different traditions already discussed. Moreover, what has been said about the Anglo-American writers is confirmed when their works are compared with those of the most durable of the detective novelists writing in French, Simenon. His detective novels are remarkable in terms of this present exercise in comparative ideology because they take a formula common to all three traditions and generate meanings that are recognizable as uniquely French. The fact that Simenon is by origin Belgian is significant in this respect because it implies a relationship to France not dissimilar from that of Chandler to the United States. Both writers produce popular literary works that appear to be in the mainstream of two distinctive national cultures, in part because they combine an insider's knowledge of the countries they represent with the distance of the outsider.

Historically, the role and perception of the police in French life have been different in important ways from what one finds in either Britain or the United States. In both English-speaking countries early opponents of the creation of centralized police agencies claimed to find confirmation of their fears in French police practice from as far back as the *ancien régime* and in the revolutionary and Napoleonic periods. On the other hand, Poe located his Dupin stories in Paris in part because of the prestige enjoyed early in the nineteenth century by the French police organization and its investigative methods. Dupin may be an anti-Vidocq, but in order for Poe's point to be effective, Dupin had to be shown beating the successors of Vidocq on their own turf.

Moreover, the attitudes of both distrust and wonder expressed in other countries found an echo inside France itself. But among the majority of Frenchmen it seems likely that throughout the nineteenth century the feeling of hostility predominated for a number of reasons. First, from the reign of Louis XIV, at least, policing was in many quarters associated with political policing, including the surveillance of the conduct and opinions of individuals, as well as with the pursuit of criminals. From the time of the lieutenant generalship of the Marquis d'Argenson at the beginning of the eighteenth century, in fact, the large-scale employment of police spies and the drawing up of dossiers on suspected private persons seems to have become established practice.

In this respect the role of the police inspectors under the *ancien régime* has been summarized by J.P. Stead as follows:

> They made inquiries into cases where a *lettre de cachet* might be required; they secretly investigated denunciations and petitions received by the police. They had their own *mouchards*, spies. They reported the state of the public's opinion of the government to the Lieutenant-General, valuable agents in the business of political police. They attended that magistrate to give a regular account of their activities and also kept an eye on foreigners and on hotels and lodging houses. Registers of visitors were already being kept and these they were supposed to inspect everyday.[1]

In his memoirs Saint-Simon noted of the Marquis d'Argenson, who was at the head of this police organization, "He had so imposed order on the innumerable Parisian multitude that there was not a single inhabitant whose conduct and habits he did not know from day to day."[2]

And another lieutenant-general of police under Louis XV, Antoine de Sartines, had a similar reputation. According to the chronicler of eighteenth-century French life, L.S. Mercier, "If this Magistrate were minded to tell the philosopher all he knows, all he learns, all he sees, and to share with him certain secret matters in which he alone is well versed, there would be nothing stranger or more instructive from the philosopher's pen: he would astonish all his colleagues. But this Mag-

---

1. *The Police of Paris* (London: Staples Press, 1957), p. 36.
2. Quoted by Stead, p. 40.

istrate is like the Grand Confessor: he hears everything, repeats nothing and is not surprised to the same degree as another man would be by some kinds of crime.''[3]

To Argenson and to Sartines there was already attributed some of the mythic power of omniscience which under the Directory, Consulate, and Empire was associated with Fouché as minister of police. In a fascinating work that details the manic zeal and intricate bureaucratic practices of the French police from informers and gendarmes to *commissaires de police,* Richard Cobb has written, ''If ever a regime could have claimed to have thought of everything, that of late eighteenth-century France could surely have done so. For the police had not only traced, and so circumscribed, every possible source of violence, tumult, and crime; they had also worked out model case histories for the commonest forms of sexual misbehavior.''[4]

As a result, from the beginning of centralized organization in modern times, the police in France were frequently perceived less as an instrument of the law than as the repressive force of order of the central government itself. And such a view continued to have widespread currency through the alternate waves of revolution and reaction that characterized French political life down through the nineteenth century and into our own time. If, from Argenson to Fouché and beyond, policing has been widely associated with surveillance and political control, criminal law enforcement itself has also been seen as seriously compromised by apparent involvement with the criminal underworld, especially after Vidocq. The fact that the man who was head of the *sûreté* under the Restoration and briefly again under Louis Phillipe was himself an ex-convict suggested to respectable citizens the unreliability of the agents of the law. Fouché and Vidocq achieved a mythical stature in their time, therefore, both because they could be identified with the ideal of omniscience and because they represented respectively the idea of a political police and a criminal police. In the eyes of the opponents of the various regimes in particular, the different branches of the police organization often managed to combine repression with corruption.

3. Quoted by Stead, p. 57.
4. *The Police and the People: French Popular Protest, 1789–1820* (Oxford: The Clarendon Press, 1970), p. 25.

A literary reflection of the widely divergent attitudes toward crime and its prosecution in France, of what I referred to earlier as "the battle around the crime," is to be found in the works of Stendhal and Balzac. Whereas the former was a political liberal as well as a romantic, the latter was a conservative who, at least from the mid-1830s, fiercely defended the idea of a political system founded on the alliance of throne and altar. And as a result of their profoundly divergent political beliefs, Stendhal and Balzac express antithetical attitudes toward crime and its policing in their novels. From Julien Sorel to *la duchesse* de Sansevarina and Lamiel, Stendhal persisted in making heroes and heroines of those who commit spectacular crimes. Like Fourier he found in certain kinds of criminal acts the expression of a noble energy in an age of repression. Stendhal's novels suggest, in fact, that where there is flagrant social injustice, crime may have the character of a positive political act.

If Stendhal is a representative voice of the French libertarian tradition, however, Balzac is among novelists an uncompromising spokesman for authoritarian order. As his *Country Doctor* in particular suggests, Balzac was preoccupied with a planned economy and with the harnessing of individual energy in the cause of state power. Thus, in spite of his professed legitimist sympathies, the model of the state he invokes in his utopian novel is a Napoleonic one. Where in Stendhal there is a form of heroization of the criminal, in Balzac the authoritarian leader and the policeman are heroized. Vautrin's demonic genius for gathering information and for controlling conduct is by the end of the *Comédie Humaine* coopted in the service of established society. Moreover, if the scale of Balzac's ambition in literature has lent credence to the claim that he was the Napoleon of the novel, his passion for documenting the social geography of France and his own air of omniscience also suggest an analogy with the police power of Fouché / Vidocq. Balzac's myopic realism is in its own way a reflection of "the infinitely small of political power" to which Foucault has referred in discussing the establishment of "permanent, exhaustive omnipresent surveillance."[5]

A very different image of the *sûreté* was projected in the 1860s by a writer friendly to the Second Empire such as Maxime du Camp. In

---

5. *Discipline and Punish*, pp. 213–14.

his *Memoirs* du Camp is full of praise for the head of the department and underlines the changes that have occurred since the time of Vidocq. According to du Camp, the new police agents led the life of classic civil servants instead of that of adventurers with criminal records. "Nearly all the detectives are married men with families," he wrote, ". . . and the regularity of their morals is in violent contrast with the life they are obliged to lead."[6] This image of the detective is reflected in Gaboriau's Lecoq novels of the 1860s and points ahead to the solution adopted by Simenon to the problem of creating a sympathetic detective hero in a country that has so frequently prided itself on its contempt for *le flic*. But Simenon had a model even closer to hand in Louis Lépine, the *préfet* of police in Paris for almost twenty years prior to World War I. Opposed on principle to political policing, he was popular and highly visible. He projected an image of efficiency with a genial face and the touch of the common man: "He regarded it as his mission to make the people of Paris like their police."[7]

In the sphere of popular literature of that same period before World War I, perhaps the best loved of heroes, at least in middle and upper-middle-class milieux, was Maurice Leblanc's Arsène Lupin. The "gentleman burglar" is not, strictly speaking, a detective, but like Raffles, the British equivalent, he embodies heroic qualities similar to those possessed by the classic detective. Furthermore, although ostensibly outside the law, he commits crimes only against those who are themselves defined as at least morally criminal. As Boileau and Narcejac have noted, Leblanc set out to create a character who would be as French as Sherlock Holmes was presumed to be English. He is, therefore, the embodiment of a certain French ideal that combines elegance, charm, wit, vivacity, and strength of character. Moreover, this ideal had a special appeal at a particularly difficult moment in French history, namely, that period after the defeat of 1870, when there was a widespread sense of humiliation and concern at apparent national decadence. Arsène Lupin was created "in the image of a certain France, humiliated by the defeat of 1870, chauvinistic, ready to revenge itself in any way, romantic, as generous as Gavroche and as

6. Quoted by Stead, *The Police of Paris*, p. 125.
7. Stead, p. 151.

witty as Cyrano."[8] Moreover, his behavior is calculated to make a clear ideological statement of a kind associated with the nationalist right: "Patriotic, with an element of Déroulède and a Barresian movement of the chin, he is terrible in revenge and not content with defeating his adversary, he makes him appear ridiculous. He is a fencer, like Cyrano. . . . Crazy about style, pedantic over points of honor, more sensitive and punctilious than a musketeer, he also experiences emotional outbursts worthy of a Parisian street urchin."[9]

The success of Leblanc's Arsène Lupin novels, in fact, is an illustration of the way in which popular literature often amounts to the imaginative replay of historical events in which a recognizable national hero is triumphant over enemies who proved more obdurate in reality. And in a more indirect way something similar might also be said about Simenon's Maigret in the post–World War II period.

At first sight what Simenon seems to offer in his Maigret novels is a compromise between the extremes of the classic British and American hard-boiled traditions. His detective novels are in a distinctly more realist mode than those of the golden age British authors, and the point of view he adopts is lower-middle class rather than upper. Yet, unlike Hammett's or Chandler's novels, Simenon's offer relatively little action and a minimum of violence. And they are written in the third person in a neutral workmanlike language that avoids the poles of the overly formal or the pugnacious vernacular. It is an efficient, occasionally evocative French that blends the traditional virtues of the written style with the suggestion of conversational ease. That is, it employs swift verbless notations, an occasional familiar word, and a rhythmic variety that adapts itself easily to description and action sequences as well as to reflective passages and Maigret's internal commentary.

Simenon's deceptively unadorned narrative style, like Hammett's and Chandler's, is nevertheless in the image of his detective hero. Maigret is constructed out of a language that is neither tough nor ostentatious but unpretentious, understated, supple, and open to the sensuous impressions of the external world. If Maigret embodies the qualities of an idealized average Frenchness that is very different from the

---

8. Boileau-Narcejac, *Le Roman policier*, p. 129.
9. Ibid., p. 132.

aristocratic and chivalrous conduct of Arsène Lupin, the incarnation is achieved by means of a language that possesses similar qualities. Maigret does not wisecrack or talk tough any more than he condescends; he watches, waits, reflects, sniffs, comments briefly, shrugs his shoulders, and returns home for dinner.

The problem Simenon faced was to invent a sympathetic detective hero for a reading public broader than that to which Maurice Leblanc appealed and that included working and lower-middle-class readers traditionally hostile to *le flic*. Simenon's solution was to create this policeman in the image of French ordinariness including an element of the time-honored French tradition of the *frondeur*. We do not need Simenon's own reminders in a work such as *When I Was Old* to perceive his preference for "characters who are ordinary rather than exceptional men."[10] Maigret, even when he is represented as famous, is not represented as superior to others. He is neither upper class and eccentric nor physically tough. Nor is he equipped with the masterly intellect of Dupin / Holmes. On the contrary, his ordinariness consists to a large extent in his reliance, for crime solving, chiefly on his intuitive understanding of human behavior. He is an embodiment of the faith in folk instinct that, in spite of Descartes, is as important an element in the French egalitarian tradition as it is in the American. It is a tradition to which Simenon himself has invariably acknowledged his attachment—"I can only trust instinct" (p. 105).

At the same time, Maigret is a construct that invites the reader's identification and approval because he does what average Frenchmen once did, enjoys what they enjoyed, believes what they believed. And nowhere is this more obviously true than in the fondness expressed for a private life centered on the family. Maigret and his wife are an expression of Simenon's belief that in the history of human societies "the couple up to the present, anyway, remains the basic cell" (p. 300). In effect, Simenon seems deliberately to ignore the fact that the commissioner and Madame Maigret constitute the archetypal French petit bourgeois married couple, which hardly seems to have been updated since French romantic writers and caricaturists began mocking the stereotype from the 1820s on. Maigret's encounters with criminals in high and low places are conceived of as no more than

10. (London: Hamish Hamilton, 1972), p. 32.

periodic interruptions, required by duty, of what is a well-regulated bourgeois life, complete with *cuisine bourgeoise*, a glass of *marc* or Armagnac and a pipe, conversations in bed with an increasingly middle-aged wife, dinners with a very few loyal friends, visits to local cafés, and vacations in the future retirement home at Meung-sur-Loire. The variations played by Simenon on the irony of crime chiefly involve contrasting it with domesticity. Predictably enough, the best known of the French detective novelists combines crime with the pleasures of the palate.

There is, in fact, nothing disturbing about the way in which Simenon has his detective grow old on the job like any other career civil servant. Maigret's ability to look forward to his retirement is an expression of an acceptance of the order of things. In the same way that Sergeant Cuff has his roses, Maigret will have his kitchen garden and his fishing. The tough heroics of the American private eye, on the other hand, make it difficult to reconcile the idea of age and dignity. Unlike a civil servant, an aging warrior is without self-respect because he has survived his role and his power of sexual attraction.

The good life in the Maigret novels is represented, then, as the well-ordered life. Simenon endlessly insists on "the importance of traditions, of habits, of rituals."[11] The characteristic ambience of cherished domesticity is brilliantly established in the opening paragraph of *Maigret se fâche*.

> Madame Maigret, who was shelling peas in a patch of warm shade that was made gay by the rich blue of her apron and the green of the shells, Madame Maigret whose hands were never inactive even at two o'clock in the afternoon on the hottest day of a sweltering August, Madame Maigret, who was watching over her husband as if he were a doll, grew anxious:
>
> "I bet you are already going to get up."
>
> Yet the deckchair in which Maigret was lying hadn't made a sound. The former Commissioner of Police had not uttered the smallest of sighs.
>
> It was doubtless because she was so used to him that she had seen an imperceptible expression cross his face that was brilliant from sweat. For it was true that he was about to get up. But out of a kind of respect for humankind, he forced himself to remain there.[12]

11. *When I Was Old*, p. 262.

12. *La Pipe de Maigret précédé de Maigret se fâche* (Paris: Presses de la Cité, 1949), p. 7.

It is significant that a short story by Simenon entitled "The Tepid Compote Dish" and published in a little magazine when he was seventeen offers a similar description of an everyday domestic scene. "What is important," Simenon himself has noted half a century later, "is the theme, the sunny courtyard of our house on the Rue de L'Enseignement, in the morning, at around ten o'clock, with my mother, in the kitchen, making preserves. On the table, in a shaft of sunshine, a dish of tepid prunes. The smell all over the house."[13] A similar fondness for the qualities of well-ordered bourgeois life may be illustrated from *Maigret a peur:* "The odor of the house had not changed and that was another thing that had formerly aroused Maigret's envy, that odor of a well-run house where the parquet floors are polished and they know how to cook."[14]

The strengths that Richard Cobb admires in Simenon are apparent in such passages. In Cobb's view, Simenon is a bad social historian to the extent that he shows little awareness of change but a good popular historian because he is remarkable in "the observation of habit, routine, assumption, banality, everydayness, seasonability, popular conservatism, especially in leisure, eating habits and clothing, the pattern of the week, that of the weekend, that of the grandes vacances."[15] And it is undoubtedly true that Simenon's popularity is to a considerable degree due to such celebration of ordinariness and the familiar routines of private life. What is also noteworthy is that he invariably manages to remain this side of the picturesque. In this respect the representation of Paris in the Maigret novels is characteristic.

Maigret himself is created in the image of an average Frenchman of the interwar years not least because he comes of rural stock—his father was the manager of a country estate—but he lives in the city. Maigret is archetypal because he is a Parisian with roots in the country and a nostalgia for the values of traditional rural life. Yet the view of Paris projected through him is quietly celebratory rather than hostile. It is nevertheless noteworthy that Simenon's Paris is no "moveable feast"—"Local color exists only for people who are passing through."[16]

13. *When I Was Old*, p. 102.
14. (Paris: Presses de la Cité, 1953), p. 21.
15. *Tour de France*, 183.
16. *When I Was Old*, p. 41.

Simenon's Paris has its seamy side and its derelicts, its criminal classes and even its corruptible politicians, but it is nevertheless no landscape of chaos like Chandler's L.A. It inspires affection, not disgust; it is characterized more by its unostentatious beauty and variety than by its patches of squalor. And this variety is woven into the texture of *quartiers* that have the quality of urban villages. Maigret on his forays is made responsive to the sounds, sights, and smells of the Seine and its bridges, the *grands quartiers, hôtels louches*, cafés, railroad stations, and unexceptional little streets throughout the changing seasons of the year. In the Maigret novels, Paris appears mellow, generous, forgiving, a home for millions of very ordinary people as well as for criminals, and is also the capital of civilization. Finally, Paris represents continuity in its own way as much as *la province* does. Like Maigret himself, therefore, it expresses a superficial skepticism which is the mask of a deeper faith. And what is true of Paris is true for the representation of French life in general. Into the 1960s Simenon's novels still offered the decor and attitudes of old Jean Gabin movies. And nothing demonstrates the mythic status of Maigret more than this unchangeability in radically changed times. As Richard Cobb notes, "We are stuck eternally in the Third Republic. That is why Simenon is so reassuring to people of a certain generation. It's a cosy, slippered world."[17] It is also why the signs seem to suggest that Simenon's reputation is in eclipse. Popular heroes tend to date quickly, and the staid heroics of Maigret are unlikely to appeal to a generation raised on James Bond.

Given the familiar national myths out of which Simenon constructs his image of enduring Frenchness, it is perhaps also fitting that he chooses to make Maigret's marriage childless for two reasons. First, Simenon's unpretentious detective hero acquires by the end the mythic status of a father figure of the nation. He is the ideal combination of sternness and tolerance, order and understanding, affection, loyalty, devotion to duty, and of that wisdom which derives from wide human experience. Maigret is a gently authoritative, pipe-smoking patriarch. And his stature is confirmed by the fact that standing at his side is an ideal average woman whose role is defined as that of guardian of the home and lifelong companion. Together they represent the ideal of

17. *Tour de France*, p. 182.

order and continuity within a marriage that has the traditional well-defined sex roles.

Second, it is fitting that the Maigrets have no children because, given the traditionalist attitudes they illustrate, it is difficult to conceive how within the framework of the detective formula such traditionalism could have survived the experience of educating children in the decades following the thirties. Mythic fathers risk murder by the hand of mythic sons.

Finally, Maigret appears sympathetic to a French public because in spite of his status as a *fonctionnaire*, he is also conceived in the image of the *frondeur*. That is, Simenon sets him up as an individualist who is skeptical of authority and ready to challenge orthodox opinions. Maigret is, therefore, an antibureaucratic bureaucrat, a policeman with a human face who gets things done his own way in spite of red tape and conventional superiors. Yet he is basically accepting of centralized institutions, unlike the private eye, including particularly those of the *police judiciaire* and the law. They may be susceptible to abuse and even corruption, but their role in maintaining a civilized order is not challenged.

In other words, like all detective heroes Maigret supports a particular version of law and order. But Simenon takes care to make the point again and again that the severity of the law is tempered in his hero's case with charity and with a class loyalty that expresses itself in a lower-middle-class point of view. Simenon's criminals may come from all walks of life, but they are carefully selected and their degree of guilt is usually a function of their life circumstances. Thus, where a certain amount of sympathy is shown for lost adolescents, old people, tramps, petty criminals, and the underprivileged in general, the upper-middle classes, landowners, industrialists, speculators, and respectable gangsters are judged harshly. The attitudes exhibited by Maigret in his detective work are, in fact, expressions of what is assumed to be a Gallic tolerance for manifestations of ordinary human weakness. At their most sentimentally humanitarian, such attitudes can reach the conclusion arrived at by Simenon himself—that "there are no criminals."[18] What is not tolerated, on the other hand, is the abuse of privilege, class prejudice from above, cowardice, cruelty,

18. *When I Was Old*, p. 112.

and insensitivity to the sufferings of others. Nevertheless, it is symptomatic of important cultural differences that crime solving for Maigret does not have the character of a crusade, as it does for Marlowe, but is a job to be done, a form of work, before and after which life offers a variety of simple pleasures.

The fictional universe of the Maigret novels appears apolitical in the sense that although Simenon was writing at a time of momentous historical and political events, from the depression and the Popular Front through World War II, such events are almost entirely ignored, as he himself was aware.[19] Yet because he was the inventor of the realist detective novel of manners in a distinctly French mode, the expression of ideological commitments is never entirely absent from Simenon as it seems to be from Agatha Christie. The distant influence of Balzac is unmistakable in slim *études de moeurs* that might be grouped under such rubrics as *Scènes de la vie privée, Scènes parisiennes*, and *Scènes de la vie de province*. Apart from the swift evocations of physical milieus, all his Maigret novels are characterized by notations on manners that make sharp distinctions among the social strata of French life in a way that recalls classic realism rather than comedy of manners. Thus, when Simenon represents a provincial town as in *Maigret a peur*, unlike Agatha Christie he does not hesitate to underline social antagonism and class prejudice.[20] Like the English author, he builds such provincial novels around the characters of the *châtelain* and his family, the doctor, lawyer, schoolteacher, shopkeepers, artisans, and servants, but the traditional political tensions between the classes are often not only made explicit, they are built into the story of the crime in a way that is alien to Agatha Christie's work. Moreover, Maigret's own loyalty to the *peuple* is invariably emphasized.

19. In 1961 he noted, "Strange? I've never written about the war of 1939 (except *Le Clan des Ostendais*, which is rather special)" *When I Was Old*, p. 207.

20. The precise description, full of hostile innuendo, of a French country gentleman at the beginning of *Maigret a peur* is typical in this respect: "He could have been the local count or the owner of the manor house, the important man in a village or in any little town. He was wearing a light tweed golfing suit and a raincoat of the kind one only sees in expensive shops. . . . In spite of the heat, he had not taken off his tan gloves, for people of that type never take off their gloves in trains or cars. He must have been sixty-five years old. He was already an old man. Isn't it odd how men of that age are so concerned with the details of their appearance? Strange that they still seek to distinguish themselves from ordinary people?" (pp. 8–9).

In general, Simenon's attitude to cataclysmic events like war and depression seems to be that, like crime, they are a form of disorder and should be ignored if they cannot be contained: "Basically, threats of catastrophe rather stimulate me to write . . . as a way of detachment, because personal life must go on."[21] And in the novels Maigret himself is the guardian of personal life against the evil of criminal chaos. He is the projection of his creator's own "instinctive reaction against disorder" (p. 139) that operates on the level not only of fictional character but also of form.

It is no accident if a typical Maigret novel is a slim, concentrated, and shapely work without subplot and with a limited cast of characters. Although apparently attracted by the idea of writing a picaresque novel, Simenon recognized that there is something alien to his taste and values in a sprawling form that illuminates the richness and variety of life in the world. His judgment on the genre suggests the gap between his work and the Anglo-American tradition that runs from Collins to Chandler.

> In a picaresque novel, what counts most is the picturesque, the differences between men, the warts, the crossed eyes, the stammers, the limps, the phenomena of every kind. Each thing that grafts itself onto man as certain little white shells onto the mussel shell.
>
> It is the accidental. The fortuitous.
>
> But, in spite of myself, I always come back, not to the differences, but to the resemblances. (p. 57)

Instead of an interest in the grotesque particularity of things, we find the classical preoccupation with what all men have in common, human nature. Instead of creative exuberance, we have formal control.

Under the circumstances Simenon's claim to be a social anarchist must appear strange. In trying to justify such a claim, he is led to the point of paradox in asserting that he is an anarchist who believes himself duty bound to follow society's rules. It is a paradox that the Maigret novels themselves resolve by coming down on the side of the rule of a law that is humane and paternalistic. In this respect the figure of Maigret is a striking embodiment of a political myth that implies a commitment to social order within the context of the centralized re-

21. *When I Was Old*, p. 320.

publican state. Maigret is the ideal Frenchman of the political philosophy of Third Republican radicalism—the independent, fundamentally private, freethinking, republican, and patriotic little man, whose philosoper was Alain:

> . . . at the heart of the radical who is always ready to obey, there is a radical spirit that never obeys, which refuses to believe, which examines and which discovers in fierce liberty something that nourishes the immense friendship of humanity. And that something is equality. The spirit of equality is, on the one hand, resistance, the refusal to applaud, cool judgment; on the other, it is faith in man, hope in an educational system and in a culture equally available to all, and horror of any regime under which man is a means and an instrument for man.[22]

The long-standing French faith expressed here provides the ideological core from which Simenon derives his fictional detective's behavior. Maigret is the lower-middle-class hero of an egalitarian but pre-socialist left, the artisan as policeman.

In France and outside it seems likely that Simenon's popularity has been in large part due to the reassurance provided by the fictional incarnation of *la France éternelle* that is his hero. In spite of *débâcle* and occupation, postwar self-doubt, social strife, and the destructive impact of economic prosperity on traditional living patterns, as long as Maigret survived the implication was that nothing fundamental has changed.

22. Alain, *Propos II* (Paris: Bibliothèque de la Pléiade, 1970), p. 917.

11

Formula and Reassurance

The detective novels of Simenon, like those of Doyle, Christie, Hammett, and Chandler, illustrate how a writer may make acceptable the idea of policing, first, by demonstrating the need for it on account of the prevalence of crime, and second, by creating agents of law enforcement who conform to a recognizable cultural ideal. In all cases an effort is made to reconcile the reader to the spectacle of the exercise of power. The British and French authors, at least, achieve this in part by making power appear gentle. Through its agents it is represented as enlightened, tolerant, and humane. The twentieth-century writers in the genre, in fact, find themselves to be heirs to a nineteenth-century tradition that had already contributed to the "moralization" of potentially marginal classes by making heroes of those who combat delinquency and villains of those who defy the law. Moreover, alongside the "heroization" of the policeman in his various official and nonofficial guises, detective novels also reveal an effort at a specific form of "moralization" of the reading public that might be called "patriotization." And such "patriotization" finds its clearest expression in the modern spy thriller. It is present, however, in more subtle ways from the very beginning of the detective novel. An ideal of Englishness, Americanness, and Frenchness comes to be embodied in the different incarnations of the detective in such a way that it constitutes a reaffirmation of national self-worth.

Thus, works in the genre provide a form of reassurance to the extent that they represent the victory of a recognizable national cultural hero over an adversary. Reassurance at the victory is experienced either as in a game, where it is simply a question of someone who wears "our uniform," or as in a novel, where the reader readily identifies with a character because of his physique, appearance, way of life, values, and purposes. The feeling of relief comes not only from the elimination of a threat, making possible the restoration of well-being, but also from the recognition of the superior qualities of the cultural stereotype who carries the action through.

This does not mean that one national reading public is necessarily excluded from enjoying popular works produced by a different national culture. On the contrary, the worldwide success of many of the authors discussed in these pages suggests that the truly popular writers in the genre know no frontiers in spite of an apparent identification of their works with a single national culture. It seems that as long as no conflict is created in the reader's mind between those cultural values with which he identifies and those which a fictional hero acts out, there is no problem in making the necessary adjustments. Thus, provided he does not recognize in James Bond an ideological enemy, a German, a Frenchman, or an American might enjoy the secret agent's victories as much as an Englishman does. It would, however, be more difficult for a Russian or a Chinese to do so.

In fact, not only do the national cultural ideals that find expression in a Holmes, a Marlowe, or a Maigret not limit their authors' appeal in countries other than their homeland, it seems that such stereotypes constitute an important element of the appeal. It is reassuring in a different way to find one's expectations about the English, the Americans, and the French confirmed in one's reading. The evidence suggests that the international audience which continues to read detective fiction still enjoys its Englishmen upper class and urbane, its Americans lean and tough, and its Frenchmen skeptical, tolerant, and worldly-wise. Such cultural stereotypes seem to confirm that the world may be known once and for all; in the face of apparent change, Englishness, Americanness, and Frenchness go on forever. The attraction of popular literature resides not least in the authority with which it offers the certainties of myth for the confusions of history.

And what is true for the detective heroes is equally true for those mythic landscapes that are Doyle's London, Chandler's Southern California, and Simenon's Paris. The gestures made in the direction of mimesis by such authors are often cultural references designed to trigger recognition by means of the same metonymic figure used by tourist brochures when they signify London and Paris with the silhouette of the Houses of Parliament and the Eiffel Tower respectively. Like Des Esseintes, the decadent hero of Huysmans's *Against the Grain*, who on his first projected visit to England abandoned his journey in an English inn at Calais, the fans of detective fiction prefer the England of the literary imagination to the banality and complexity of the real thing. The most popular authors in the genre are the distillers of familiar national essences.

Detective novels provide reassurance, then, not only because they deal in identifiable good and evil and end up punishing the latter but also because they propose a world of fixed cultural quantities. They effectively suppress the historical reality that they seem to represent and draw for solutions to the problems posed on cherished, but frequently anachronistic, cultural values. In one way or another a mythic national past is made to appear adequate to the difficulties faced by the national community in the present.[1] And from the chivalric codes of Conan Doyle and Maurice Leblanc to the cult of an individualism ratified by the gun in Hammett and Chandler, examples of such faith abound.[2]

The continuing success of the detective story in one medium or another can be explained in part by its capacity to absorb into itself the changing anxieties of the times and make them appear innocuous. It touches on each new generation's fears because it is sufficiently flexible to allow good and evil to wear as many masks as the human imagination can conceive, from slant-eyed Chinese and long-nosed

---

1. Richard Slotkin comes to a similar conclusion in his discussion of the stereotyped images of the frontier hero encountered in popular American literature: "Such images were developed as responses to problems, as symbolic means of reducing the complexities and ambiguities of the American situation to a simple, satisfying formula. This method of problem solving does not proceed by the difficult path of study, experiment, argument, and full intellectual engagement with a dark unknown. Rather, it replaces the troublesome and problematic facts of the real world with a counterworld of pseudofacts. The reader is thus given a new world to perceive, more consistent than the real one and more in line with his own hopes, fears, and prejudices." *Regeneration through Violence* p. 466.

2. Richard Slotkin suggests that one important difference between major American writers and popular writers in their representation of the myth of the hunter is that the former, unlike the latter, are never content with using the wilderness "merely as an occasion for exhibiting the superiority of certian cultural assumptions and class types." *Regeneration through Violence*, p. 515.

Yankees to Aryan and African beasts, imperialists, terrorists, and extraterrestrial beings.

The detective story supports an ideological system, then, on the level of both its formulaic constants and its surface variables; it always celebrates a form of heroic action, but the heroic qualities deemed important under different historical circumstances vary greatly. The question also arises whether beyond both its deep ideological constants and its surface ideological variables a detective story does not inherently support a given world view simply by virtue of the fact that it exists as a readable story.

In this connection, as was suggested above, the detective novel is found to be satisfying by its fans first because it plays the reading game according to well-established rules. Thus, not only does it begin by raising a conventional problem for which it goes on in due time to supply a conventional solution, it also goes out of its way to make explicit the terms which guarantee the reader's comprehension. Moreover, of all existing novel types none provides an example of such perfect closure as the detective novel. Like a sentence, it is a hierarchical verbal structure that binds a subject to a predicate and ends with a highly visible period. Its strong beginnings are matched by equally positive endings. In the move from mystery to clarification and from crime to punishment, a sense of mechanistic inevitability is communicated that has the reassuring force of a law. A detective story may be regarded as a pleasure machine in part because of the predictability with which it engages our fear and then goes on to exorcise it with such finality.

Even apart from the readable story of a crime solved, however, a detective novel reassures because, as Roland Barthes has taught us, whenever it is narrated the world does not go unexplained. And what is true of narrative in general is particularly true of formulaic narrative. A formula story like the detective novel satisfies not least because it is a device for explaining crime, a way of recuperating a violent and apparently random act through its integration into a meaning-conferring system. In addition to the particular fictional events they report, therefore, works written in a formulaic genre always retell the story of a well-ordered world, even if it is a partly evil world.

Viktor Shklovsky's opinion that the primary function of art is defamiliarization has been widely shared by twentieth-century literary critics. Yet, since popular formulaic literature imposes well-known shapes on fresh material, the effect achieved is precisely the opposite. In spite of the emergence of new attitudes and a new investigative technology in the detective story between writers as remote from each other as Doyle and Fleming, the genre ends up making the strangeness of the present familiar by means of the various formulaic characteristics discussed here. On the level of the reaffirmation of national mythical values and of fixed cultural quantities, as well as on the level of an asserted narrative order, the detective story functions as a literature of reassurance and conformism.

PART III:
BEYOND DETECTION

12

The Professor and
the Detective

That detective fiction embodies a particular world view is corroborated in a different way by a representative essay to which I am in-
debted for the title of this chapter.[1] In her 1929 article Marjorie Nicolson anticipated the opinion, expressed in the preceding chapter, that
detective stories are experienced as reassuring because they project the image of a cosmos subject to the operations of familiar laws.
She did not raise the matter as a question of ideology, however, but
in order to explain the source of the pleasure she and many of her
academic colleagues found in the genre. Consequently, although her
essay accounts for the satisfaction some readers take in the hidden
logic, revealed at the denouement, of apparently random events, it
disguises as much as it explains about the appeal of most detective
novels.

We do not usually derive much pleasure from listening to someone
else assert what we hold to be familiar truths except under circumstances such as those that sometimes obtain at religious or political meet-
ings, where those truths are ritualistically asserted in order to reaffirm
communitarian bonds. The pleasure associated by fans of the genre
with the works discussed in this book for the most part lies elsewhere,
as I have suggested in earlier chapters and as I hope to reaffirm in a
different way in this chapter.

Yet the case made by Marjorie Nicolson is an interesting and
suggestive one. She finds that detective novels appeal to academics

---

1. Marjorie Nicolson, ''The Professor and the Detective,'' in *The Art of the Mystery
Story*, pp. 110–27.

because they afford an escape not from life, as is usually assumed, but from literature. And by literature she meant particularly the contemporary avant-garde novel of early modernism, Joyce and company. She claimed that the taste for the detective story was the expression of a preference for objectivity over subjectivity, mind over emotions, belief in an orderly universe over metaphysical pessimism. Finally, having defined the two methods employed by fictional detectives as the "Baconian" and the "intuitive," she opens her concluding paragraph with the sentence, "Yes, those are the only two methods both in scholarship and in the pursuit of criminals. For, after all, scholars are, in the end, only the detectives of thought" (p. 126).

Although the analogy drawn in the last sentence is not developed, it does imply that there is both romance and risk in the scholar's work and, at the same time, it confers intellectual respectability on the figure of the mythic investigator. The affinity perceived between the two roles was obviously suggested by the type of fictional detective Marjorie Nicolson favored, namely, the cultivated and often erudite gentlemanly amateur of the classic tradition. In Poe's earliest version of the type, in fact, the character of the detective could hardly be closer to the traditional image of the scholar; Dupin is persuaded only reluctantly to give up for a time the *vita contemplativa* in his bachelor apartments in order to test theory in practice and to apply the gentle power of knowledge.

Part of the pleasure Marjorie Nicolson derives from the classic detective story clearly lies in the way it celebrates the type of the scholar / adventurer and the life devoted to scholarship as a form of heroic adventure. A further implication of the phrase "detectives of thought" concerns the activity of problem solving as the enterprise which all academic disciplines have in common with each other and with the work of detection. This implication deserves to be explored more fully by anyone interested in the mythic drawing power exercised by the genre over the popular imagination in universities and outside.

Doyle's biographers tell us that he was inspired to create a detective hero who was a diagnostic genius by the example of a professor of medicine under whom he had studied as an undergraduate. Stripped of his eccentric trappings, Holmes represents the application of scientific method to police work, the first fictional criminologist. He is therefore a hero in the mainstream of the Western intellectual tradition, and the affinity perceived by Marjorie Nicolson reflects the common view of the activities of the intellectual researcher. Whether the task in hand is the decipherment of Linear B, the search for a cure for cancer, the interpretation of a sonnet, or the construction of a model representing the structure of the genetic code, it involves that well-known process of observation, inference, and the construction and testing of hypotheses which has been associated with the advancement of knowledge since Bacon. The script, the disease, the poem, and the unknown operations of the genes are, like the corpse in the locked library, enigmas to be explained or stories demanding to be told.

What Doyle's fictional model celebrates particularly, however, is the heroism inherent in the scholar / researcher's work. If Holmes is heroic, it is chiefly because he possesses the intellectual's power to produce coherence. Like the scholar / researcher, Holmes takes the fragments and finds the hidden pattern; he establishes relationships where none had previously appeared. His implied motto, "Give me your clues and I will build you a theory," might well be the slogan of the whole academic profession. From Newton to Hegel, Darwin, Marx, Freud, and Einstein, our most highly regarded intellectual heroes have been system builders and producers of order on a grand scale. And the degree of greatness attributed is in direct proportion to the quantity of disparate data converted by mind into pattern.

In the same way, from Dupin on, the Great Detective's crime-solving powers lead to victories for intellect far more than for morality. He triumphs not only over evil but also over apparent contingency and irrationality, which from a traditional theological as well as an aesthetic point of view are the same thing. The appeal of the great intellectual synthesizers resides in their power to offer in a desacralized universe new systems of belief or alternative theories for the operation of macrocosmic wholes in place of earlier theological schemes. And on the level appropriate to popular fiction the Great Detective fulfills a similar mythic function. He is the guarantor of that cosmic purposefulness which was challenged by the twentieth-century literature Marjorie Nicolson disliked. She therefore looked to the detective story for the reaffirmation of traditional beliefs: "our science and our theology, our ethics and our metaphysics, are based upon a belief in implacable justice, in the orderly operation of cause and effect, in a universe governed by order, founded on eternal and immutable law'' (p. 125).

The ideal version of the detective hero's role expressed by Marjorie Nicolson, if not her value judgment, is by now broadly accepted as the more or less explicit world view of the formal genre.[2] That there is also specific similarity between the operations carried out by literary critics and by fictional detectives has been less often remarked, but it is worth noting because it explains further the force of the detective / scholar analogy. And it is not simply a question of the detective work of traditional literary history, from the editing of manuscripts to the tracking down of sources and the establishment of biographical facts. The similarity also concerns the textual interpretation associated with modern critical practice at least since New Criticism.

A critic's attitude toward a work of literature is comparable to that of a detective at the scene of a crime. A novel, like a corpse, is approached by professionals as an enigma requiring a solution. It, too, is assumed to be in need of a mediating intelligence if its true story is to be told. The activities of both literary critic and detective involve a process of selecting from a multiplicity of soliciting signs those that may be organized into an interpretation. A critic, and every reader by virtue of the fact that he is engaged in the act of reading a literary work is ipso facto a critic, seeks to solve the crime / problem of the novel's meaning by collating all the material as it is furnished to him in its sequence in time. And he organizes and reorganizes his theory of that material in the light of the continual flow of fresh evidence that is the text right up to the denouement. The critic's essay is the report of an investigation leading to the (re)construction of a literary work.

If a traditional critic operates like a literary detective, the detective behaves like a well-trained critic to the extent that he also (re)constructs a whole out of more or less disparate material for the purpose of conferring a meaning. The similarity between the two kinds of activities will seem less surprising, however, if it is recalled that both roles have a single mythic antecedent. Oedipus combined both functions.

2. See the more recent essays on the relations between postmodernist fiction and the detective story by Michael Holquist, "Whodunit and Other Questions: Metaphysical Detective Stories in Post-War Fiction," *New Literary History* 3, no. 1 (1971–72): 135–36, and William V. Spanos, "The Detective and the Boundary: Some Notes on the Post-modern Literary Imagination," *Boundary* 2, no. 1 (1972): 147–68.

As a detective he was successful in solving the crime of his father's death. And as a riddle solver he demonstrated the sensitivity to the ambiguities and levels of meaning in verbal utterances that we expect of the literary critic.

In fact, the formal detective story in particular is constructed on a principle similar to that of the riddle. In the same way that the latter depends on a form of punning, a detective novel presents the reader with a set of data that either appear to be meaningless or suggest an obvious but wrong interpretation at the same time that they conceal the true one. The riddles posed by detective stories have more often been situational than verbal, but in all cases there is the same need to interpret a given sign or series of signs, whether they take the form of an utterance, a gesture, an expression, or a collection of inanimate clues. As Viktor Shklovsky pointed out, the title of the Doyle story ''The Speckled Band'' is in itself a riddle suggesting the false solution of the involvement of a ''gang,'' when in reality a ''ribbon'' is meant.[3] At their most formal, on the other hand, situational riddles are of the kind invented by Poe in ''The Murders in the Rue Morgue,'' namely, How and by whom could a double murder have been committed in a locked room apparently without an alternative means of egress?

It is a question for which the detective hero provided an answer after having first brushed aside the false solution suggested by the circumstances themselves or by various foils in the role of false detectives. The mechanism is the same as in the obscene folk riddles to which Viktor Shklovsky also referred.[4] After a moment of hesitation a less obvious, inoffensive answer is substituted for the implied obscene one. A modern equivalent would be, ''What is hard and long and full of se(a)men?'' Answer, ''A submarine.'' In any case, like the priest interpreting his oracle or the traditional literary critic with his difficult text, the task of the true detective has been to cut through ambiguity and rescue sense from nonsense.

The detective novel is popular among both academics and the gen-

3. ''L'Histoire à Mystères,'' in *Théorie de la littérature*, ed. Izvetan Todorov (Paris: Editions du Seuil, 1965), pp. 156–57.

4. ''The Mystery Novel: Dicken's *Little Dorritt*,'' in *Readings in Russian Poetics: Formalist and Structuralist Views*, ed. Ladislav Matejka and Krystyna Pomorska (Cambridge, Mass., and London: M.I.T. Press, 1971), p. 220.

eral public in part because it is a vehicle for expressing the age-old human faith in the existence of important meanings to be revealed, in life as well as in literature, and in the power of the riddle solver to reveal them. The world we confront is not yet that realm of surfaces of which Robbe-Grillet dreamed but a universe of Baudelairean correspondences that still beckon their interpreters on.

It is in some such spirit that Marjorie Nicolson, like so many authors before and since, attributed a heroic purity of motive to literary sleuths. Yet, in order to arrive at such a position, it is necessary to ignore certain fundamental characteristics of the literary detective's activities. The attraction of the detective hero resides at least as much in the fact that he has a license to pry into secret places and that, as a consequence of his great intelligence, he always ends up asserting his mastery over others as well as over the previously unknown. Power and penetration are the two fundamental qualities inherent in the role of avenging investigator. Thus, although riddle solving may be fun, it is not always undertaken for the purest of motives and is sometimes dangerous, as we know from our myths. Like academic research in general and literary criticism in particular, it can give rise to the breaking of taboos and is less innocent than it first appears.

Marjorie Nicolson and, more recently, Michael Holquist have thus emphasized the affirmation of rationality and order as the primary appeal of detective fiction. And the conclusion they reach confirms the traditional view of the genre. Yet it is important to understand that such a conclusion is in part conditioned by the critical approach adopted. An implied premise of this study is, in fact, that any explanation of the genre's appeal will always vary to some extent according to a critic's method.

In common with the mainstream of twentieth-century Anglo-American criticism, both Nicolson and Holquist confer meaning on a work by adopting the point of view of its end. Although the attempt to see a work in its wholeness is not only legitimate but indispensable, such an exclusive approach gives rise to the creation of the passive equivalent of the omniscient author—the omniscient reader. To begin one's critical account of a work only after one has completed it is often to forget the importance of one's former ignorance. That affective experience which is the activity of reading fiction needs also to be taken into account. Reading is in the first place a working through, a form of suspenseful consumption in which what one is about to consume always remains more or less mysterious.

Chandler himself was very aware that as far as the reader's emotional involvement in a novel is concerned, "the part is greater than the whole. The scene before the eyes dominates the thought of the audience; the normal individual makes no attempt to reconcile it with the pattern of the story. He is swayed by what is in the actual scene. When you have finished the book, it may, not necessarily will, fall into focus as a whole and be remembered by its merit so considered; but for the time of reading, the chapter is the dominating factor. The vision of the emotional imagination is very short but also very intense."[5]

The explanation that finds the appeal of detective fiction in the affirmation of order is founded on the traditional implied metaphor that regards literary works as systems existing in space. Such an attitude is an expression of the tendency to deduce from a book's existence as a physical object the conclusion that the novel it contains is itself an artifact available, like a building, for visual inspection. If in order to explain a work's meaning, the critical approach adopted spatializes a literary work of art, it will tend to produce a text in the absence of a reader. If, on the other hand, literary works are looked upon as occurrences rather than as objects, then the only text is the text in the reader.[6]

The critical choice involved is, in effect, a choice of roles. One can choose to be either the cartographer of the New Critical and Formalist traditions or the traveler of the reader-centered approach. One can either chart the ground covered after the fact, and preferably from the air, or present the record of a journey. To choose the first approach will be to distance and objectify a text, to choose the second will be to concentrate on the reader's involvement and affect.

For analyzing a popular genre like the detective novel, the reader-centered approach is helpful because it affords a more plausible explanation of the genre's appeal to the great majority of its readers. Reader-centered criticism makes clear that the readers of detective fic-

5. "Twelve Notes on the Mystery Story," in MacShane, ed., *The Notebooks*, p. 40.
6. See Stanley Fish's important essay, "Literature in the Reader: Affective Stylistics," *New Literary History* 2, no. 1 (1970): 123–62.

tion indulge in their pastime not simply to have comforting beliefs reaffirmed but in the interest of their pleasure. To make what Stanley Fish calls "experiential sense" of a text is to realize that the pleasure of detection is, like all pleasure, distinctly more primitive than the invocation of rationality suggests.

Like traditional fairy stories, detective novels typically involve a loss and a recovery, a criminal act and the act revenged, an exposure to danger and a return from danger. And the pleasure of reading them is keenest where a reader is appropriately responsive to the threat. No one who is reading properly is a professor of literature when he reads, if being a professor means practicing detachment. The point is that the enjoyment of the return from danger at the denouement presupposes a more or less protracted stage of pleasurable tension. It involves the experience of fear, however attenuated, and the willingness to be led with a mixture of anticipation and reluctance to the bottom of that fear. The reader reads in order to experience the excitement of being played by the novel he holds in his hand in the same way that the concertgoer allows himself to be played by the interpreted score. Except in the most ratiocinative and, therefore, least popular works in the genre, there is always the time for exposure to a form of danger that often has the character of a taboo and is the detective novel's equivalent to entry into the giant's castle or into the forbidden wild-wood of fairy tale.

In short, the reading experience itself suggests that the affirmation of rationality with which the detective story traditionally ends overlays irrational fictional premises and that the relief provided by the former depends largely on a responsiveness to the latter. This phenomenon is confirmed by three fundamental features of the genre, the first concerning its status as game, the second the character of the detective hero, and the third the reader's behavior.

Detective stories have traditionally been associated with games such as crossword puzzles and bridge as a means of passing time agreeably in disinterested exercises of the intelligence. And the point I am making about reader pleasure in the exercise of sympathetic power is perhaps best illustrated in connection with games, since academics as a group continue to derive at least as much pleasure from the mental calisthenics of certain sedentary games as they once did from the reading of detective stories.

The connection between the pleasures of play and those of solving mysteries was first made by Edgar Allan Poe at the beginning of *The Murders in the Rue Morgue:* ''The mental features discussed of as the analytical, are, in themselves, but little susceptible of analysis. We appreciate them only in their effects. We know of them, among other things, that they are always to their possessor, when inordinately possessed, a source of the liveliest enjoyment. As the strong man exults in his physical ability, delighting in such exercises as call muscles into action, so glories the analyst in that mental activity which disentangles.''[7]

Poe points here to the pleasure experienced in the activity of those problem-solving faculties that are also exercized by academic research in a supposed spirit of detachment and objectivity. Yet we are by now aware that neither game playing nor research is exempt from at least some degree of self-assertive egotism, as I noted earlier in my chapter on the erotics of narrative. The exhilaration of which Poe speaks is related in part to that experience of insight and mastery already referred to as characterizing the performance of fictional detectives. In fact, all our best-known games in the West are competitive and involve a testing by an adversary that exists either as another person or as prescribed difficulties to be overcome.

Chess, bridge, and crossword puzzles are characterized both by the demands they make on the intelligence and by a hidden emotive intensity that is inherent in a rule-governed competitive activity devoid of all physical expression. Chess may be among the most cerebral of games, but, as in such macho play as poker and football, satisfaction comes to the winner from the establishment of dominance. Chess, too, is war by another means as the nomenclature of the pieces suggests. It involves the attempt to defeat an opponent through the superior deployment of equal firepower in a predetermined space. And no one who has experienced the quickening of the pulse that can occur in the implementation of a plot to capture the king would deny the game animates buried responses more appropriate to a war party or a hunt. It seems that only an activity capable of arousing the strongest feelings could explain the protracted concentration normal in a game of chess.

The lesson of chess is that nothing excites intellectuals quite so

7. (London: Everyman, 1908) , p. 378.

much as when minds lock horns. That is why the Fisher / Spassky world championship match briefly turned the game into a major spectator sport, with the additional attraction that the opponents were representatives of the two rival superpowers. When Fisher and Spassky faced each other across the chessboard, they were viewed as the champions of two competing ideological systems. As things turned out, in the suitably exotic locale of Iceland, the CIA was once again victorious over Smersh.

The reference to the world of James Bond here is deliberate because the connection between play and the detective's role is at its most explicit in Ian Fleming's novels. The prowess and temperament of the gamesman are qualities possessed to some degree by all detective heroes, but nowhere is the generalized game-playing power related to actual skill at games as obviously as in the James Bond thrillers.

As Umberto Eco has noted, "The books of Fleming are dominated by situations that we call 'play situations'."[8] There are the formal games themselves, such as baccarat, golf, and bridge, which occupy an important place in many Bond novels. And thematically linked to them are the various testing situations in which Bond is placed in his role as secret agent, testing situations that themselves resemble games insofar as they involve more or less formalized moves and countermoves. It is characteristic that in *Casino Royale,* for example, Bond's task is not to kill the enemy agent Le Chiffre but to destroy him by beating him at baccarat. The antagonists may face each other across the green baize of the gambling table, but the scene is a shoot-out between hero and villain just as much as if it had occurred in a Western street or a city alley. It even includes the conventional Western motif of having Le Chiffre's henchman attempt to shoot Bond in the back with his walking-stick gun.

Sport, as we know, is often not much fun. Yet even at its grimmest, it is conducive to certain forms of pleasure. And in the spy stories devised by Fleming in the fifties and sixties, the formal game concerned is both the grimmest and most thrilling of all, namely, the manhunt. Bond is a gambler who plays for the highest stakes. The power of cool calculation he displays at the moments of greatest risk is the supreme quality of the chess and poker player as well as of the big

8. "The Narrative Structure in Ian Fleming," p. 51.

game hunter and soldier. As Lévi-Strauss has confirmed from his readings in North American Indian mythology, "To win a game is symbolically to 'kill' one's opponent."[9] The game of Waterloo was won on the battlefields of Eton.

The second feature of the detective novel isolated above as a clue to the more primitive source of reader pleasure concerns the character of the detective hero. What even a cursory examination of the formula reveals is that from Dupin and Holmes down to Philip Marlowe, Lew Archer, and even James Bond, detective heroes, like all problem solvers with a mission, are obsessive types. The heroic role imposed by the formula condemns them to single-mindedness, even where, as with Maigret, they are equipped with character traits that suggest they know how to enjoy life apart from detecting. The tension Simenon in particular sets up between the character and the role accounts for some of his detective's relative richness; it also confirms the rule. The essential type has the power of concentration of the hunter. By definition, a detective is a detective only when he is in pursuit of human quarry.

The Poe / Doyle tradition established the figure of the amateur of genius for whom crime solving itself is a hobby. Yet the point about hobbies is that they are often the sole objects of genuine enthusiasm in an individual's life, and the excitement Holmes is shown to derive from unraveling confirms this. In spite of appearances, a Holmes does not know how to relax any better than a Marlowe or a Bond does, because his hobby is both his real work and his chief passion. As Doyle makes clear in *The Sign of Four,* when the Great Detective is not detecting he suffers from the spiritual malaise of the nineteenth-century decadents, ennui. And his only refuge from such a condition apart from work comes through the artificial paradises of drugs (cocaine) or romantic art (solo violin playing).

If Holmes does not turn to sex, it is not simply because of the constraints imposed by Late Victorian morality but also because celibacy is the condition of heroic single-mindedness and allows the alternate gratification of the chase. In this respect the hard-boiled detective is no more than a modern version of his classic precursors. Spade, Marlowe, and Hammer, in spite of their well-advertised power over

9. *The Savage Mind* (University of Chicago Press, 1966), p. 32.

women, are fundamentally as celibate as Holmes, and their best "highs" are analogous to those stimulated by the hunt. Sex in the hard-boiled tradition is usually no more than a disappointing come-on, with the result that the sex objects evoked are far more often eliminated than made love to.

Finally, as far as the typical reader of detective fiction is concerned, it is worth repeating W. H. Auden's characterization of what is involved: "For me as for many others, the reading of detective stories is an addiction like tobacco or alcohol." It is an addiction he recognized above all through "the intensity of the craving."[10] Not only are the genre's heroes obsessive types, then, its readers are compulsive consumers.

The reading of any fiction of a certain length presupposes a form of compulsion, and it is one rooted in the linear, end-oriented character of traditional narrative. In the same way that most people who catch the beginning of a TV drama have to overcome a psychological resistance in order to turn the set off, an experienced reader who completes the first page of a novel is often impelled by an urge to read on, often in spite of himself. The desire stimulated by the printed page is less to know what happens *next,* as E. M. Forster put it, than to know what happens *in the end.* A half-read book, like a half-seen film, represents a state of psychological suspension such that the reader or spectator accepts the idea of noncompletion only with the greatest reluctance. And the reason for this is that reading fiction is a form of stimulation from which relief is available only in an end. If, as I suggested in chapter 5, reading fiction is an erotic activity, then the pain of a broken sequence is the pain of desire first aroused and then frustrated. It can be explained only as a form of coitus interruptus.

The fact that detective novels are traditionally devoured at a single sitting and often under conditions such as a train journey, which make other kinds of mental activity impossible, confirms the genre's power to excite, if not necessarily to satisfy. The reader of a detective story, in his rush to know who did it and how it was done, is tempted to behave like Roland Barthes's hypothetical night-club spectator, "who

10. "The Guilty Vicarage," p. 146.

jumps on to the stage to help the dancer strip faster."[11] Barthes's implied point is that striptease excites most when it occurs as formulaic theater;[12] the garments should fall in a measured, preordained order from outer to inner and from the extremities to the sexual center. Under such conditions striptease holds out the promise to reveal all in the end with the stimulation of froufrou on the way.

Similarly, those who are tempted to skip when they read detective novels usually do not do so because they know that much of the satisfaction of reading comes from the excitement produced by waiting. They recognize that the pleasure derived from narrative fiction depends on the postponement of pleasure and that the expected joyous release from tension, which is the knowledge furnished at the denouement, is frequently disappointing. As in all fiction the end that is the goal of a detective novel is a threat as well as a promise, since it also signals an end to pleasure.

The triggering of the compulsion to know is, then, a fundamental genre characteristic because of the dominant role played by the hermeneutic code. The mysterious threat embodied in the strong beginnings, coupled with digressive material that is often not intrinsically satisfying, makes the average detective story more end-oriented than almost any other type of narrative. This characteristic also explains another distinguishing feature of the genre. The great majority of detective novels are instantly forgettable and discarded as soon as they are finished; they are books to leave behind in vacation cottages.[13] If they still constitute a large proportion of the throwaway literature available at airport and railroad kiosks, therefore, it is because the whole point of reading them is in that state of pleasurable suspense which depends on not knowing the outcome. As with popular literature and movies in general, it is commonly assumed that a knowledge of the end spoils the pleasure because a revealed secret has little

11. *Le Plaisir du texte*, p. 21.

12. "Pornography is perhaps the most completely formulaic of literary structures." Cawelti, *Adventure, Mystery and Romance*, p. 14.

13. "I forget the story as soon as I have finished it, and have no wish to read it again. If, as sometimes happens, I start reading one and find after a few pages that I have read it before, I cannot go on." Auden, "The Guilty Vicarage," p. 146.

power to excite the imagination. The shadow of a monster is always more terrifying than the full frontal image of a monster. The red glow of dozens of eyes in Doctor No's tunnel is diminished as a threat as soon as the creatures are named, even if the name is "tarantula."[14]

In effect, the detective novel, like melodrama, is a genre in which the writing up of a menacing reality precedes its writing down. In contrast to tragedy, it represents events lived not under the threat of an end but under the promise of an end. It is therefore a commonplace that the final unmasking in a detective novel and the hero's rational explanation of events hitherto mysterious are mostly experienced as disappointing.[15] And the reason for this lies in the naming process just mentioned; to find a name for a mystery is to bring it under the control of knowledge and put an end to the play of fantasy. The moral of detective fiction is similar to the one Hannah Arendt invented for the Eichmann trial. What its denouements reveal is the banality of evil.

In short, to locate the appeal of the detective novel in the spectacle of reason vindicated by reality, and moral order reaffirmed, is to be guilty of at best a half-truth. A criticism attentive to reader response cannot fail to locate the genre's attraction above all in its pleasure-centered construction. To read a detective novel is to submit oneself to a sequence of experiences planned by an author in ways discussed earlier to promote reader pleasure. And it is important to realize that the pleasure is not in the end but in the process, not in the final reassertion of order but in the halting and suspenseful approach to it. The best detective stories are those that maintain a doubt in the reader's mind by threatening to remain insoluble right up to the moment they are solved. A final explanation is pleasurable only if it appears as important in its context and comes as a welcome relief from tension. Otherwise, it is a bore.

Moreover, if we are to believe the testimony of James D. Watson, the Nobel Prize winner and author of *The Double Helix,* stories of scientific discovery take similar forms and engage similar passions. In its own naive way Watson's book confirms that critique of knowledge

14. "The main thing is not to give the reader the opportunity of recognizing the object. Once an object is recognizable, it no longer frightens us." "The Mystery Novel," p. 224.

15. See Wilson, "Why Do People Read Detective Stories?", p. 233.

which Michel Foucault finds both in Aristotle ("The intrinsic desire for knowledge in Aristotle relies upon and transposes a prior relationship between knowledge, truth, and pleasure") and in Nietzsche ("knowledge is an 'invention' behind which lies something completely different from itself: the play of instincts, impulses, desires, fear, and the will to appropriate. Knowledge is produced on the stage where these elements struggle against each other").[16]

In his foreword to Watson's book, Sir Lawrence Bragg points out that "the latter chapters, in which the birth of a new idea is described so vividly, are drama of the highest order; the tension mounts and mounts toward the final climax. I do not known of any other instance where one is able to share so intimately in the researcher's struggles and doubts the final triumph."[17] Sir Lawrence's comments are a tribute to Watson's story-telling ability and take for granted the fact that the material is organized into a traditional story form—the very words "struggles," "doubts," and "final triumph" suggest, of course, the structure of conventional melodrama. Thus Watson involves his reader in a scientific pursuit drama that has a mystery to be solved, obstacles to be overcome, distinguished "rivals" to outwit (Linus Pauling), suspicious colleagues to convince (Rosalind Franklin), and a deadline in the form of an urge to be first with a solution. As Watson himself acknowledges through his choice of words, the search for an appropriate structural model for DNA was experienced by the Crick / Watson team as "a race," involving "glory" for "the winners" in the concrete form of the Nobel Prize. There is nothing fanciful or belittling, therefore, in finding in this account of a major scientific breakthrough a tale of constructed suspense and peripeteia, with a background of exotic European locales such as Cambridge and with a gallery of "characters," including especially Francis Crick, who plays the immodest Sherlock Holmes to the sly but equally brilliant narrator, James D. Watson's Dr. Watson.

From the point of view I am adopting here, however, it is important to note that, as the author himself suggests, the ultimate triumph of

---

16. *Language, Counter-Memory, Practice: Selected Essays and Intervies,* ed. Donald F. Bouchard (Ithaca: Cornell University Press, 1977), p. 202.

17. *The Double Helix: A Personal Account of the Discovery of the Structure of DNA* (New York and Scarborough, Ontario: New American Library, 1969), p. vii.

reason occurs only after a passionate and protracted search that engages in its protagonists a whole complex of emotions. Moreover, Watson affirms that the path followed by him and his colleague is not atypical of the way scientific research is done: "I do not believe that the way DNA came out constitutes an odd exception to a scientific world complicated by the contradictory pulls of ambition and the sense of fair play" (p. 10). In Watson's story, in any case, the search for the molecular structure of DNA turns out to be motivated less by the disinterested pursuit of truth than by the excitement of the scientific chase, the stimulus provided by competing scientists, and the honors that accrue to the men who are first past the post. Above all, however, there is the far from simple pleasure to be found in problem solving itself. In this respect Watson's autobiographical story confirms Thomas S. Kuhn's influential view that what he has called "normal science"—the kind of activity conducted by a given scientific community in conformity with the norms of a current paradigm—is itself a form of "puzzle solving."

According to Kuhn, whatever the initial motivation for wanting to become a researcher in a given field may have been, the reason a scientist attacks his problems "with such passion and devotion" is "the conviction that, if only he is skillful enough, he will succeed in solving a puzzle that no one has solved or solved so well. Many of the greatest scientific minds have devoted all of their professional attention to demanding puzzles of this sort. On most occasions any particular field of specialization offers nothing else to do, a fact that makes it no less fascinating to the proper sort of addict."[18] In a scientific context the choice of Kuhn's final word here—a word that echoes Auden's in connection with the reading of detective stories—may come as a surprise. Yet it is not surprising if applied to those who enjoy solving jigsaw puzzles, crossword puzzles, and chess problems. And it is in such cerebral play that Kuhn goes on to find an appropriate analogy for the rule-governed puzzle solving of "normal science." In all cases—in puzzles, science, and "the science of detection"—the activity is addictive to the extent that the outstanding solution becomes for the participant a matter of urgency and is pursued with an intensity similar to that which characterizes a hunt.

18. *The Structure of Scientific Revolutions* (Chicago and London: University of Chicago Press, 1970), pp. 37–38.

A similar view of scientific observation is to be found in Emerson's gloss of Thoreau's writings. He detects in the latter's naturalist pursuits of observing, collecting, collating, and explaining a sublimated hunt: "His determination in natural history was organic. He confessed that he sometimes felt like a hound or a panther, and, if born among Indians, would have been a fell hunter. But, restrained by his Massachusetts culture, he played out the game in this mild form of botany and ichthyology."[19] In four lines Emerson points to the hidden connections between scientific research, hunting, and games. It is no wonder, therefore, that in the past, at least, professors as a group have enjoyed formal detective stories. Academics are problem solvers who have managed to make a profession out of a passion and who understandably recognize in the activities of the Great Detective a form of heroic enterprise with which they fully identify.

Among those who have attempted to play metasleuth and explain why many millions of people throughout the world have such an appetite for detective fiction are the psychoanalysts. And the advantage of their approach is that it does assume such reading is undertaken to gratify submerged desire.

The classic case for a psychoanalytic interpretation has been put by Geraldine Pederson-Krag in her essay entitled "Detective Stories and the Primal Scene." Her view is that the detective story narrates in an appropriate symbolic language that evades the censure of the superego the forbidden mystery of sexual relations between adults:"The mystery story attempts to present a more satisfying, less painful primal scene from the stand point of the unconscious."[20]

Accepting the validity of the specific analogy perceived between parental love-making and literary murder presupposes a leap into psychoanalytic faith. But whether or not one makes that leap, the identification of the topos of a mysterious and dreadful scene as the most significant defining characteristic of the genre seems crucial to an understanding of the detective novel's power to grip a reader. In novels as different as *The Moonstone, The Hound of the Baskervilles,* and *The Big Sleep,* what the reader looks forward to in the end is the re-

19. Quoted by Slotkin, p. 519.
20. *Psychoanalytical Quarterly* 18 (1949): 212.

construction in its circumstantial wholeness of that crime whose clues
are scattered throughout the novel like *disjecta membra*.

There is, of course, a sense in which, because of the potency of the
original affect, all secrets are sexual and all pleasure erotic. The Bible
itself authorizes us to consider that the curiosity to know is a sexual
curiosity, and knowing, a carnal activity. And the Bible's authority in
the matter is confirmed by the myth of Oedipus insofar as it is one of
the earliest known stories to propose a connection between sex and
detection, between the activities of the riddle solver and those of the
incestuous son. Yet the trouble with the proposition that violent crime
is not violent crime but censured sex is that it is reversible. Love making is also a killing, with its weapons, offensives, counteroffensives,
penetrations, bleedings, and, sooner or later, its victors and van-
quished. Making love is the closest most of us ever come to commit-
ting murder. And the theory of the Oedipus complex alone legitimates
the assertion of the anteriority of Eros over Thanatos, an anteriority
challenged by Freud himself in *Beyond the Pleasure Principle*.

Furthermore, the reader's responsiveness to the representation of
the two staples of all our literature, sex and violence, is dependent on
a formal structure common to both. Sex and violence may also elicit
a similar squeamishness. Young children, at least, close their eyes to
explicit sexual activity on the screen in the same way that they shut
out too graphic violence. The appetite that is fed by stories as different as popular romance and pornography, classic detective novels and
thrillers, seems to respond to a common form of manipulation, even
if it is not fed by a common sado-erotic source. In literature, at least,
the power of intercourse and murder to arouse and fix the attention are
roughly comparable. And they are explicitly joined in the crime that
has perhaps the most powerful emotional charge of all, the sex crime
of rape.

From the eighteenth-century novel of manners on, the genre of the
novel has always owed part of its appeal to a taste for more or less
elevated gossip. The claim it makes on a reader's interest has been
inherent in an implied promise to report at length on other people's
private lives. And the detective story has exploited the reader's pru-
rience more thoroughly and consistently than almost any other category of fiction except pornography itself. The crime is a gap by means
of which the reader is permitted to enter the closed world behind the

yew hedge or the apartment door. The detective story gratifies because it legitimates activities considered taboo in its readers' lives.

Through the mechanism of the morally upright detective hero, the detective novel allows its readers to pry and peep, to enter locked houses, and to open drawers and cupboards in other people's homes. In this a detective has an advantage over almost all other fictional heroes because he has a license to look in and under beds, open private correspondence, and eavesdrop on intimate domestic scenes. And the reader enjoys without guilt the luxury of watching without being seen. Most traditional novels offer some of the pleasures of the keyhole, but apart from various forms of erotica none does so more systematically than the fiction of detection. The secret of its power resides to a large degree in the trick that makes of voyeurism a duty.

That such a duty is implied appears in the representation of the search through other people's lives as goal-oriented and morally necessary. The search gathers as it proceeds a succession of hints and pointers, mysterious stains, fingerprints and footprints, torn clothing, dried blood spots, murder weapons, and mutilated bodies that challenge the imagination's ability to invent scenes of fitting sado-erotic power. Everything is designed to point in the end to the secret of secrets, that is to say, to the original act that put the skeleton in the cupboard. And the scene to which everything points has been described by Aristotle as well as by Freud. It is both the scene of suffering of the *Poetics* and the original trauma of psychoanalysis.

Geoffrey Hartman defines the scene of suffering as follows: "to solve a crime in detective stories means to give it an exact location: to pinpoint not merely the murderer and his motives but also the very place, the room, the ingenious or brutal circumstances."[21] The scene itself antedates the discovery of the corpse or its equivalent that is the beginning of the novel proper. But it is the scene to which a detective novel sooner or later returns, the original bloodletting that sets a series of moves and countermoves in motion and has to be reconstructed before justice can be done and the series end.

As is apparent from the three very different novels discussed in chapter 2, it is not uncommon for the solution of the crime to depend on the reenactment of the original scene of suffering. Thus, in the first

21. "Literature High and Low," p. 204.

of the English detective novels, Franklin Blake is made to establish the precedent of acting out precisely the circumstances leading up to the theft of the jewel, thereby proving that his apparent guilt is real innocence. Collins has been so often imitated because actual reenactment is a way of fulfilling the need to recapitulate the scene of suffering, whose advantage in terms of the production of suspense is obvious. More commonly, the detective himself releases the group from the trauma of crime by reconstructing the location and circumstances of the scene verbally. And the result is usually anticlimactic.

In this respect the similarity between the parts played by the Great Detective and by the creator of psychoanalysis, at least in his role as hero of his case histories, is too obvious to need emphasizing. The similarity has, of course, been wittily exploited by Nicholas Meyer in *The Seven Per Cent Solution*—a work which confirms W. H. Auden's opinion that "the *gnosis* of a concrete crime and the *gnosis* of abstract ideas nicely parallel and parody each other."[22] The camp taste that has recently made a hero of the late Victorian detective enjoys the suggestion that Freud's genius and method have something in common with those of the fictional Holmes. But the serious point on which Meyer's novel touches is that Freud himself has become a mythic figure on the same footing as Sherlock Holmes and for similar reasons. Both are cultural heroes of late nineteenth-century science; both restore on the basis of often fragmentary evidence what Peter Brooks has referred to as "the seamless web of signification."[23] The lesson of Freud from *The Psychopathology of Everyday Life* on is the lesson Sergeant Cuff teachers Superintendent Seegrave in *The Moonstone:* "At one end of the inquiry there was a murder, and at the other end there was a spot of ink on a tablecloth that nobody could account for. In all my experience along the dirtiest ways of this dirty little world, I have never met with such a thing as a trifle yet" (p. 136). The science of detection is founded on the intellectual power that reconstructs the past on the basis of an ink spot. It presupposes the belief that the world is so organized that every clue has its cause, every signifier its signified. The fundamental ideological principle of the

22. "The Guilty Vicarage," p. 150.
23. *The Melodramatic Imagination*, p. 79.

genre is the rationalist one of the traceability of crime, and a similar faith relative to mental illness animates psychoanalytic therapy.

In the context of this study of a narrative formula and its appeal, however, the most interesting point to note is the formal similarity between a detective story and a psychoanalytic case history. If it has long appeared legitimate to interpret literary works in the light of psychoanalytic theory, more recently it has appeared useful to apply critical thought to the verbal forms through which the theory itself is communicated. The value of such an approach lies in the understanding it affords of how, before it is anything else, a case history is a narrative formula with all the characteristics of such formulas. Moreover, what is most striking about the case history is the number of features it shares with the detective story. The attraction both "genres" exert appears to proceed from similar formal causes. And although they appeal for the most part to very different audiences, many academics enjoy stories of both kinds.

Like the detective story, the psychoanalytic case history is a mystery story that is dominated by a combination of the hermeneutic and proairetic codes. On the one hand, it opens by raising a problem whose solution is furnished at the end. On the other, it names the sequence which is the passage from a loss to a restoration. If, in line with Propp, therefore, one looks for the opening lack, which sets the story in motion and requires the summoning of a hero, it is to be found in the loss of mental health. And before the latter can be restored and a cure proclaimed, certain obstacles have to be overcome that require the intervention of a problem solver. Further, the functions generated by such a story type give rise to the roles of investigating analyst and patient / victim. As a consequence of the concept of the divided psyche central to psychoanalysis, however, the patient / victim doubles as his own villain. The latter's role in the traditional tale is performed here by the enemy within.

Like a detective story again, a case history is the story of the recovery of a story. It is the account, narrated this time in the first person by the analyst, of a psychic adventure that begins with the arrival of a suffering stranger in the analyst's consulting room. But the story proper starts with the description of the corpse of the neurosis and goes on to tell of the slow process of clue gathering, made possible by a variety of investigative techniques, which leads in the end to the diagnostic explanation of the mysterious symptoms and of the causal chain linking them all to the observed neurosis. Finally the cure itself presupposes as a crucial element the reenactment of the original trauma, or scene of suffering.

A psychoanalytic case history is, then, not so much a whodunit as a how-and-at-what-moment-was-it-done. It does, however, appeal on its level to a similar voyeuristic interest in other people's intimate lives. Nothing in a detective story or even a pornographic novel is as private as the contents of someone else's unconscious.

Moreover, if nothing in detective fiction turns out to be as exciting as a Freudian psychoanalytic tale, it is in part because Freud reverses the movement which leads from hideous appearances to banal causes. Starting from apparently random and frequently innocuous clues, he uncovers the blocked libidinal drives in which they originate and the extraordinary mechanisms responsible for the blocking. Yet, because of the power and irrationality of the forces at work, the discovery of a hidden rationality in apparent psychic contingency does not give rise to a straightforward sense of relief as does the denouement of a detective novel. Freud's late writings, at least, project instead a vision of Joycean complexity and a tragic sense of the precariousness of the whole human enterprise. In its own way Freud's work anticipates many of the central issues raised by the writers discussed in my last chapter.

13

Antidetection

If, as I suggested in the previous chapter, in popular genres from gothic novel and melodrama to the detective story and spy thriller, the writing up of apparent mysteries of human experience precedes their writing down, a major tradition in twentieth-century fiction has been characterized by an antithetical movement. While they often employ the forms and even the materials of the detective story, writers as different as Henry James, Kafka, Robbe-Grillet, and Borges have suggested how the apparently familiar may turn out to hide a mysterious and often threatening face. The difference, stated in its simplest terms, is between an art which embodies the perception of reality as extraordinary and even monstrous and one which discovers over and over again a hidden banality governed by familiar laws. In the fictions of the serious modernists the investigations conducted by a variety of protagonists lead not to the reaffirmation of a hidden order satisfying both to reason and morality but to a core of doubt. Where the detective story has pursued the goal of perceptual refamiliarization, much of the serious fiction of our time has been committed to the task of defamiliarization, often by means of a more or less explicit parody of the detective genre. In lieu of a conclusion, therefore, it is illuminating to contrast that affirmative world view for which Marjorie Nicolson praised detective fiction in her time with the very different vision of the highbrow literature that has borrowed its outward forms. The contrast will, I hope, suggest the limits of a genre that by now must have almost as many detractors among professors of literature as it once had defenders.

I have suggested in earlier chapters that the art of the popular detective novel derives from the rhythm of desire. That is, it begins by stimulating desire, proceeds to tease it through a technique of progressive revelation interrupted by systematic digression, and finally satisfies it, however unsatisfactorily, in an end that reveals all. In contrast, the tendency of much modernist fiction in the twentieth century has been to stimulate in order not to satisfy. Even where it remains readable in the Barthean sense, such fiction offers endings that are not denouements of the traditional kind or, in the case of James, the solitary satisfactions of retreat and renunciation. In the most consciously parodistic of the writers mentioned above, Robbe-Grillet and Borges, the fiction operates like a trap to catch a reader. In place of the pleasure machine of popular fiction that returns its reader to the safety of his point of departure once the thrilling circuit is completed, many modern tales are machines without exits. The end brings neither revelation and the relief of a concluded sequence nor, *a fortiori,* the return of order to a community and confirmation of human mastery. However, this does not necessarily mean such endings disappoint.

Disappointment is, of course, the familiar reaction of a whole class of readers to the denouements of detective novels. Edmund Wilson's complaint is typical: "It is not difficult to create suspense by making people await a revelation, but it does demand a certain talent to come through with a criminal device which is ingenious or picturesque enough to make the reader feel that the waiting has been worth while."[1] Disappointment is also the reaction of a very different class of readers when they are deprived of the kind of denouement to which the detective story formula has habituated them. And an important feature of the creative task undertaken by both Borges and Robbe-Grillet in parodying and reinventing the detective story genre concerns the preparation of a disappointment for this second class of reader.

It follows that even the *nouveau roman* was not the writable text Barthes dreamed of in *S/Z* because it still relied for its effect on reader expectations learned from the reading of traditional novels. Its power to disturb depends on a reader's attempt to solve the problem of its meaning in terms of the two sequential codes, the hermeneutic and the proairetic. As Bruce Morrissette first showed, Robbe-Grillet's early novels were still recuperable through the application of traditional crit-

---

1. "Why Do People Read Detective Stories?", p. 233. MacShane quotes Chandler on the subject as follows: "the trouble with all these situation or plot stories is that at the end you suddenly feel as if you had been drinking city water while you thought you were drinking sparkling burgundy." *The Life,* p. 138.

ical techniques. And what is true for the *nouveau roman* is more obviously the case for the works of James, Kafka, and Borges. They depend for their very different effects on a reader involvement similar to
that which obtains in the reading of traditional detective stories. As
such, they are equally examples of manipulated desire.

In his discussion of the metaphysical detective story, Michael
Holquist makes the point that the detective story gave the postmodernists a structural principle comparable to the one that myth had given
the early modernists. Yet the examples of James and Kafka suggest
that insofar as it is characterized by a prolonged effort on the part of
an investigator to establish elusive truths, the detective story structure
has informed serious fiction for a good deal longer. Since the eighteenth century the mystery story, if not the detective story proper, has
been available to communicate suspense in the presence of the unknown even if it went on to relieve it at the denouement.

In the same way that Peter Brooks has made a convincing case for
seeing in James's fiction "the melodrama of consciousness," it is
worth considering briefly the way in which a typical Jamesian novel
takes the form of a detective story of the moral life. Both his novels
and his tales typically concern the exploration of an unfamiliar reality
by an investigator struggling to make sense of ambiguous data. In
James's case, however, the investigators are not worldly-wise special-
ists in crime but innocents, and the discovery of crime itself, most
commonly in the form of adultery, occurs not at the outset but late in
the work. The surprise of crime in James is ironic in a different sense
from that in the formal detective novel.

The way in which the pursuit of knowledge inadvertently leads to
the uncovering of infamy behind the brilliant display of civilized manners is perhaps most obvious in *What Maisie Knew*. With a directness
missing from the later works, the author announces, "It was to be the
fate of this patient little girl to see much more than she at first understood."[2] And the body of the work is dedicated to the gradual closing
of the gap between "seeing" and "understanding" started here. It is,
however, characteristic of James that even at the end doubt persists as
to the amount of knowledge crystallized in Maisie's awakened consciousness.

2. (London: The Bodley Head, 1969), p. 27.

What relates James's short novel to both melodrama and detective fiction is, on the one hand, the presence at its center of persecuted innocence in the shape of a young girl and, on the other hand, the effort in a world where mysterious crimes are committed to discover their nature and their perpetrators. James's richly metaphorical prose serves constantly to remind the reader of the threats to which his reluctant young investigator is exposed: "Everything had something behind it: life was like a long, long corridor with rows of closed doors" (p. 45).[3] As such gothic imagery suggests, the presence of hideous crime in a context of manners characterizes James's fiction as well as Agatha Christie's. The difference is in the moral seriousness of the issues engaged: "There was literally an instant in which Maisie fully saw—saw madness and desolation, saw ruin and darkness and death" (p. 183).

In general, it is also true, as the above quotations suggest, that the hold James's fiction exercises over a reader resides in its power to promote suspense. Not only is a sympathetic and more or less defenseless innocent exposed to unknown dangers, the promise is held out, as in all fiction dominated by the hermeneutic code, of important revelations to be made—"Everything had something behind it." Yet the force of such revelations here is in the end to frustrate desire. James's major works are typically structured on an almost unbearably halting approach to the realization of some rich dream, which is followed by a more or less swift destruction of it. The denouements celebrate victories that have the character of defeats. They show not so much evil eliminated as evil finally recognized but to be endured; *Portrait of a Lady* is, in spite of its surface of manners, as chilling a story as *Bluebeard*. Characteristically, the denouements involve the assumption at the greatest personal cost of responsibility for choices originally based on a misinterpretation of cultural and human data. Isabel Archer's American innocence is not permitted to unburden her of a moral commitment.

---

3. James's wording here anticipates Macherey's comments on the gothic novel, where the fact that characters and passions are always ambiguous is an "essential motif in their interpretation." Macherey adds, "Every meeting is deceptive and it is in this fact that the possibility of salvation resides. The virtuous pirate and the loyal robber represent the duplicity to be found in every human being." *Pour une théorie de la production littéraire*, p. 42.

Further, James's novels are frequently centered on courtships that go unconsummated or marriages founded on deceit. And they incorporate a subtle and protracted flirting that, owing to the refined codes of the actors involved, gives rise in the central reflector to a precise, eroticized attentiveness to posture, articles of dress, gesture, inflection, and nuances of speech. The most mannered of societies demands an avid and informed reader of its signs, if its messages are to be accurately decoded. That is why the peculiar Jamesian irony derives typically from limiting his narrative point of view to American strangers to European society. Their alien reading habits make them accident-prone.

The fact that James's fictions so often involve the effort to understand a complex reality also has important consequences for their form. For the most part his novels, like detective stories, are characterized by a dramatic organization founded on the central importance of peripeteia and scenes of suffering and recognition. The scene of recognition occurs typically in James as a sudden insight that comes to his central reflector consequent upon an act of seeing; a couple is surprised close to each other in a stance connoting intimacy. And, whenever it appears, the Jamesian equivalent of the scene of suffering is offered with even less circumstantiality. It is not reconstructed but hinted at. It comes about as the result of a chance encounter, fresh information supplied by gossip, or previously known circumstances suddenly revealed in a different light. Its power in James lies in its remaining largely implicit; the adulteries mostly concerned tend to appear evil partly because they go undescribed.

A work that offers a characteristic example of such Jamesian motifs and among the mature novels comes closest to being a tale of detection is *The Ambassadors*. Strether's heroic role in the novel is that of an investigator and rescuer who, as in many a tale, undertakes a difficult journey in order to make good a loss. He is dispatched by a mother in order to bring back a son apparently in thrall to the sirens of femininity and luxurious foreign living. Strether's task is to restore the boy to family and to virtue. The role requires a detective because Strether has to find out what is happening to the boy, the nature of his entanglements, and the best means of effecting a rescue. It is a typical stroke of Jamesian irony, however, that he establishes a conflict between role and character. Far from the worldly sage of the classic detective tradition, Strether, like Maisie, is an innocent stranger. He arrives prepared to be shocked and even do battle, and is instead seduced. *The Ambassadors* is, then, the story of a failed mission and of a seduction. Strether is a reluctant detective who finds himself unprepared for European difference. Since he is decidedly not at home in Paris, he is for a long time condemned to misreading clues that later pose no problems to the boy's sister, the worldly-wise Sarah Pocock. Strether's problem is the central Jamesian problem of understanding what one sees. Confronted, like Holmes, with the enigma of faces and gestures and with comings and goings among the unfamiliar artifacts of an old civilization, he fails to perceive properly the pattern in the data. He allows himself to be taken in by civilized geniality, deceived by one woman, and distracted by another. As a consequence, he is quite understandably dismissed by his original client.

Yet the significance for James of Strether's failure to live up to his role is in the qualities of character such a failure under such circumstances presupposes. In the context, Strether's weakness as a detective is a sign of his strength as a human being. His abortive quest permits at the same time a moral and sentimental education. The foil of Sarah Pocock confirms the sense communicated by Strether's generous blunders that the detective of the popular genre is even at his most genteel always a rampaging bully. As James's title indicates, there is more than one ambassador in his work, and the coercive energies of Sarah Pocock are reminders of what is required by the single-minded pursuit of solutions. To remain satisfied with savoring the civilized show or with making subtle moral distinctions is to give up the detective's role.

James's novel may be described as a work of antidetection, then, because it finds virtue in the failure to complete a given investigative task. It is also a novel that stimulates desire but concludes by refusing to fulfill it. The denouement typically involves an act of self-denial. Strether's seduction has to be for James a seduction without loss of honor. Since he is offered so much in the person of Maria Gostrey and the obstacle to his entering into possession of it is so apparently slight, Strether's renunciation makes him, like so many a Jamesian hero or heroine, a model of moral scrupulousness. James does not give the reader the apparently fitting union that he wants but forces him instead to acknowledge a heroism of the heart and conscience. Rather than risk following desire to the moment of fulfillment and, therefore, to potential disappointment, James prefers in his denouements to leave his readers with a sense of awe for what is the ethical equivalent of martyrdom. The richness for the imagination is in the courage and in the loss.

The presence of hidden truths and the power to stimulate the desire in a reader for satisfactory resolutions are what James's love stories have in common with his ghost stories. And in both cases what is missing in the end is the satisfaction of desire that comes from "knowledge," whether that knowledge take the form of knowledge of a woman, as in a wedding, or knowledge of the facts of a crime reconstructed in its logico-temporal sequence for the delectation of the reader, as in the recognition scene in the library of the formal detective story. And it is because such ghost stories as *The Jolly Corner* and *The Turn of the Screw* fail to account in rational terms for the mysterious evil they represent that they reveal a side to James's art which anticipates features of postmodernist fiction. But what is incidental in James is central in the works of Borges and Robbe-Grillet. They project a vision of a labyrinth in the absence of a labyrinth-solving great mind.

Taken together, these two writers suggest that a world of forgotten relationships and of signs reluctant to declare their meanings is as great a threat to a human order as is a world of surfaces. Whether we like it or not, the work of sign reading goes on under the most adverse of conditions because man is an interpreting animal. Not only do they offer ghost stories without ghosts, therefore, and detective stories with or without detectives, in Robbe-Grillet's case at least they force the issue of readability without which there is not only no solution to the crime / problem but no crime / problem posed. There is still a problem, however, but it is one faced by the reader. In the *nouveau roman* the latter is made to assume the investigative task of learning how to read again in the face of the deliberate dislocation of the hermeneutic and proairetic codes.

If the labyrinth is the presiding metaphor for human experience among such postmodernists as Borges and Robbe-Grillet, however, its contours were first imaginatively explored by the writer to whom they both owe their greatest debt, Kafka. And it is in *The Trial* that Kafka projects the nightmare vision of the law itself as a labyrinth to be solved. Of his three novels it is therefore the one which, from its outward appearance at least, has most in common with the detective novel.

The Trial contains an apparent crime and a definite suspect as well as the trial of the title. The disturbing originality of Kafka's novel, however, is in his employment of an ironic economy measure. His story is told from the point of view of a suspect who also struggles ineffectually to be his own private investigator. Joseph K. is forced by the law to go in search of his own elusive crime in order to prove his innocence. Kafka returns to the predetective story tradition of the criminal hero, but the radical faith associated with literary apologies for the outlaw's lot at the turn of the eighteenth century is absent from the twentieth-century writer. The law in The Trial is not corrupt and therefore potentially reformable but unfathomable.

In effect, Kafka's novel embodies the experience of the uncanny in the form of a common nightmare. Joseph K. is accused of a crime of which he is apparently innocent. He seems as guiltless as Franklin Blake in The Moonstone or as Hitchcock's "wrong men," but unlike the heroes of such popular works,[4] his ignorance also extends to the nature of the crime of which he stands accused. Moreover, Kafka does not simply exploit a common fear in order to exorcise it in his denouement; in The Trial there is no end to nightmare. In the same way that Gregor Samson wakes up one day transformed into a bug and remains a bug until he dies, Joseph K. finds he has become a guilty man overnight and discovers also that it is a condition for which in his universe there is no recourse. The scandal of The Trial is in the absence of that ideal of balance traditionally associated with justice. If Crime and Punishment is a novel that suggests in the symmetry of the two terms of its title the existence of a moral order, The Trial uncovers no evidence of the operations of such an order. In Kafka's title the absence of a first term implies a monstrous asymmetry. Punishment may occur in the absence of identifiable crime.

The suggestiveness of Kafka's novel resides in its power to accom-

---

4. Peter Brooks has shown how central "the dramaturgy of virtue misprized and eventually recognized" is in the aesthetics of melodrama. The Melodramatic Imagination, p. 27.

modate itself to interpretations on a variety of levels, from the psychological and the political to the metaphysical. It coolly depicts an individual nightmare subsequently corroborated by history for a whole race. Its general significance is perhaps best suggested by Borges's short story "Tlön, Uqbar, Orbis Tertius." In summing up the significance of the imaginary, ideal land of Tlön constructed as the result of the collaboration of so many great minds, the narrator comments: "Ten years ago any symmetry with a semblance of order—dialectical materialism, anti-Semitism, Nazism—was sufficient to entrance the minds of men. How could one do other than submit to Tlön, to the minute and vast evidence of an orderly planet? It is useless to answer that reality is also orderly. Perhaps it is, but in accordance with divine laws—I translate: inhuman laws—which we never quite grasp. Tlön is surely a labyrinth, but it is a labyrinth devised by men, a labyrinth destined to be deciphered by men."[5] The labyrinth represented in Kafka's *Trial* is experienced by his protagonist precisely as if it were designed "in accordance with divine law." The anguish Kafka evokes is that of attempting to decipher what must always remain undecipherable on human terms. *The Trial* is perhaps the supreme antidetective novel because its theme is the seeming lawlessness of the law itself.

In *The Trial* there are strange peripeteias but neither the recognition scene nor, in spite of Joseph K.'s effort to reconstruct it, the scene of suffering that the reader of the detective formula requires for his satisfaction. Instead, he experiences the anxiety and frustration of an incomplete sequence; there is the closure of an execution, but the mystery of Joseph K.'s crime goes unsolved. Worse yet, the work raises the chilling possibility, but never quite confirms it, that enforced self-scrutiny will in the end bring any man to acknowledge his guilt because the original crime is the crime of existing, of having been born one's father's son. *The Trial* gives an affirmative answer to Roland Barthes's rhetorical question: "Isn't every story a form of the Oedipus story? Isn't all narrative a search for one's origins, an expression of one's encounters with the Law, an involvement in the dialectic of tenderness and hate?"[6]

---

5. *Labyrinths* (London: Penguin Books, 1970), p. 42.
6. *Le Plaisir du texte*, pp. 75–76.

Another way of promoting the reader's disorientation is not to omit the long awaited scene of suffering but to produce it in an unexpected form. This way is chosen by Borges in his short story "Death and the Compass" and by Robbe-Grillet in *The Erasers*. The reconstruction of the scene of suffering in those works is perfect because it is the crime of which it is supposed to be the solution; the recognition scene and the scene of suffering are one and the same. In *The Voyeur*, on the other hand, the scene of suffering—"that one definitely visualized scene to which everything else might be referred"[7] in the detective formula and from which it derives its power to hold the reader—is the famous hollow center around which the novel is constructed. And for that reason no novel illustrates better than *The Voyeur* the nature of the reader's expectations in detective fiction. Robbe-Grillet largely relies for his success on reading habits that are inappropriate in his novel. Without warning, he changes the rules of the reading game and leaves the reader to discover for himself what the new rules are.

Reading is a living through, the experience of suspension between a known beginning and an end that is always in some sense looked forward to as an end to contradiciton and uncertainty. Seen in this way, a novel resembles a baited trap that entices the reader with the promise of a reward. And the reward traditionally offered in a detective novel is a revelation and a reconstruction in which everything is seen to fit after all. In *The Voyeur*, however, Robbe-Grillet baits the trap in such a way that the reader is enticed but is never released from contradiction. The expected "solidarities" among parts, to which Barthes refers in *S/Z* and which underline as often as possible "the compatibility of the circumstances concerned"(p. 162), fail to materialize. Instead, the reader finds himself in the position of desiring to witness the rape / murder of a girl, since denouement is possible only through the reconstruction of that scene of suffering. By withholding the "reward" of the scene of suffering, Robbe-Grillet's novel cunningly obliges the reader to acknowledge the voyeuristic character of the activity he is engaged in. If in *The Erasers* the detective is the criminal, in *The Voyeur* the reader is. The work's title is therefore an accusation. The hollow center is designed to show that the voyeur is

7. Hartman, "Literature High and Low," p. 207.

not so much the fragmented consciousness, locatable intermittently as text within a containing text, but the reader himself.

In the essay quoted above, Pederson-Krag writes: "In the gradual revelation of clues that make up the bulk of the narrative, the reader is presented with one significant pleasure after another, a protracted visual forepleasure. Finally, the crime is reconstructed, the mystery solved, that is, the primal scene is exposed" (p. 212). The shocking originality of Robbe-Grillet's novel resides in the absence of such a scene consequent on the dislocation of the two chronological codes.

Borges also is an author of verbal traps for unwary readers. But, unlike the novels of Robbe-Grillet, which teasingly exploit the sado-erotic imagery of the popular thriller, the tales designed by Borges appear innocuous at first sight and are characterized by a scholarly sobriety of tone. Borges harks back to that romantic tradition of the speculative essay and the fantastic tale to which Poe himself belonged. Typically, his stories begin with a paradox that seems open to reduction by reason, but instead they explode into scandal and defeat. If a reader experiences any pleasure at all under such circumstances, it is a pleasure that comes from an appreciation of the subtle irony associated with the violation of a formula. Borges's tales have the appearance of essays devoted to philosophical musings, but the relationships they uncover have the startling suggestiveness of the best surrealist conceits. They are relevant here, however, because they make clear the connection between the activities of scholarship, game playing, and detection. In "Death and the Compass" the connection is made explicit.

Given the task of solving a series of murders, the Dupin-like detective, Lönnrot, searches for the hidden symmetry by devoting himself to the study of cabalistic and Hasidic texts. As a result, he eventually finds a solution to the murders only to learn that the murderer planned that he should. His reasoning powers prove in the end to be just adequate to conspire in his own defeat. The labyrinth that he solves is merely a human labyrinth woven around him by one Red Scharlach in order to lead Lönnrot on to his death. Furthermore, the crime involved is a crime of reason; it involves a checkmating by an intellectually superior adversary. Yet it is judged by Lönnrot an imperfect crime because the labyrinth constructed by the criminal to trap his victim lacks the beauty of simplicity. Before he kills the detective, therefore, the murderer promises that the next time they meet he will capture Lönnrot in a labyrinth composed of a single line instead of four.

From a formal point of view an important feature of Borges's tale is that it ends not with a solution but with mystery enhanced, not with a denouement that functions as a closure but with a sudden bursting through the circle of logico-temporal norms within which it had operated up to that point. The end offers not the assertion of mastery and a return to order but the surprise of impotence. Borges's detective is not and never will be adequate to his investigative task. As in *The Erasers*, therefore, the recognition scene is also the scene of suffering.

The intricate web in which Borges's anti-Dupin is trapped reveals its diabolic rationality. More often than not, however, the experience of Borges's narrators and scholar / heroes is of a universe which abounds "in pointless symmetries and in maniacal repetitions" (p.113). If they find a path through the labyrinth, it is only to discover that the exit is really an entrance, that the labyrinth solved is no more than a labyrinth within a greater labyrinth. Problem solving is shown to occur, as on a chessboard, only within predetermined and therefore artificial limits. In Borges's fictional universe a checkmate achieved in accordance with the traditional rules of the game turns out to be a suicidal move on a suddenly expanded board. Consequently, if one writer stands out as the great modern anti-Freud, it is Borges. There is, perhaps, pattern without design, symptoms wihout causes, fortuitous order.

It is also no accident that his fiction equally as much as the formal detective story is largely dominated by the hermeneutic code. A problem solver is confronted at the beginning with a problem that he then proceeds to investigate. That is, the tales tell the story of an attempt to recover a hidden or forgotten story. But in the baroque hall of mirrors that Borges devises the effort of recovery invariably fails. His researchers find themselves facing a spectral reality composed of an endlessly receding series of repetitions and reproductions. The maniacal pursuit of meaning and order conducted by his scholars, mystics, and detective goes on. The images beckon, but the patterns that form instantly dissolve. Thus, in the end, the investigator finds he is without the instruments required for distinguishing the mirror from the wall and with no vantage point from which to comprehend the architecture of the whole.

Borges takes the familiar trope of the book as mirror of the world and stunningly reverses it. His tales raise the question how, as in "Death and the Compass," one can tell the tracker from the tracked or the reader from the read. Like Don Quixote himself, characters and readers are faced with the uncanny possibility that they are appearing in works that have already been written. The prefigurations, echoings, and repetitions that Borges's investigators stumble upon project the image of universal culture as a gigantic echo chamber without origins or ends. In his tales the possibility raised by Poe that "the universe is the plot of God" is once again canvassed. As such, it must always remain resistant to human hermeneutics.

It is perhaps fitting to conclude a discussion of the detective story formula with these brief comments on Borges, then, because his own stories mischievously undermine faith in historicity and in the logico-temporal sequences of the well-told tale. The proliferation of clues and of apparently random symmetries makes it impossible to exhume the simple story that, as in detective fiction, would disclose meaningful pattern and signal an end to nightmare. In Borges's stories no equivalent is found to the scene of suffering or original bloodletting, from which all that follows is the logical consequence and to which an end may be set through a painstaking reconstruction. What he offers is the appearance of purposefulness without an understanding of purpose, clues to the great mystery of being but no Great Detective to gather them into a meaningful pattern.

A major weakness of popular detective fiction is that it insists mechanically on denying the strangeness it first evokes, and it does so by trivializing it. From Poe to Fleming and Freeling the formula is unsatisfactory, finally, because it is founded on a deception. The horrors which it suggests have typically the same status as those to be found in a fairground haunted house. They are shown in the end to be the result of trickery, a matter of lighting and papier-mâché masks. The effects evoked are out of all proportion to the causes. A typical detective story is therefore also like a riddle or a conjurer's trick because once it has been explained, it loses all further power to stimulate the fantasy. The reason why run-of-the-mill detective stories do not warrant a rereading is that almost all the pleasure for the reader is in their hermeneutic dimension, in the suspense of not knowing. Such novels are mere *textes de désir*, with little of the rich digressive play which characterizes *textes de plaisir*. Moreover, even where, as in *The Big Sleep*, the horror revealed turns out to have a greater shock value than the preceding effects themselves, there is a loss of tension by reason of the fact that the crime itself is solved. Chandler's denouement may afford a sense of relief; it is also in spite of its strength disappointing because we are most alert when attuned to the promise of truths *about* to be revealed. Postcoital sadness occurs because there is for the moment nothing more to know or feel.

At the end of a short essay entitled "The Wall and the Books," Borges makes the point with characteristic delicacy: "Music, states of happiness, mythology, faces belabored by time, certain twilights and certain places try to tell us something, or have said something we should have missed, or are about to say something; this imminence of a revelation which does not occur is, perhaps, the aesthetic phenomenon" (p. 233). It is also apparently "the scientific phenomenon." In response to a question concerning her research, a scientist interviewed on the program *Nova* gave the following answer: "It's like a very exciting detective story. . . . You think you've understood it but then something else happens and you realize you haven't." And a second scientist added, "What we don't know is much more exciting than what we know."[8] Now that we have been to the moon, it is clear that all the drama was in getting there.

In its own way, therefore, the popular detective formula feeds our appetites for strong novelties, but because of its framework of certainty it leaves us bored in the end. Consequently, some of our major twentieth-century novelists have been at pains either to contrive the defeat of their detective or to banish him altogether from stories that

---

8. Televised on April 2, 1980. The point was not, of course, lost on Conan Doyle: "Like all Holmes's reasoning the thing seemed simplicity itself when it was once explained. He read the thought upon my features, and his smile had a tinge of bitterness. 'I am afraid that I rather give myself away when I explain,' he said. 'Results without causes are much more impressive.' " "The Stock-broker's Clerk," in *The Complete Sherlock Holmes*, p. 363.

rediscover original strangeness. The pleasures such authors offer are associated with the experience of awe and of still unsatisfied desire. If, as has been suggested here, detective stories traditionally take the form of a striptease, in Borges's work every garment that falls discloses new and unexpected garments. In his stories the promise of pleasure persists beyond the end because the final G-string never falls.

Index